SEMINARY
A SEARCH
Paul Hendrickson

SUMMIT BOOKS | NEW YORK

SUMMIT BOOKS and colophon are trademarks
of Simon & Schuster, Inc.

Manufactured in the United States of America

10 9 8 7 6 5 4 3 2 1
10 9 8 7 6 5 4 3 2 1 Pbk.

Library of Congress Cataloging in Publication Data

Hendrickson, Paul
    Seminary, a search.

    I. Hendrickson, Paul. 2. Ex-seminarians—United States—Biography.
3. St. Joseph's Preparatory Seminary (Russell County, Ala.) I. Title.
BX4668.3.H46A37 1983   207'.761485   82-19481
ISBN 0-671-42030-5
ISBN 0-671-63586-7 Pbk.

Portions of this book first appeared in *Esquire* and *Playboy*.

FOR MY MOTHER AND FATHER

CONTENTS

ACKNOWLEDGMENT

All the events in this book are true, but not every name is real. Although this is a work of nonfiction, it is also a subjective and personal account. Many people and several institutions came to my aid. I am indebted to the Alicia Patterson Foundation for funding the first part of my research. I am particularly indebted to four people: Jim Silberman, president and editor in chief of Summit Books, who took over the project midway and helped me to see the whole, not just the parts; Shelby Coffey, a deputy managing editor of the *Washington Post,* who shouted and inspired from the sidelines; Elizabeth Kaplan of Summit Books, who attended to a thousand tedious editorial details; and Cecilia Moffatt Hendrickson, who knew, when I didn't, that it could be done and who didn't waver in love or enthusiasm. Also I must thank Ben Bradlee, executive editor of the *Washington Post,* who first convinced me that writing about the seminary was not an obscure project. To all those ex-priests and former seminarians as well as current men of God who allowed an old associate to come back into their lives, I can only be lastingly grateful.

Introduction

In the winter of 1948, when I was three and a half, my mother gave birth to a premature child, alone, late at night, in an upstairs bedroom of a rented Illinois farmhouse, with phone lines down and a snowstorm brawling outside. My father was on a flight for his airline and had taken our only car to the airport. Stranded, with two young boys in the house, two and a half miles from the nearest neighbor, twelve miles from St. Mary's Hospital in Kankakee where she was supposed to have her baby eight weeks hence, my mother made the bravest decision of her life and delivered the child by herself. Both calm and terrified, she instructed my brother Marty, who was five, to get towels and sheets from the basement and to bring pans of hot water. She instructed me to bring tea bags and drinking water and then stand downstairs on the landing and turn the lights on and off. She told us both to pray very hard to Baby Jesus. She closed her door and some hours later a child was born. We are unsure how long he lived, but my mother feels he lived long enough for her to baptize him and name him David Hendrickson. The next evening, the flat, fallow fields of Illinois heaped white and peaceful, my father copiloted a DC-3 into Midway Airport on the south side of Chicago, got in the employee bus, which took him to his car, and drove home to his family. He found my mother propped up in bed. "I had the baby," she said. "What?" he said, his voice and legs beginning to buckle. "Look in the closet," she said. My father went over to a small

11

storage space near her bed and pulled out a narrow cardboard box with a lid on it. Inside the box, wrapped in white sheets, was something very small and dark; it almost looked charred. My father put the lid back on the box, called for a doctor, arranged for a nurse, and sometime later that night drove to a funeral home. A day and a half later a Chevrolet driven by a rueful twenty-nine-year-old husband pulled out of Illinois headed for Ohio. On the back seat of the car sat an infant's coffin. The coffin and its contents now lie in St. Brigid's Cemetery in Xenia, Ohio, the town where my mother grew up. The grave is marked by a small, flat, pinkish stone, and standing over this stone in wet grass on certain fine autumn days, I have been able to understand how the glorious is sometimes a synthesis of the joyful and the sorrowful. In a way, the story of an American seminary, and my part in it, starts there.

PART ONE

THE GIFT
ONCE GIVEN

My dwelling, like a shepherd's tent,
Is struck down and borne away from me.
You have folded up my life
Like a weaver, who severs the last thread.

—Isaiah 38:12

From
My Mother's Sleep

———

When I came out I was twenty-one years old, a virgin, scared stiff. I had never met a Jew; I had never been on a date; most of my cultural heroes had "Saint" affixed to their names.

TIME SQUEEZES, presses flat, like something I left in a leather book. The school, I like to think now, was an archipelago of prayer and learning, with barns and woods and toads and amused unlettered Negroes lapping at us on every side. Its formal name was St. Joseph's Preparatory Seminary, but everyone called it Holy Trinity. This was the name the founder had given it forty years before. It stood a couple of football throws back from Guerry Preuett Highway, in a tangle of kudzu, along the Chattahoochee River, past a rise in the road called Red Level, out into the scabbed red dirt and fragrant scrub-pine of Russell County, Alabama. In the twenties Holy Trinity had been an old plantation. When I got there, in the late fifties, you could still see chain gangs in striped suits and leg irons working in the ditches by the road out front. The year before I came, the Ku Klux Klan burned a cross on the seminary lawn in the middle of the night. Turned out it was just some drunked-up Phenix City, Alabama, boys with white hoods and a Jeep and a kerosene-soaked crossbar wrapped in gunnysack; but the story got on the wires. My freshman year a reporter came out from town, looked around, and wrote: "Spread out to the horizons are lush green patches of spring wheat and oats and fat cattle grazing and tractors plowing in the black loam, for these are men and women of the soil as well as the spirit." Actually the loam was pretty sandy. But you knew what he meant.

We got up every morning at five-thirty, except on Sunday, when there was a sleep-in until six. "Wretched puckies," we called them. We meant eyeballs. Wretched puckies were what our eyes felt like every winter morning in the frigid Sunny South. Getting up and into my clothes and struggling out to the unheated jakes. No time to shave—just eleven minutes to pee and wash my face and maybe squeeze a zit in the narrow little cracked mirror over by the door. Then, the one-hundred-yard bolt across the walk to chapel. Finding my pew in the dim holy light. Trying to make my mouth work for morning prayers. Trying to stay awake for the meditation period, back nudged against the wooden back of the pew. Drowsiness, head gliding toward my breastbone: *snap!*—the sudden jerk awake.

Afterward: breakfast in the refectory at long wooden tables covered with oilcloth. Inside that narrow room with its bank of tall green windows was fuel. Warmth, too, though the heat that rammed out at us from the single gas blower above the prefect's head was as dry as Death Valley. Nobody complained. We'd stand by our places until the priests were in. Father Constantine would doff his biretta, intone grace. Soon as we were down he might say, *Tu autem Domine miserere nobis.* The Major Silence was over. We were free to talk.

Miss Julie and Miss Elsa, our two devoted spinster cooks, would set out watery scrambled eggs in white Melmac dishes. Seconds only lasted so long; this was survival of the fastest. To this day I still eat as though the house is afire. My wife will slow me down, and in a week I'm back up to old racing speeds. On Sundays we got small, limp, shredded pieces of bacon in our eggs. We lived for Sundays, even if Sunday meant Vespers at one-thirty and ten trips to chapel instead of eight splintering our day.

In my third year, when I was sixteen, the seminary would move to a new building in Virginia; by then, the sixties—and all that word entails—had begun creeping in. But in the good years, one hundred of us lived and prayed and studied at Holy Trinity, Alabama. Most of us had come from up North, from towns named Bayonne and Florham Park and Davenport. We were parish altar boys, daily communicants. We belonged to the only "the" church, as comedian Lenny Bruce used to say with scorn. We were R.C.s. We wanted, all of us, to be priests. A few of us made it.

I was in the seminary seven years. I had gone in a few months after my fourteenth birthday. Then, on a pond-still summer afternoon in 1965, I shook hands with the most intimate friends I have ever known, helped heave a trunk into the rear of a station wagon, made a visit to chapel, rode twenty-three miles to a Central of Georgia railway depot, bought a ticket, and went home to Illinois. As easily as that, it seemed, I was no longer Brother Garret, student for the Catholic missionary priesthood. I had on that day a starchy black eighty-dollar mohair suit, white shirt, black tie, white socks, black shoes, and a burr haircut. As the train pulled off, I waved to Father Declan, the Master of Novices, who had brought me in and now stood on the platform making comic faces. I wish he'd quit, I remember thinking. On the ride home I tried to talk to a girl. She thought I was an undertaker.

For all I knew that day, my leaving was an isolated act, in tune with really nothing but its own going. I couldn't see it yet, but my departure had come at almost the exact midpoint of a confusing decade. John Kennedy had been shot, though his brother hadn't. There had been fire in the Gulf of Tonkin, though not yet on the moon. Watts was a place I wouldn't hear of until a little later on. What I had heard of on a July day in 1965 was something called the Second Vatican Council, a worldwide gathering of bishops and cardinals, called together in Rome three years before by a stubby Italian pope determined to let in some fresh air. At the moment of my leaving, the council that Pope John XXIII started in 1962 had just begun to slap at the seminary walls. In the next five years would come floods of change. On the day of my departure the choir stalls didn't yet seem bare and ruined.

•

In bed that last morning, July 15, 1965, waiting for the rising bell, lulled by muffled snoring up and down the hall, I tried to picture what the coming days and weeks might be like. The window was open, and cool five-o'clock light draped itself across my sheets and over to the habit and cincture hanging from a nail on the back of my door. My cassock badly needed rehemming, and in several spots the heavy black material had gone thin and shiny, like an old man's shin.

Lying there, I could find no concrete images of what lay ahead. My mind took me home, to my parents' living room, sitting in the chair by the bay window, coat over my arm, bag in the hallway, and then went blank. After that was a blurred middle zone, shapeless.

All I really knew was that I had two priorities: I wanted to get enrolled in a university somewhere and finish my degree, and I wanted my stomach to stop hurting. I also wanted to kiss a woman passionately. Almost any woman would do.

I wondered if I had lost my faith, my belief in God. I didn't think so, but it was a scary thought. I looked at my watch: ten after five. Through the window I could see the little building fifteen yards across the lawn where the Master of Novices slept; the building's roof stood out against a pale stream of high yellow sky. It would be a nice day, I judged. I strained to catch a sound from the farm and thought I might have heard a cow. I'd miss the farm, going down there on Saturday mornings with a wheelbarrow to get manure for the rose gardens, coming back and hoeing it into the beds till I had a fine, gritty powder. The farm was only a quarter of a mile off, but somehow it felt farther than that. Going to the farm was always a small escape.

I searched the room. It was an absurd and cramped place, no more than three paces by five. A year before, when it had first been assigned to me, the room repelled me, scared me. I could see only the deficiencies then. Now I was not only accustomed to them, but I also wished the room no other way: ceiling papered to midpoint, as if somebody had suddenly realized what he was doing and quit. Flat-green walls blotched white with primer. A hole to the right of the radiator you could put your elbow through and through which, I was certain, rodents paraded in the pitch of night. I kept my toes under the sheets.

The bell rang, startling me, a hammer hitting steel. In seven years I had never gotten used to it. Bodies stirred. Beds creaked. I got up, put on a pair of pants, went down the hall to the sinks. I came back and slid into my habit. I hoped I'd always know what it felt like sliding into the habit, snapping the three buttons at the shoulder, holding the belt in my teeth until in one swirl I gathered it around me, hooked it at my hip, and whispered, "My yoke is sweet, O Lord, my burden light." I've forgotten the rest of the prayer now, although not the feeling.

I went over to chapel. Nothing felt very different. I hung my weight between my elbows and knees and swung lightly between the two. You could kneel on bare board for hours that way. At the consecration I bowed my head and prayed for worthiness. In six weeks my classmates would be in vows. Where would I be? I went over to breakfast and sat in my old seat across from my pal Bertin Glennon. We passed each other food while another novice read aloud from the *Lives of the Saints*. Then I went to my room and started packing. That wasn't hard. I put into a trunk and suitcase my five or six pairs of black straight-legged wash pants, my several sport shirts, my underwear, the dozen or so books I had been allowed to keep as a novice. I didn't pack my breviary. Someone could have that. I took off my habit and folded it neatly on a chair. We used to kid that the habit hid a multitude of sins; we didn't just mean wrinkled wash pants and T-shirts with yellow holes. I put on my one white shirt, got into my mohair suit. My parents had bought the suit the summer before at a department store in Elgin, Illinois. Six months from now I would hock it for five bucks on Olive Street in St. Louis. "Don't much get a call for a preacher's suit," the pawnbroker would say, pushing the money under the window.

After lunch I said goodbye to my classmates. They were in colloquy, having their thirty minutes of talk and relaxation before going back to work and the Minor Silence. It was the moment I dreaded. I had participated in this ritual dozens of times over the years, but from the other side. Somebody else was always going; I was staying. Not this time. No matter who you were or what face you tried to put on, leaving the semi-nary seemed funereal and awkward and somehow shameful. Nobody quite knew what to say. A trunk on the front step was the equivalent of a hearse. Some boys managed to light out early while the rest of us were in chapel or doing morning chores. The priests preferred it that way, I believe. Better on morale. Let's not start a run on the bank. Once, somebody left, got as far as the Atlanta airport, came back. They let him stay. Usually you just saw an empty place in the refectory. "Where's Digger?" somebody would say. "He left," somebody else would answer. Nobody ever said for where; just "He left," as if everything else were outer space. They still say it that way. "He left."

I shook hands, moving around the room, making talk. Somebody gave me a two-handed shake, not quite a hug. Somebody else whispered, "You won't have to slur the middle one," and immediately I understood. It was a joke we had about the three religious vows—poverty, chastity, and obe-dience. We always said that on Profession Day, when it came time to kneel at the altar and cup hands with the superior, we were going to slur the middle vow so it came out charity. I was going to miss my chance by six weeks.

There was only one thing left: making a visit to chapel. We had a custom, a rule almost: anytime you went off the prop-erty or came back, the first thing you did was go to the chapel. On a soft September night eleven months earlier my family had watched my investiture in this building. Afterward, me in my new habit and name, standing outside in moist dark, with screech owls calling and bullfrogs answering and the moon like alabaster, my six-year-old brother Mark jumped into my arms. "Garret the carrot," he said. I went in now, brushed my fingers across the sponge in the holy water font, made the sign of the cross, and genuflected. This old wooden building, with its plain amber windows and wainscoted walls and smooth dark pews that were milled from timber up on the hill, framed our lives. Nothing since has seemed so holy.

I came outside and stood on the step. The afternoon felt webbed with quiet. You could almost hear the bees in the hive boxes up by the pool. I didn't know all the reasons why I was leaving something I loved so much. Maybe I would know that later. I helped one of my classmates lift my trunk into the back of the car. I slid into the front seat. Father Declan got in, started the engine. When he turned off the front drive onto the highway, I didn't look back. I am trying to do that now.

In Green Wood

The place was sacred and it was cruel. I remember warm
May nights in the pergola, ten or fifteen of us sitting in
a U on green benches around the water cooler, when I
thought: nobody gets out of here alive. There was a
certain gleeful genius in us for spotting a ripe vulnera-
bility, a hidden defect, then exposing it to group light.
Maybe someone had a harelip, as someone did. Maybe
someone had a bed-wetting problem, as someone did.
Usually our knife sessions were more good-natured than
vicious, though every once in a while something went
wrong. Then it was as if a man sitting in a tower in a
railyard had switched us onto another track. Then our
little cruelties were like child savageries: they had to run
their course, as if in proof of a Newton law that when a
thing is in motion it stays in motion. But there were
other moments, too, of an almost iridescent softness.
Several times a day we went to chapel to murmur in half-
dreamy unison, "O most precious blood of Jesus/Oozing
from every pore/Grant us the grace to love Thee ever
more and more." There was music, a loving willing
witchery, in that cadence. . . .

SOMETIMES it almost seems as thin and gauzy as a dream. We
never got to go home at Christmas. Our letters, both coming
in and going out, were opened and read by the Prefect of
Discipline. (Letters from girls were confiscated.) We slept in
creaky dorms, in metal bunks, on rude wooden floors. Our
showers were a couple of cement-block rooms slick with
algae, and the "jakes" were three long rows of hoppers bolted

to wooden runners on cracked concrete flooring. They had
flimsy green plywood dividers, no doors. The boys who had
jake duty that week would come along with buckets of indus-
trial-strength ammonia and swab the place while you sat
there. You could raise your feet or get your socks disinfected.
We'd lean forward past the plywood dividers to talk to one
another up and down the stalls. Even in my own house it is
hard for me to sit on a toilet now without wanting to bolt the
door.

We went to school six days a week, with Thursday and
Saturday afternoons off for work and play. Classes began at
eight-thirty, running until noon, cramming in our Latin and
trig, biology and Greek, the odd dirgeful joys of Gregorian
chant. Latin was first; everything bowed to getting your thirty
lines of translation prepared. We began with composition
and syntax, went through Caesar, Cicero, Virgil, Horace,
Ovid, Seneca, Livy, Saint Augustine. In our third year we
began studying two languages a semester; in our fifth year,
three languages, plus English, chemistry, religion, chant, and
mathematics. That added up to twenty-two credit hours, and
after that the language blitz slackened off some. But there
was never enough time.

Before noon every day we were back in chapel. "Hitting
the kneelers," we spoke of it among ourselves. The days,
despite their pace, could seem a solemn glide. In the afternoon, following class, there were fifty precious minutes of
recreation. You might sit in the rec room, listening to Lester
Lanin or Billy Vaughn or the Kingston Trio on the hi-fi,
watching breezes billow curtains, maybe reading a Daphne
du Maurier novel (*Catcher in the Rye* would come later, under
the blankets), while up at the pool others were splashing
wildly. Or you might run your head off down at the gym,
trying to shoot the eyes out of the basket, as I did, with something approaching pent-up frenzy. The rest of the day, save
for supper and thirty minutes of "colloquy" afterward, belonged to chapel and study hall.

At four o'clock every afternoon we showered. The Prefect
of Discipline would come through in his habit, reading his
breviary, sidestepping puddles. "Eight minutes, gents," he
would say. "Custody of the eyes, gents." Father Constantine
had been Prefect of Discipline a long time. He could be hard

as stone, and he needed to be, too, for there was fundamental anarchy conspiring against him—the institutionalization of the occasionally pious adolescent. Father Constantine wore gum-soled shoes and loved sneaking up on seminarians. He was surprisingly light on his feet, and one of his favorite pastimes was sneaking up on you and flicking red-hot ashes from his cigarette down your shirt collar. Riding herd year after year on a building of boy seminarians had bled him of his patience, I think. When I knew him you didn't want to ask the wrong question, especially when he was annoyed: he'd bear down on you with a tight-lipped grimace. The real grimace was in his eyes. But he could be outrageously funny, too (though sometimes I think we were guffawing out of sheer relief), as well as self-deprecating and surprisingly sentimental. He was town crier, grim reaper, stick in our lives.

At four twenty-five it was the warning bell. And then, hair plastered down, perspiration still beading temples from pumped-up body heat, underarms coated with Mennen Speed Stick, one hundred postpubescent divinity students in white socks, black wash pants, and white T-shirts got down to their translations with a Cassell's Latin-English dictionary (and "trot," if you could keep one hidden), to their French and history and Euclid, all of which were essential to converting heathens. So ran our gripes.

At nine-thirty every night, at least until we were eighteen and had reached the college department, the lights went out. Then it was Major Silence. To break it was a sin. To get caught breaking it could mean three gigs, which meant jug, which also meant Saturday afternoon with a swing blade in the field below the gym we called the Swamp. My sophomore year I practically slept at the Swamp, and with good reason. There were lots of ways to earn a trip down there—falling asleep in chapel several mornings in a row, electrocuting a frog in biology lab, failing to pass bed and locker inspection too many times in one week. For inspection the blankets were to be folded, military style, at the foot of our beds, sheets pulled tight enough to bounce a prefect's coin (though this was more legend than carried-out test). The prefect went up and down the aisles while we stood not quite at attention. A crucifix was on every pillow. If you had committed an impurity the night before (and this presented a whole other dread in the confession box the next morning) you were liable for the smirks of your peers. Nobody talked about masturbation much. But it was there, hovering. There was a myth among some of us that if you didn't touch it you could go to communion in the morning.

If ours was an odd kind of holy terrarium, if there were vague, dim, sexual innuendoes and stirrings, I knew or wanted no other. I was in love with the place. It was alive with spirit, and for all its seeming shroud at times, there was something perfectly linear about it, too: we each hoped to be a fisher of men. Our energies flowed toward one goal.

Only something got in the way. By the close of the sixties, my seminary was effectively dead. In 1973 it locked its doors. I was long gone by then, from the seminary and some other things, separated from my first wife, about to file for divorce in a Michigan court, out of touch and time with old classmates and priestly feelings, on edge, struggling to find a writing voice, living for the space of stories I got in newspapers, killing off everything around me that breathed of church or religion.

I am writing these words this morning, a not particularly gloomy thirty-eight-year-old ambivalent believer who has twice married. I am writing from the second floor of a rented town house in Washington, D.C. I have lived here for five years. Outside, sycamore leaves are drifting down. It is a Sunday and a cooling autumn morning is on my skin. It feels like silk.

A decade of days, a cycle of seasons. I went in in '58, left in '65, got married in '69, got divorced in '74, got married again in '79. In the seventeen years since I quit the seminary and have gotten myself to this Washington, D.C., morning, I have left more cities and jobs than I should have. I don't go to church regularly anymore. I have wriggled through a number of other departures and changes and off-seasons. And yet, wherever I go, almost whatever I do, I find that the seminary comes softly clacking along behind, like a child's duck dragged on a string.

Close to nine hundred boys went through my religious Order's seminaries in the forties and fifties and sixties. Almost all of us are out in the world now. Some got to the major seminary, were ordained priests, only to jump from the boat later. Some of them jumped in rage, some of them jumped in desperation. Some jumped out of ennui, some jumped out of loneliness. Of all of us who were there, for however long, maybe 8 percent made it to priesthood, maybe 2 percent are priests now. Any cost accounting would be brutal, though that of course is irrelevant: dollars are earthly.

Somebody became a rug baron in Ecuador. Somebody runs an Off Track Betting Parlor. Somebody runs an FBI SWAT team, or did, the last time I checked. Someone helped install a phone system in Egypt. Someone may be in the CIA but won't say it. Someone is a junkie; someone is gay; someone is a clinical psychologist. Somebody manages a 7-11 store, somebody went to Las Vegas to help probate an alleged will of Howard Hughes. Somebody is a professor of Russian. Somebody became Ronald Reagan's Secretary of Labor—and found himself accused of having Mafia ties.

And somebody else, an old lanky hero of mine, went to Vietnam as a chaplain and ended up winning the Medal of Honor. His name is Charlie Liteky, and one day the President of the United States decorated him in the White House. A little while later Charlie left the priesthood. He has since seemed to wander the earth, although not aimlessly. For a time he lived on an island in Florida, in a scrap-wood cabin that looked out to an infinity of sea. When I found him, he was living in a cheap hotel on Eddy Street in San Francisco, trying to write a novel.

In my own class, twenty-one boys from eleven states, each boy thirteen or fourteen years old, began their first year of studies for the Catholic missionary priesthood at Holy Trinity, Alabama, on a wilting August afternoon in 1958. One of us is a priest today. His name is Father Bertin Glennon, and he works in the coal camps of eastern Kentucky. The rest of us wandered off somewhere along the thirteen-year route to ordination, or shortly afterward, as did most of the classes above and behind us.

In the last several years I've been out to California and down to Florida and no farther than a ten-minute subway ride from my own house, and what I've found in almost every instance is a piece of a musty dream, each piece fitting into a huge puzzling puzzle. The first time I called up Jim Franklin I recall his saying almost tonelessly and without detectable self-pity, "I have no past." It was as if it were a cold, hard fact.

Franklin, who was two years behind me and has an almost mystic Celtic capacity to enjoy seedy taverns and ill weather, is a high school English composition teacher in Detroit. He said he is in Michigan now because that's where he left the Order. He left in the late sixties, when the walls seemed to be caving in, and not from Vietnam or assassinations, though these were some of it. "I didn't want to be the last one out," he said. He also said he wonders sometimes if he didn't make a mistake. On noon hours now he'll slip into his school's chapel and just sit there. But he doesn't think of himself as tragic.

The seminary comes back to me at the damnedest times in the damnedest ways. The other day I heard a fire bell and immediately thought of Goofy. Since we lived in rudely made tinderbox buildings in Alabama, fire drills were one of the prefect's special little tortures, especially in the dead of a winter night. We would be warned of a coming drill before going to bed. We might be asleep for an hour or two and then a blood-curdling alarm would set off. We'd have maybe three minutes to get dressed and stumble in silence out to a field opposite the gym.

One late autumn night—it might have been one or two o'clock—we were huddled beside the gym waiting for Father Constantine's dismissal when we spied a lone figure loping in the moonlight toward chapel, trying to put on a tie. It wasn't Ichabod Crane at all, but a freshman named Bill Portier, from Tenafly, New Jersey, whom somebody had nicknamed Goofy, after the Disney cartoon character. Goofy was long-legged and skinny and terribly bright in school, although he could be slow in other ways. He had slept through the fire alarm, come awake, seen an empty dorm, figured he had missed the rising bell, and taken off for chapel in flight against fury.

We watched this apparition. Then Father Constantine, who almost never summoned anyone by nickname—though he knew most of the names—boomed, "Uh, Goo-fee, down here." The apparition swerved left and the entire school broke Major Silence.

Today, Bill Portier is a theologian with a doctorate from a

Canadian university. He is married to a former nun and teaches at a college in Maryland. On the night I stopped to see him he was hunched over a typewriter trying to fashion an article for a theological journal from a seven-hundred-page dissertation. Bonnie, his wife, was off teaching, the kids were in bed. Since he lasted a few years longer than I had, I asked what the place was like when suddenly everybody began leaving. "We thought if we could just get out into the secular university, all our problems would be solved," he said. "What happened in the end, I think, was an irresolvable clash of world views. The priesthood suddenly seemed deontologized, demystified."

After a while I brought up his old moonlit lope. "Aw, shit," Goofy said, screwing up his face, sounding fourteen and straight out of Tenafly, "don't put that in."

I've also found most of my old role models, the priests who taught us. It was their Order and we were merely aspiring to it. They called us the *spes gregis:* hope of the flock. Some of these men don't wear religious garb anymore and aren't called Father except by their kids. These days, my old seminary college prefect, Father Ambrose, who was always a whiz with electronics, is a service rep on hospital X-ray equipment. His name is Bob Benzing again and his lunch is out of a sack. When I caught up to him he was married to a shy, intelligent black woman and was living in an inner-city neighborhood in Toledo, Ohio. "It's an old neighborhood," he said on the phone, and then repeated it when I asked if I could come by.

He was fifty-eight, still reed-thin and jerky in his movements, though his hair had grown past his ears. His daughter, Elizabeth Jane, had been born two months earlier. "We're losing our buttons," he said when I walked in, sticking the infant over his head, making faces at her, the old raucous half-asthmatic laugh perfectly intact. Father Ambrose didn't leave the priesthood because his Church wouldn't change. He left because he had fallen in love, which came after a tour in Botswana for the Peace Corps. He went to Africa for the Peace Corps as a priest and afterward came home and met Marian in Chicago. And now he repairs X-ray equipment and takes out the garbage at midnight. *Proceso,* the Spanish might call it.

On the night I visited Bob, he talked of money worries, of

the nightmare vision of ending up on welfare, stuck off in a room somewhere with no work and growing kids. "We have to believe in a provident God who's been provident thus far," he said. He said that nearly his whole life it had been a mystery to him how people got up and went to work every day. He talked of a powerlessness, of being "the recipient of other people's decisions, the people who get on jets and travel around on these big images of themselves." As he said it he drew in the air a large, round, weary, invisible loop. That night he made dinner—hamburgers, fruit salad, sweet potatoes—and ate the last half of it while his two-year-old, Caroline Maria, nodded on his lap. "These memories are alive in us; we live with them," he said.

It is that way for me, too. In the New Testament, in Saint Luke's gospel, there is a place where the writer wonders what something will be like in the dry wood. I wonder that about my life, about all our lives. For as Saint Luke suggests, the dry wood must in some sense reflect, finish up, what was begun in the green.

The Seed: 1950-1955

When I was nine my mother gave me a card with a quotation on the back. The quotation was by a man named Lacordaire, and though it wasn't really a prayer I sometimes said it as one. In time I had the holy card memorized: "To live in the midst of the world with no desires for its pleasures; to be a member of every family, yet belonging to none; to share all suffering; to penetrate all secrets; to heal all wounds . . . to teach and instruct; to pardon and console; to bless and be blessed forever. O God! what a life, and 'tis thine, O priest of Jesus Christ."

It was better, I figured, than playing for the Yankees.

FIXED POINTS. We lived then in Kankakee, sixty miles below Chicago, far enough away for a city that big to be mostly an idea. Chicago in my mind meant Marshall Field and Company at Christmastime and an annual visit to the Museum of Science and Industry. Mostly, my horizons ended at the two ends of Court Street. At either end of this flat east-west Midwestern avenue began great continental plates of corn and soybeans, or so I like to imagine now. In between were my house and the CYO (Catholic Youth Organization) and St. Pat's Church and school and rectory and convent. St. Pat's Church, a squat sandy building administered by the Clerics of St. Viator, seemed huge to me, a basilica where men held gleaming cups and flowed through candlelight. By fourth grade, at age nine, I was up there with them, their acolyte. I went back to visit my boyhood church not long ago and was stunned to see that it was so small.

My father was an airline pilot. I can remember standing by the side of our stucco house next to my mother while he backed a green 88 Olds up a concrete ramp where my brother Marty and I played basketball, turned the car north in the alley, and drove off. He wouldn't be back for two or three days, and knowing this caused both loneliness and euphoria in me. There seemed no pattern to his going, no logic. Sometimes he had to leave in the middle of the night, and then I would hear him moving at the front of the house, talking to my mother, his voice waving through my sleep as though through water. Other times he left after supper, or on Sunday after church, or before Marty and I got home from school.

I remember how life in our house seemed to hold while he got dressed for the field. (He called it simply "the field," as though he were going to lift off from a cow pasture. He had grown up in Kentucky, the third child of nine, a Depression farm boy sitting on wagon tongues and craning his neck for airplanes.) It was as if each of us had a role to play in his going. I would wander upstairs to find him standing in his underwear in front of the bathroom sink, soaping his angular face with the stubby brush he had had for as long as I could remember. He'd be singing to himself, "That lucky old sun's got nothing to do but roll around heaven all day." Maybe he was already up there, streaming across the earth, belted into his cockpit of glowing knobs and dials. All I could see was a razor licking his neck in smooth, steady swipes.

"How come I can't go?"

"Got to take care of your mom, cowboy."

He had to fly on weekends a lot in those years, and for supper on a lonely Friday evening my mother would put frozen fish sticks and frozen french fries on a cookie sheet in the oven. When they came out, the stove warming our little arc of diminished family, Marty and I would kill them with ketchup. (In the seminary that first week I would glance around and see ravenous boys blitzing even their eggs with ketchup. Catholics, I think, have made the Heinz family wealthy beyond comprehension.) The next night, Saturday, my mother might take Marty and me down the street to a cafe called the Chuck Wagon, precursor to McDonald's, where the burgers, gray deathballs, came in greasy wax paper and red plastic baskets. In my mind there was no finer dining. Life was in suspension again, only at the other end, until my father got back, though at the same time my mother's lighter hand made these intervals seem like tiny holidays, respites from my father's disciplines and often harsh anger. The suspension I felt in such times seemed parallel to the snowy state the world was in. The earth was like a surplice, the night a cassock. The sun stayed low on the horizon, casting long shadows on dull colors, producing in me the surreal sensations of walking dream. On Sundays, Marty and I sometimes got to go to the matinee at the Luna. Coming home those three blocks afterward, I knew there was nothing left but supper and homework and bed. Late Sunday afternoons still depress me. By evening I perk up.

The subtle tension cutting our lives was that my father might not make it back. It was hardest on my mother, of course, and she had lived with this anxiety in starker ways a decade before when her then new husband was overseas, in the Pacific, flying P-61 Black Widows, and she was stuck in a flat with two young sons. I was less than a year old when my father went overseas; when he came back and tried to get me to run into his arms, my mother says I wobbled right past him into the arms of my "pop," who in reality was my grandfather.

In Kankakee, in the early fifties, while I swam to consciousness, my mother waited for phones to ring from the field in the middle of bad winter nights. None of us talked about this tension, though once I recall asking my father if he worried about all those lives lined behind him in rows of twos and threes. "Yes, but you don't let yourself think about them, son," he said. "What you concentrate on is getting yourself back down and they'll be fine."

Over my writing desk now are several photographs of my mother and father; the pictures have begun to come unstuck from their cardboard backing. In one photo, my mother is proudly wearing her new husband's wings. Raven hair falls in coils to the collar lace on her modest forties suit. Rita Kyne Hendrickson is only twenty-one and already the mother of two. In the photograph beside it, a young man is clad in World War II flying togs. There is a parachute on his back and his thumbs are tucked up inside the shoulder straps. The boy has a farmer's blunt hands, and you can't miss this about him. Though he is destined to survive this war, and though he will spend most of his years afterward in cities, or near them, he will remain in essential ways a country boy. A sheepskin collar is on the young man's flight jacket. His goggles are pushed up over his head, and he is wearing a skin-tight aviator's cap. He is grinning to beat the band. On the back of the photograph, barely legible, is this: "Honey, how do you like my Mae West?"

Several years ago, my father and youngest brother, who also is a pilot, flew a single-engine plane to Alaska, puddle-hopping all the way. My father was sixty-one and had been put out to pasture by his airline. He and Mark carried flares and sleeping bags and survival rations, and when they got all the way up, my father, who was at the controls, banked out over Point Barrow, spotted the Polar Ice Cap, and turned toward home. Three or four days later my mother and little sister were waiting with WELCOME HOME on a sheet.

Catholicism seemed simply there, everywhere around me, like air. It somehow didn't matter that my house was bordered by the Asbury United Methodist and St. Paul's Episcopal, a stolid gray building that looked as cold as it did empty. The minister's daughter was my occasional playmate, and it is odd to me now that I can remember nothing about her, not her name or face, except once defying mortal sin and standing beside her in her father's vestibule, peering in at the bareness. What did they do in there without a Mass? Even today entering Protestant churches makes me feel slightly sinful.

Later, when we had moved up to a suburb of Chicago (my father's work was soon going to shift from Midway Airport, on the South Side, to a onetime apple orchard on the Northwest side called O'Hare Field), I remember going to my mother upset about the fact that the father of one of my playmates wouldn't be able to go to heaven: he wasn't Catholic. She said it wasn't exactly true that Catholics were the only ones who got in. What made me feel so bad was that I would see Mr. Anderson bringing Billy and Johnny to Mass on Sunday and then taking a seat in the back and just sitting there. I was sure he wished to be one of us. It wasn't fair.

It was a tactile and sonorous and immensely comforting faith, though not one especially chained to logic. Boys got girls pregnant by kissing them with their tongues. (We were not alerted to this physiologic miracle until the last year of grade school.) Padre Pio, Sicilian monk, regularly suffered the stigmata, bleeding profusely and happily from his palms. The world was going to end on January 1, 1960. We knew this because Sister Lucy, one of the three children of Fatima, had written a letter to the Holy Father, detailing some of the things the Virgin had told her during the Portuguese apparitions. The Pope had read the letter and fainted. We knew.

Fish on Friday: it was a badge, a sign, telling the world we were different. There were other signs, too, like the obsessive ripped-off sign of the cross before a crucial foul shot in a basketball game. (Part rabbit's foot, part parochial tic.) On Saturdays the "publics" went to the YMCA and we went to the CYO, where Mrs. Africano passed out Ping-Pong balls and tried to keep a sheen of order. My brother Marty, sixteen months older and fifteen pounds heavier and always street-smarter, once fought a public outside the CYO. The fight terrified me, and as the public started to win, I began sobbing for it to quit.

We had curious Catholic words and terms—like "plenary indulgence" and "ejaculation." "My Jesus, mercy!" was an ejaculation. Supposedly, it got you three hundred days' parole from purgatory every time you whispered it. (The sign of the cross was good for three years; with holy water, seven.) All Souls Day (November 2) was the Christmas of the purgatory parole: every time you made a visit to the Blessed Sacrament, you scored a plenary. A plenary indulgence was like confession, only simpler, it seemed. During the noon hour on All Souls we would go over to the parish church, hang on one knee inside the door, tear through a prayer, go out on the front step, come right back in. If you were fast, you could get a dozen logged in fifteen minutes.

Saturday confession: I am standing in line in the back of St. Pat's in a fresh shirt, having been plucked from afternoon play by my mother. My whole family is here—mother, already forgiven, in the pews saying her penance, tissue on her head (she forgot her hat); father, in line on the other side, hands partially clasped; brother, one penitent over, rehearsing sins. The cleansed sinner ahead of me now emerges. I take the door he politely holds open for me, nod my thanks, go solemnly in, close the door, feel my way through the three feet of pitch to the wedge of cushioned kneeler, lower myself. The place is an upright coffin. I lean forward and press the tip of my nose against the finely meshed wire screen. The screen stings but feels good, too, penitential. The box is warm, furry, mysterious. I hear muffled whispering coming from the other side; can't quite make it out. A sweet-sour scent floats into me: part cheap clerical cologne, part stale musk of past sinners under rebuke.

The little wooden window on the other side is sliding shut, feet are shuffling, a body is rising. My turn. The window on my side starts to scrape open. I can feel his breath, sense his face, his quivering nostril hairs. Only the screen and something more than dark divide us. Microticks of concentration. "Yes?" a voice says softly, inquiringly, but I have already begun, ripping into it, a locomotive beginning to highball: "Bless me, Father, for I have sinned. It has been two weeks since my last confession. Since that time . . ." Somewhere in the middle, with jumbled shame, I slide in my transgressions against the sixth commandment: "four impure thoughts, one impure action." In three minutes it is done, his standard questions, my ready replies. I start the act of contrition as he starts absolution in Latin, the two voices praying as one on opposite sides of the wire. He finishes first. "Go in peace," he says, the final word cut off by the sliding window and his haunchy shift of position. Before I am out the door he is hearing another blurt on the other side.

Early in life I learned how to select a lenient confessor (you usually had a choice of two, sometimes three), the kind who gave you a penance of four Hail Marys, four Our Fathers, four Glory Be to the Fathers, no matter whom you murdered. In the new Church they would speak of penance as a celebration, a rite of reconciliation. For us it was pure purgation and ordeal, with a grocery list of sins, down to number and kind, but I see now it wasn't all bad. For one thing, the world was so good again when you were through. There is something

to be said, I think, for going to a dark box on Saturday after-
noon and externalizing your faults to a voice behind a screen.
If the faith I grew up in is easy to mock, it is easy to miss, too.
The ghetto was dark, all right, but the ghetto had its joys.

Three decades from St. Pat's and Kankakee, on a July Sunday in 1981, my wife and I are driving through St. Paul,
Minnesota. We have been visiting my parents on a lake in
Wisconsin and are now on the way to the airport. A palace
with a green dome floats in front of us. It is the St. Paul
archdiocesan cathedral. We park the car and go in. Noon
Mass is finishing. There is the melancholy crash of an organ.
I am standing just inside the door, looking at a plaque with
gilt letters cut in marble. The plaque doesn't interest me, a
smell does. The smell seems waxy and holy, full of incense
and tallow and imprecise longings. "What is that smell?" I say
aloud to my wife, as though coming from a nap. "Candles
melting," she says, shushing me, giggling. I reach up and
work my fingers across the plaque, lining its hard-edged
grooves, feeling foolish, but thinking somehow this will sustain a smell, unlock secrets.

Why, I wonder, do I seem to remember going to serve Mass
only through tunnels of winter dark? Surely I must have
served at other times, too. An alarm would go off at five
forty-five. The house is still, cold, a ship creaking under my
feet. I dress, go softly down the back stairs, let myself out
through the door the milkman uses, walk the icy five minutes
down South Harrison Street, kick snow from my boots at the
door of the church, go in, get the lights. I take down from
the rack in the sacristy one of the worn half-buttonless cas-
socks, one of the blousey starched surplices. The surplice
always has a good, burnt, newly ironed aroma in it. I get the
candle lighter down from its hook in the hall. I inspect the
taper. It is gunked with yesterday's wax. I light it and go out
into the still-dark sanctuary. Fire drips from my stick. The
sanctuary light is aglow in its red casing; it burns twenty-four
hours a day, 365 days a year. I look up at the altar. Plaster
saints with wet faces gleam down at me. I go to the center of
the altar, genuflect, move up the carpeted step. I light the
candles on the right side first. The Blessed Mother is watching me. In the sixties and seventies, entering statueless
churches and seeing burlap banners with words like PEACE

and AGAPE painted on them, hanging in the places where my old gaudy friends should be, I will feel a strange resentment. I steal a look out into the body of the church. Mrs. Cavanaugh is here, Joe Wojak's dad, maybe a half-dozen more. Mr. Wojak is a daily communicant. Never misses.

At six twenty-five Father McNamara arrives. He faces his dressing table, shoelace untied, face pulpy with sleep. First the amice around his shoulders. Then the alb, bunching it together, kissing it, pushing it over his head and down around his waist. Next the cincture rope around his waist, looping the cord. Then the stole, crossing it over his breast. Next the maniple, pinned to his sleeve. Finally the chasuble. He is robed. He puts one hand on the throat of the draped chalice, turns, nods at me. I take my place in front of him, yank the cord on the warning bell. Together we step out into the sanctuary. A clatter in the pews. Bodies rising. Father hands me his biretta, bows. The Sacrifice of the Mass, time's endless celebration, has begun.

Introibo ad altare Dei, he says. (I will go unto the altar of God.)

"Ad day-oom quee lay-tee-fee-kat you-vane too-tame may-am," I answer, the weird phonetics bobbing out of me like a devout taunt. They mean: to God Who gives joy to my youth.

In time, as I became a dependable altar boy and a lieutenant on the school patrol, various sisters began nudging me toward the idea of the seminary, though what I didn't yet know was that something in my past had already compassed me there. Grammar schools were the seminary farm team in the fifties, and sisters were the scouts. In a way, getting into a school for the priesthood at thirteen or fourteen was as easy as gliding down a stream on a raft—all you had to do was get on and go with the current. Usually the stream flowed into stone fortresses with wide lawns on the edge of burgs far removed from the world, harlots, and the devil. The scouts would nudge in various ways, some of them not terribly subtle. "Getting married is fine, but it's a diamond in your cap to go away and be a priest," one of my nuns once whispered. It made sense. It was an elitist theology, and she was merely passing on what had been passed to her: priests and sisters are first, the married state is second, the single world comes in a lagging, suspect third. I remember another nun's description of priesthood. "It means complaining of thirst—and being given gall and vinegar to drink," she told our uncomprehending class. "It's the paradox of Calvary."

I can picture the room in St. Pat's convent where the sisters ate: long, narrow tables covered with white cloth, rows of perfectly aligned plates with a white napkin rolled in a silver ring beside each setting. The room is scented, perfumed with freshly made bread. The room smells like new milk sloshing and foaming in a bucket my grandfather brought from a barn in Kentucky at nightfall. I wanted badly to see the place where the sisters slept, but couldn't, of course: not even a sister's parents penetrated this part of the cloister. The Protestants, we heard, believed that the priests and sisters had tunnels and secret passageways bored between the convent and rectory so they could have late-night sex. Just like Protestants. But what would Sister Rose of the Precious Blood look like, I wondered, sealed alone in her room, shorn of the yards of starched linen and cotton and crepe that hid her hips, sliced off her hair and ears, yoked her chin as chastely as the lady on the Dutch Cleanser can? Our biggest mystery was how a sister went to the bathroom during the day.

We took terrible advantage of those sisters, sassing them, mimicking them. They worked all day without wages—teaching, conducting altar boy practice, cleaning the church, preparing for tomorrow's onslaught in the classroom, praying. They prayed for the missionaries in China, for our vocation, for people they had never even met. Some of them were anti-intellectual and bludgeoned us with thoughtless theology, but they weren't narcissistic. I doubt if they knew the word. You can talk about what has been gained in the new Church and the new world, and it is much, but to say what has been lost is a harder task.

The pastor of St. Pat's lived across the street from the convent and came over to the grade school to hand out report cards. He was busy with the "larger" things of the parish. He and his curates had cars and golf bags and regular days off, but the sisters seldom left the corner of South Indiana Street. They were brides of Christ tortured by pygmies. "You can hang my body on a gibbet and riddle it with bullets, but I'll never give in to you, class," one sister said about every third week. She dreamed of going to darkest Africa and being strung up by savages, I think. "You're a bold, brazen article," she told me, and she was right. Sometimes, when exasperation had taken her, she'd ram down the aisle with a window pole, a knight in tears. She'd joust us with the pole and we'd stagger in mock wound.

Sisters were scouts; mothers were cheerleaders. It helped to have a devout mother of Irish ancestry, as I did, who deeply felt her heritage and knew the greatest blessing God could provide would be calling one of her boys to the priesthood. Like my father, my mother grew up with the Depression, on a farm in southwestern Ohio. She comes from Murphys and Kynes and gave up a scholarship to a Catholic women's college in Cincinnati to marry, at barely nineteen, a noncom in the Army Air Corps and bear his first son ten months later. It is a truism the Irish produce priests, or once did, the way Jews are said to produce psychiatrists and dentists—it was the family business. There is a passage in James T. Farrell's hard-bitten thirties novel *Studs Lonigan*, where the sainted Mrs. Lonigan says of her efforts to get young Studs onto the flow, "I say the rosary every night, and I offer up a monthly holy communion, and I make novenas that God will give him the call." And when violence flares, as it inevitably does, between Studs and his working-class father, Mrs. Lonigan stands by and sobs to the Virgin. It is an old cycle, so hackneyed it hurts, and I have seen it in my own family too many times. My father wasn't working class, or even Irish, but violence flared often in our family, especially between my father and his eldest son. Marty, two grades ahead, went into the seminary ahead of me and came out five years before I did, and in many ways both created and took the heat in our family. For a long while after he left, Marty wouldn't talk about the seminary. He would get up and leave the room. While I was fascinated, he was contemptuous.

I have no idea how many holy communions or novenas my mother offered up for my call, but I know she prayed nightly on her knees for me. I can see her reclined over the edge of her bed, rosary in her fingers. I remember a prayer card to the Blessed Mother she kept by her bed. It was "for a son's right choice of a state in life." Right choice meant seminary. I also remember my mother coming into my room to hear my prayers before I went to sleep. "What do you think you'd like to be when you grow up?" she'd say, tucking me in, smoothing the covers. I had stopped kissing my father good night by the third or fourth grade even as a physical affection between my mother and me had grown.

"Truck driver." I was keen on the way long-distance haulers pulled into truck stops in the middle of the night and crawled into a bunk behind them in their cab.

"I think you could aim higher," she would say softly.

Religion is rooted in an ability to hope, and if I could never be sure what my father thought about God and his faith when I was growing up, my mother's belief seemed as round and clear as the bell striking noon at St. Pat's grammar school. My mother would have two sons enter the seminary eventually, a third almost enter. (This was my brother Eric, six years behind me.) For a flicker-flash of fifties and sixties time, it seemed to me as though our family had been charmed with a version of the American Catholic dream: sons in the seminary, parents youthful and handsome. My mother was an Irish colleen, my father was Luke Skywalker. I can still remember visiting days in the seminary when the priests and brothers all seemed to be ganging around my family; afterward they would tell Marty and me how lucky we were to have parents like that.

Neither of my mother's sons who went to the seminary would finish, and three of her four sons—Marty, Eric, and myself—would eventually marry and divorce, and one of us, Marty, would marry and divorce again. For a time in our family there would seem almost a blur of quick marriages and divorces. Years after Marty and I were gone from the seminary we used to joke that, between the both of us, we had nearly enough time to qualify for an ordination and that we should petition a bishop for my mother's sake. It was a wan joke because we both knew how much my mother hoped and prayed for a priest in her family. I don't think my father ever wished us to go in the first place, but he had deferred, at least in this, to my mother's sheer joy and will. In a sense, priesthood was my mother's greatest dream. To this moment I can taste the pain of that afternoon in 1965 when I arrived home from the seminary for good and my mother said: "Well, Paul, if we knew you were coming home we wouldn't

have gone to Sears and bought a new air-conditioner for the
station wagon. We bought it specially for the trip south for
your vows." I despised her saying that; it made me feel guilty
and cheap, though I could recognize a little while later she
was only exposing *her* pain, reasoning my departure from
her own hurt feelings. My mother and I used to sit up on
summer nights when I was in the seminary and talk about
the place. She could listen for hours. Mostly that summer
after I left for good, she tried gallantly to pretend a homecoming was fine.

It seems insane now, from the haughty vantage point of
three decades, but in many ways the fifties Church was a
child-centered religion, a kiddie ministry. In 1930 there were
187 schools for the Catholic priesthood in America, but by
the middle fifties, when I was getting in, they were rising like
factories after a war, which is what some of them seemed:
assembly lines for clergy. By 1958, the year I left for Alabama, 381 Catholic seminaries, major and minor, would exist
in the country; within twenty years 259 of them would fold.
The fifties proliferation was answering, I think, the baby
boom and the Catholic rise to the middle class and a general
post-World War II premium on higher education, but also, I
suspect, the significant religious response that sometimes
comes after a people bumps its head against a stone wall of
limits: war had afforded hints of beyond. It was practically a
syllogism: Christian family life is strong; the world is in a
noncombative age; why shouldn't young men be responding
naturally to the devout life? The wider world had something
called the Beats, but the world I knew had the final ripe flex
of an old Catholic muscle: if you have talents, you should
give them back to God in the form of religious life.

So I was the beneficiary, if that is the word, of the last
pitched battle for boy vocations. The incredible thing is that
the kiddie ministry lasted so long. Catholic minor seminaries
had formally begun after the Council of Trent in the six-
teenth century. Four hundred years later, an overriding idea
stuck fast: get a vocation early, pick it ripe, "before the habits
of vice take possession of the whole man." Those are words
from the Trent Council, 1563, when it was determined that
a candidate for priesthood should be at least twelve years old

at his start and not a bastard in the literal sense. Just as iron tends to rust, just as untended soil grows weeds, so a boy will go bad unless put away in a hermetic environment—this, I think, was the logic that had stumbled into modern times. In the sixties, after Vatican Two, the kiddie ministry would begin to collapse like a mud slide, and by the seventies scores of junior seminaries, and even major seminaries, would be standing idle, shards of an earlier glory. The carnival had moved on. A few years ago a survey by the National Opinion Research Center in Chicago found that 94 percent of Catholic boys between fourteen and adulthood had never even considered the priesthood as an occupation.

And yet, while the kiddie ministry lingered, nothing in the Church seemed healthier, or at least more viable. The ministry was maintained into modern times not only by grade school sisters and parish priests and resolute Irish mothers, but by wave after wave of handsome young collared pitchmen for the diocesan and religious order schools—the Oblates, the Franciscans, the Maryknollers—fevered men who rode from grammar school to grammar school with movies and rubber-banded stacks of brochures and detachable mail-in cards in the trunks of their solid-colored chromeless sedans. They were religious Professor Harold Hills drumming through Iowa and Illinois and Minnesota to sign up a boys' seminary band, not for vulgar motives, and least of all for profit, but to perpetuate a system and extend a lineage and light the world. These young charismatic Jesus figures, some still dew-wet from ordination, could seem to a Catholic boy like a Saint Francis of Assisi and a Tom Sawyer rolled into one, not to say a Lone Ranger, who may be a bigger patron saint of fifties vocations than all the saints in the stained glass windows of the Vatican combined. The Lone Ranger myth, in a way, was at the core of the vocation pitch: dare to be holy, dare to be different.

So it was nothing, really, for the graduating eighth-grade class at Holy Redeemer, or Mary Star of the Sea, or Resurrection, to be sending off a dozen boys to the seminary in the fall. Some of these Called might be going only as far as the local diocesan day-hop seminary, while other Chosen, like me, would be riding to a seminary in a far state, rolling by rail with other similarly imbued boys (A WHOLE CAR RE-

SERVED FOR THE GANG GOING DOWN FROM CHICAGO, my mailing said), each of us with decals in the form of pennants gummed on the side of his spanking new Samsonite suitcase. My pennants gleamed: HOLY TRINITY, ALA.

I have been wondering lately why the nuns of my school worked so hard to sign us up. Maybe getting eighth-grade boys to go out into the desert of religious life was an expression of their own immaculate motherhood. I wonder now if many of them weren't hoping on some sly semiconscious level to sit one day in the solarium of a convent nursing home and be able to say to the other forms in the room: "Father's one of mine." And think if she got a bishop!

Grievous Angels

In 1957 I was a Midwestern eighth-grade boy thinking about the seminary with a father who flew airliners. It did not occur to me, nor should it have, I suppose, that priest and pilot are really two opposite symbolic ideas, the one celibate and renouncing, the other sexual and adventuring. Nor was I consciously aware that, nine years before, in January 1948, when I was three and a half, something traumatic and terrifying had taken place in our family, and that this covered-up event had lodged in me, like unseen slivers, anxieties about birth and death and sex which had been growing and shaping and bonding themselves ever since.

THOUGH IT IS possible, even likely, I would have entered a seminary after grammar school in any case, I now believe that the awful history of one winter night, when I was three and a half, and the arousal in me of that history nine years later, in 1957, when my mother became pregnant again, all but cinched my decision to go in, to *flee* in.

But I never really knew it, nor fitted all the parts, until five years ago at my maternal grandmother's funeral. Until then all my conscious mind knew—would have sworn—in the matter of a stillborn child named David Hendrickson, was that once, years before, when I was small, my mother went away to a hospital to have a baby but didn't come home with my baby brother because grieving angels had come for him and taken him instead to heaven to be with Baby Jesus. This was the family myth I had grown up with. The one fact I was absolutely certain of in the myth was that my mother had given birth to the child in St. Mary's Hospital in Kankakee, Illinois. Beyond this I had long been familiar with a hazy heroic story involving my mother and her performance of an emergency baptism on a delivery table in front of doctors and nurses, then sinking into sleep. I couldn't say how I had come to this story, only that I was certain of its truth.

The truth is that there were no hospital and no doctors and no painkillers, and that my mother gave birth to the child at home, by herself, with my father away, and my older brother and me trying in vain to help through a night of cries and torments. The truth has always been there inside me, I presume, as real and tactile as a rubbing you might make on a monastery wall. But because the story was too awful, too awesome to be deciphered or even viewed, I buried it, covered it up, like my dead brother, and what I didn't bury I reinvented.

I learned the truth, which is rarely pure and seldom simple, to paraphrase Oscar Wilde, at the funeral of my last grandparent. Nonna, my mother's mother, died near midnight on Easter Sunday, 1978. She was not only my last living grandparent, she had been far and away my favorite grandparent, and I didn't get there in time to see her go. But I like to think now that the real story of David Hendrickson's birth and death was a gift Nonna sent to me from the other side of life, though she actually had nothing directly to do with my finding out.

The real story fell out because of something I happened to say to my youngest brother, Mark, a few hours after Nonna's wake, the night before we buried her. Mark and I and a first cousin were sitting in a tavern on the outskirts of Xenia, Ohio, the town where Nonna had lived most of her life. Had I not been sitting in that bar, and had I not made this chance remark, I suspect I might have gone on indefinitely with my writer's smug, vague, and pleasant sense of doomed indifference. But Nonna's funeral provided both an unearthing of a story and a jolting from indifference.

She died on the day the Saviour rose. I knew in a general way her heart was failing, but no one called to tell me it was failing fast. The truth is, Nonna had lived so long and stub-

bornly in her little white frame house behind the library on
Edison Boulevard in Xenia that I couldn't quite imagine her
going at all. There were times when I thought she would bury
the rest of us first. She had become terribly arthritic and
irritable in her last ten or fifteen years, and I couldn't stand
to be around her more than a day or two. But there was
something about her independence, her flinty, damnable independence, that never failed to stir me. Her husband, the
man I had called "Pop," had died in 1950, and she had carried on with few public tears. Once I wrote her into a story
that got picked up by the wire services. I said she was nasty
as a mule, and she didn't take it amiss the next time we talked.
She was eighty-odd then and probably some mules were
kinder. A couple of years earlier, in 1974, a tornado had
come rolling into her town one April afternoon, killing thirty-
two people, ripping a hole the size of a man's torso in her
Chevy, sailing pieces of slate from the library roof through
her dining room window and into her walls, unearthing a
giant fir that had stood in her front yard since 1935. I was
working at a newspaper in Detroit that year, and I drove
down as soon as I heard. A few days later I wrote a newspaper story about Nonna and the tornado, describing how
she had spent the first night on a cot at the local YMCA, only
to rise about midnight to point a hickory cane at a National
Guardsman and tell him, look out, sonny, she was going
home. She liked that one, she said.

On Valentine's Day, 1978, I called her from an airport
lobby. It was six weeks before she died. I said I was sorry I
hadn't remembered to get a card out to her for Valentine's
Day, but that I hoped she knew I loved her very much. I said
I intended to be over to see her soon. It was our last conversation. It seemed only a day later that my father was calling
from a hospital corridor to say she was dead.

By Easter Monday afternoon, most of my family had gathered in Ohio. Mark had driven over to Ohio from the University of Illinois, where he was in the aviation school, and I
had flown over from Washington, where I had taken a job
the year before at the *Washington Post.* I hadn't seen my kid
brother in nearly a year, and the talk in the tavern was warm
and rambling and only now and then laced with sadness. I
don't recall how it came up, but suddenly I found myself with

the strongest urge to talk about Baby David Hendrickson, the brother none of us knew. We always referred to this mysterious child in the same way—Baby David. Maybe I had the urge to talk about him because David lay buried in the cemetery, in the same plot, where we would bury Nonna in the morning. I turned to my cousin and said, "Baby David Hendrickson was the infant my mother had in 1948. The baby was born in St. Mary's Hospital in Kankakee. We were living then far out in the country in an old farmhouse. Nonna came to stay with Marty and me while my mom went to the hospital, and after the baby was born my father had to leave for several days on a flight. Mom baptized the kid herself in the delivery room of the hospital."

Mark looked across the booth at me. He is a sensitive, quizzical adult, fourteen years my junior. "That's not true, Paul," he said lightly. "Or at least I don't believe it's true. Hell, I wasn't even alive yet, but Dad once told me the whole story. The baby was born at home, and you and Marty were there alone with Mom. Mom couldn't make it to the hospital because Dad had the car and the phone was out and there was this big snowstorm and all the neighbors were too far away. She thought she'd die if she tried to walk to help. So she had it herself."

I felt dizzy, as I sometimes do when I have to go to an ear doctor and he shoots pressurized water into my middle ear to drain the wax. "Hey, are you all right?" Mark said.

The next noon, after we had buried Nonna, I was due to return immediately to Washington and my job at the paper. I asked my father to drive me to the airport in Dayton. As soon as we were around the corner from Nonna's house I began telling him what had happened the night before. He must have sensed the urgency in me, for he didn't say anything, just kept nodding and not looking over much and chewing his lip a little. When I was done he began to tell in painstaking and painful detail all he knew about that night, all he was able to piece together from the time he walked into the house. He talked in a monotone, in thin, strained words. He finished as we neared the airport. He found a spot to park and kept the engine running. "I remember when I drove in, the snow was piled so high I could hardly find the road. I got into the house and either you or Marty met me at the door and said, 'Daddy, Mommy's been real sick while you were gone.' I ran upstairs and there she was, propped up, with her hair combed. But there was death in the room. She had done her best to clean up the afterbirth. When she told me she'd already had it, and to look in the closet, I thought I was going to faint. I called for the doctor and got a nurse and called her father in Ohio. After the horse gets out of the barn, I'm great at shutting all the doors."

He paused. "It's not something we ever wanted to talk about around home very much, but I don't think we would have denied it, had it ever come up. You and Marty never asked, and while I guess we thought that was a little odd, we just let sleeping dogs lie. It was a family secret."

He paused again. "There are so many damn mysteries to it. Why did the phone lines go out and the electricity and heat stay on? She didn't want me to go. She said she had intuitions, premonitions, the baby was coming. We had just been to the doctor a few days earlier, and he had examined her and said he was convinced the baby wouldn't be premature. She asked me not to go on my flight, and when I reminded her what the doctor had promised, and told her I had to go, she said she wanted to take you and Marty and go up near Chicago and stay with some friends until I got back. But I discouraged that." He seemed to suck at his teeth; it made a flat, low whistle. "I should have listened to her, Paul. She knew. Your mother was braver than I think I could have been. I doubt if I could have made it through that night. I've replayed it a thousand times. I've had to live with the fact I wasn't there on the night she needed me most."

What my father didn't say, but what I knew, was that he had been with his airline only a few years. He was a copilot out of the war trying to make his way up. Canceling a trip for any airline pilot is serious business, but if you're low on seniority and you cancel at the last minute, it could jeopardize a career. My father made a judgment call based on a doctor's hazardous guesses and his own convictions. And the call was wrong.

Only recently have I been able to talk out that night with my mother. On a visit home a while ago I took my parents to dinner at a place we have been going to off and on since I was in grammar school. Afterward we came home and my father went upstairs to watch the news. My mother and I sat facing each other in the living room, in the bay window, which is where the two of us had sat on the afternoon sixteen years before when I came home from the seminary. She looked as pretty as I'd seen her in several years. She had on a soft blue sweater, and she sat with her feet crossed and pulled up modestly to the base of the chair. After a while my father came down. My mother was sniffling a little then, and I was hiding my tears, and while my father didn't join us in that, he took a chair on the other side of the room and listened. "I knew something was wrong—I just wasn't gaining any weight," my mother told me. "By five o'clock that afternoon I found the phone was out. By seven I knew the baby was coming. I just knelt right on the steps and prayed as hard as I could. By ten o'clock I was having contractions. I told Marty to get all the sheets and towels and hot water he could get and bring everything upstairs. I didn't want him to turn on the stove so I told him just to let the faucet run a real long time. I told you to get me tea bags and two glasses of water, one of which I would use for a baptism, if I needed to do that. Then I told you to stand downstairs by the sunroom and keep turning the lights on and off in the hope someone might see it. It was all I could think to do. I had thought about trying to bundle the two of you up and trying to walk to help, but I was afraid I'd have the baby by the side of the road. The drifts were too high, and I was afraid you and Marty wouldn't make it, and I knew I couldn't carry you. So I decided it would have to be this way. I think I finally got Marty to go into his bed about midnight, but you kept coming into my bedroom and saying, 'Mommy, what's wrong? Are you sick?' I kept trying to tell you I just didn't feel very well, but that if you went to sleep everything would be fine in the morning. I don't really know if you ever went to sleep. The last part of it is so hazy. But I remember the baby was born at ten minutes after five."

My mother wants to believe there was a flicker of life in her child, and perhaps there was. She tried spanking it to life, she said. She cut the cord. She dipped her fingers in the glass of water by her bedside. "I didn't give him a middle name. I just said as quickly as I could, 'I baptize you David Hendrickson in the name of the Father, the Son, and the Holy Ghost.' "

The next morning, exhausted and pale and very much in control, she told Marty and me to come to her room, she had a small job for us. She had already wrapped her dead child in sheets, had covered his head. In the closet was an altar candle box a priest had given her only several days before, when she had gone to church to get her throat blessed. "It was a long white narrow box, just like a little coffin. I put David in the box, put the lid on it, and told you and Marty to carry it very carefully over to the closet. There was nothing much else to do then but wait for your dad to come home. He got in that evening."

I asked her why the story had so long been kept a secret, but I think I already knew the answer. "It was years before I could tell anybody about it. I guess it was a combination of shame and embarrassment and sorrow. I don't think I told anybody the whole time we lived in Kankakee, when you and Marty were growing up, and even after we moved up here to Wheaton I could barely mention it. Only a couple of years ago did I tell Mary Wilson, and she's one of my best girl-friends. We were talking about cemetery plots when it came up. I don't think I'll ever completely be over it. But it's okay now."

The morning after I learned this story, my mother and father and I drove over to Aurora, Illinois, where my dad keeps his single-engine Debonair, and the three of us climbed into a clear, cold, wind-whipped May morning. Spring had come to the Midwest, and it was lovely. We flew over lands smoothed by ancient glaciers, freshly turned by plows. We landed in Wisconsin, had breakfast, turned around, flew back. "We're the jet set," my father said, laughing, taking her down. He landed his little craft right on the money, like snapping off salutes. He had on a blue baseball cap with CAPTAIN braided on the brim. My mother sat in the back.

I have tried in vain these last several years to locate that 1948 night in my memory, and though I have alternately cried and cursed and prayed, nothing of it comes, not the towels, not the hot water, not the sheets, not the phone that wouldn't work, or the light switch, or the snowstorm, or my mother's cries. I *do* know I have no trouble recalling events and places that predated that night. I have memories and fragments of memories that go back to when I was two years

old and we were living in Miami. (My father had just begun
with Eastern Air Lines.) And I have a precise memory of the
night we moved into that farmhouse outside Kankakee: we
cooked on a hot plate in the living room, the four of us—
Marty, me, my mother, my father—bunched around the little
burner. My father made us scrambled eggs, I remember.

Oddly, or maybe not so oddly, my brother Marty, who was
five the night the baby came, says he has the same erased
memory and blunted feelings. In all our years of growing up
together, the two of us never talked of it, never rubbed the
stone that might have flint-sparked a memory. Only once
since I have known the truth have I tried to bring it up to
Marty. He said he couldn't remember. I let it drop. Marty
and I aren't close anymore, and talk doesn't come easily between us.

A while ago, on a January weekend, I took a plane to Chicago without letting my parents know I was going to be in the
vicinity, rented a car, and drove down to Kankakee. It was a
miserable weekend. I drove out into a snowy countryside
trying to find the farmhouse we lived in that long-ago winter.
It was lost. It was as if the real farmhouse, like the real story,
preferred to stay as hidden as the one in my memory. I kept
going down endless look-alike gravel roads, the radio on,
finding nothing.

Sometimes I think I can see myself on a landing, madly
flicking a light, though probably this is just sympathetic response and guilt—a man's need to help a scared boy help his
stricken mama. The boy wants desperately to be doctor, husband, nurse to his mother in this hour of her terrible need,
but he is ill equipped for any of it. So he stands on a step and
flicks a light and prays to Baby Jesus, a witness.

I guess I didn't always want to be on a step, or anywhere in
the house, which is one possible reason why a three-and-a-
half-year-old, standing in the lurch between truth and fantasy, between cries of birth labor and what surely sound like
the primal cries of death, would have wiped the night from
his mind and invented a new antiseptic version, one with
doctors and nurses and painkillers.

And nine years later, in 1957, when his mother inexplicably became pregnant again—what then was the boy to think?

I can picture that day in 1957 when I learned she was going

to have another baby, as if it were in daguerreotype browns, motion-frozen in a still photo. My mother was the one who said it. She was sitting in the dining room, and my father sat to her left. This in itself was odd, as she was in the place where my father always sat when he was home. My mother had on a crisp fall suit and her hair looked freshly set. Had she just come from the beauty parlor? Through the window that framed her head I could see our oak trees, and beyond them the summer house and orchard. The grass around the house was still green although August had scorched the rest of the yard. I had just begun eighth grade. Marty was a sophomore at Holy Trinity. It was the first week of September, 1957. I had just come in for lunch.

I took a seat, reached for a sandwich.

"We have something to tell you," my mother said.

I looked up.

"Your father and I are going to have a baby."

She said it and I felt sliced with fear. Why do I recall the precise texture, the exact stab, of this fear? Because of the surprise and shock with which it struck me, I guess. I simply knew my mother was going to die. It was heinous, needless. I didn't know where this feeling came from, or why I was having it, only that I was sure. In seconds the fear had climbed to terror. I still have no idea whether my parents read the alarm that must have been all across my face that noon, but if they did, they didn't say anything. And neither did I. I kept on eating my sandwich, drinking my milk. I wanted to hide behind the glass, climb inside it.

What I should have been able to do at that moment, but somehow wasn't, was blurt out my fear—that I didn't want her to have a baby because I was afraid she would die having it. But I didn't. I couldn't. I knew that would have sounded absurd, nonsensical. Mothers had babies all the time, and they didn't die. At thirteen I was already woefully adept at hiding my real emotions in order to always seem sane and normal, and in this I was the perfect seminary candidate. So I shut up. But I wonder now if the instinctive censure of my own feelings had to do with an ultimate child secret: sex. That is, I knew my parents had gotten together and made love, which meant a baby, which in my mind meant death, and this fact embarrassed and shamed and confused me into silence all at once.

For the next year and a half, well into my first year at Holy Trinity, I lived secretly with night terrors, though by then the object of my terrors had long switched to something else: from death in childbirth to stark sleeplessness. In fact my fears had seemed to transfer almost immediately—from a fear that my mother would die having her baby to a fear of being unable to fall asleep when I went to bed at night. Sleep was something I had never given much thought to. I didn't even know the word "insomnia." Sleep was something that simply happened after you said your prayers and hopped into bed. It was like being thirsty and going to a faucet to take a drink of water, except of course when it was Christmas, when you weren't supposed to be able to sleep because of your excitement. At Holy Trinity my first year, I would lie awake for hours on my back on an iron cot in a dormitory glimmering with my night fantasies, fifty or sixty boys snoring all around me, my imagination stoked like a draft furnace, my brother Marty one dorm over and a seeming thousand miles away, my eyes fixed, *bored*, on the white cross atop the chapel. The cross was outlined with bulbs, like an actor's makeup table, and stayed on all night as a beacon for cars out on the highway. It was my beacon, too, and it came through the window beyond my toes. While my sleeplessness held, I was unable to mention anything of it to my brother, to any of the priests, to any of my classmates. I was afraid, I think, of being sent home. I was afraid they would think something was terribly wrong with me. Eventually, though, like water dripping steadily on a stone, there came a blemish in my fears, the slightest reduction of my pain. The sleeplessness diffused, and then went away. Every night I would say over and over to myself: "So what if you don't get to sleep?"

And the year before, in eighth grade, all during that long lonely fall and winter of my mother's pregnancy, I couldn't tell anyone, either. Once, maybe a month before the baby was due, I tried to hint at what I was holding inside. I already had made application to the seminary by then, had taken a physical and gotten letters from my pastor and school principal. Every day my mother and I waited for the mailman.

One night we were folding clothes in the basement behind the furnace. I bumbled toward the admission that I couldn't get to sleep at night. "You're getting to be an old fuddy-duddy, Paulie," she teased me easily. I loved her more than anyone else on earth. And I couldn't tell her. I was afraid she would think I was crazy.

That night, while my mother and father slept at the front of the house, I lay in my room at the back, listening to the walls as they expanded and contracted, nothing mattering but getting to sleep. The fear that I could not get to sleep prohibited any chance of my doing so, at least until two or three or four o'clock, when in spite of myself I fell through some black shaft of unconsciousness and exhaustion. But while I was awake I prayed fervently for one thing: that if she was to have this baby, the baby, and not she, would die. This baby was faceless, nameless. I had no feeling for the amorphous brother or sister coming into my life. The fears I felt in those hours, moving from my back to my stomach and then to my side and then to my back again, seemed without subject or object or predicate. The fears were too big to reason with.

What was happening, I believe, was this, and of course in hindsight it seems so plausible, linear: the announcement of the coming baby so caught me off guard that I was shocked into a sleeplessness, and within a few days this completely new experience of being unable to fall asleep became my primary fear, substituting for the baby fear, and in fact taking over most everything from that point onward. Only recently has it occurred to me that my refusal to go to sleep for so long was perhaps a symbolic way of keeping myself alive, if not my mother, inasmuch as sleeping can represent to an unconscious imagination the symbolic state of death. Until lately I had always thought of my sleeplessness as an arbitrary substitution for the larger fear, and yet I wonder now, and even as I wonder I grow weary of my own voice, my own theorizing. It may be all of this, and it may be none of it. But the deeper question, unanswered until a few years ago, at Nonna's funeral, was why a presumably normal thirteen-year-old eighth-grade boy should have been so unreasonably convinced that if his mother were to go ahead with a pregnancy it would surely mean her death. Where had the idea come from? It came, of course, from a terrifying night nine years before, and though I had no conscious memory of that 1948 night, it was there inside me, lapping at my psyche as surely as the moon sucks at the tide.

A dream. A brightly lit stage. I am standing alone before a drawn red curtain. Out beyond harsh floodlights are people I can't quite make out. It is both hazy and dark out there, though I think I recognize some people. I am out there, too, which means I am able to watch myself. Now tiny cannons are exploding. They are being fired at me, and though their charges don't hit me, they explode all around me, causing me to feel dizzy and nauseated. Even worse than this are the voices in a low, sardonic drone, the laughing, that I hear coming from beyond the floodlights. The people out there are laughing at *me*, talking about *me*. The more they drone, the dizzier I get.

This jumbled dream, recurrent in my childhood, puzzles me. Sometimes I still get fragments of it in my sleep. Even now I can't recall all its details. More than once when I was young, I remember waking from the dream and going into my parents' room, slipping between their sleeping forms. Several times when I was small I tried explaining the dream to my mother. But the telling made no sense. It didn't even seem that scary.

I see now there may well have been a resonance of death through my entire childhood: church death and family death. Why does the heft of cathedral tunes seem so sad? I think of February and suddenly I can sense the cool, waxy feel of a pair of crossed candles scissored against my throat on the feast of Saint Blaise, patron of throat disease. I think of Ash Wednesday, and I think of the grit—the light sandpaper scrape—of ashes rubbed into my forehead in the sign of the cross on the first day of Lent. Remember man, that thou art dust and unto dust thou shalt return. Lent was redolent of suffering, somber and empurpled, breeding Easter out of the dead land. The statues were draped in violet during Passion Week. "O Sacred Head surrounded/by crown of piercing thorn," we would wail. "O Sacred Head so wounded/reviled and put to scorn."

I remember a Kentucky funeral when I was ten or eleven. I can see the front bedroom of my grandmother Hendrickson's farmhouse outside the little town of Morganfield. The room is cloying with the smell of cut flowers. The flowers are in white vases and the vases are on white stands and the stands fan out around a gleaming box inside of which, wearing a thin smile and a blue suit, sleeps my Uncle Gerald, not yet thirty years old. Gerald, wildest of my father's eight brothers, has drunkenly smashed a car into the side of a bridge and killed himself. He leaves behind a wife and two babies. We are gathered now for the closing of the casket. My grandmother Hendrickson kneels on a red-cushioned kneeler in front of the box. She has on her Sunday hat and dress, and her face is rouged and her eyes are red welts. Her stockings are normally turned down below her knees as she does her household chores, though not today. Relatives crush in on all sides of her—maybe thirty-five or forty people trying to get into the small room. I am squeezed beside her, into the silky folds of her dress. The box is at a level with my eyes. She is sobbing, and the sobs cut through the terrible smell of the flowers. "Take a look," she cries, nearly hysterical. "See what liquor does? I want all my children and grandchildren to see what liquor does."

The mother owns the heart, the father is the eagle. A few days after I learned my mother was going to have another baby, due in the spring of 1958, my father took me fishing. The day had been planned for several weeks, and we drove to the Fox Lake chain in northern Illinois with another pilot who flew for the same airline as my father. The man had a boat and we pulled it along behind us. In the early September air was that distinct Midwestern tang and color that are suddenly there, a week or two after Labor Day, and which hang for only three weeks or so before starting to dissipate into the general bleakness of October. On the way to the lake I sat in the back of the car listening to talk of flying. For four nights I had lain awake. How could my father be so nonchalant about my mother's pregnancy? Didn't he know what this meant?

After we had put the boat out on the water, and had wet lines, and were digging into the sandwiches my mother had sent along, I said, as casually as I was able, "Dad, wonder if Mom gets sick having her baby?"

His pilot friend was listening; for once I didn't care what other people would think of me.

"No," he said, "hardly ever happens."

I pressed an inch further. "But I've heard stories about mothers dying on the delivery table. Something goes wrong; they have to operate. If there's ever a question, which one do they try to save first?"

This time he looked over. His gaze seemed to float into me.

"Depends, Paul. But there's almost no chance of that happening, of that question coming up. I promise you. Your mother's in fine health. Maybe once in ten thousand times does something like that come up."

We are victims of what bores us and what torments us: even Saint Thérèse, the stainless Little Flower, could say on her deathbed in her final hours of agony: "I am assailed by the worst temptations of atheism." My father's assurances did nothing to relieve me.

In October, Holy Trinity's vocation director came to my parish. His name was Father Walter, and he was young and looked athletic and spoke with a gruff, blunt friendliness. I liked him right off. Father Walter showed a movie to the eighth-graders in the school auditorium. The movie was narrated by actor William Bendix of films and television's "The Life of Riley." The movie was all about a boy's life at Holy Trinity. "Chattahoochee," Bendix said of the river that flows near the seminary. "Sounds like somebody with a bad head cold." Father Walter passed around some literature. There was a booklet about the seminary with a boy on the cover in an argyle sweater. The boy was standing at a blackboard and holding a piece of chalk under a question mark. There were three words chalked on the board: Going His Way? On page eight there was a cartoon of a zooming train with the caption: ALABAMA HERE I COME. On the last page were a couple of sentences I read over and over: "Your thoughts about the missionary priesthood came to you because of God's grace; they are the work of the Holy Spirit in you. When God gives something He expects you to make use of it."

After the movie my eighth-grade nun told us to close our eyes, and that those boys who felt called to speak to Father

Walter privately should raise their hands and come forward. Four or five of us felt called. Father Walter was waiting for us in the auditorium kitchen, amid ketchup bottles and old bologna wrappers. It was a kind of makeshift confessional. He took us one at a time. When I went in he knew that I had an older brother already at Holy Trinity. Immediately I had a leg-up.

"So do you think you have a vocation, pal?"

"Yes, Father."

"How do you know?"

"I just feel it."

"Sure?"

"I think so."

"Your vocation is not your brother's vocation—you know that, don't you, pal?"

"Yes, Father."

"What about all those Janes up there in your class? There aren't any of those in the seminary."

I felt embarrassed. I said I could do without them.

Father Walter knew Marty well, and that helped my case. He also knew I already had visited Holy Trinity with my parents the previous Thanksgiving, in Marty's freshman year, when I was in seventh grade. I had loved that visit to the seminary. I got to sleep alongside Marty in the dorms. I played Ping-Pong games with his classmates in the rec room. I went on a Saturday hike to the river. I knelt beside Marty in his pew in the chapel. Brother Urban had given me cookies one evening in the refectory and asked if I might be coming to the seminary, too, when I finished eighth grade. After that visit, I think, my selection of a school was foregone. Holy Trinity seemed like year-round camp with some holy stuff thrown in. On a more visceral level, though, I wonder if I wasn't being drawn to the South herself, to a lush, sultry, overgrown frontier. I can remember stepping off the airplane with my folks in the Atlanta airport and entering the old hangarlike terminal. There were murals of plantations and cotton bales and turban-wrapped Negroes on the walls of the Dobbs House Restaurant. Afterward I sat on a metal-rimmed chair with my trousers rolled while a crinkly-headed old man with shiny palms worked over the tops of my shoes, rubbing the polish into the leather with his fingers. It was my first shoeshine. In Chicago we had left Midway Airport in a snowstorm. But down here the sun and spring were out. In late November. People were mowing lawns.

Several days after my talk at school with Father Walter, he came to our house for dinner. My father liked him, and this further helped. Father Walter said he wanted to know once more, for the record, if I really felt sure about the seminary. I practically stood up and shouted yes. Okay, he said, better begin making official application. I went upstairs to do homework, and the three of them sat in the dining room, continuing to talk. But I knew I had won. After that evening my father was on the downside of any argument to get me to stay home and go to the new Catholic high school up the road.

A month or so later, three or four other eighth-grade boys and I went for a weekend to a seminary run by the Divine Word Fathers in Technie, Illinois. We arrived late on a Friday night. I was led down a subterranean corridor to a room with one straight-backed chair, a white-framed bed, a luminescent crucifix. I lay awake that night staring at the crucifix. I was a budding contemplative, trying to warm myself by faith's fleshy heat.

The baby came, on schedule and without complication, on March 23, 1958. In another two months I would complete grade school. A week before Mark's birth I had received my official acceptance to Holy Trinity. I can remember almost nothing of the night my mother went to the hospital. My father took her early, and when he came into my room some hours later, I was in the middle of dreams. He roused me. "I said it's a boy, son," he said, shaking me. "His name is Mark Kevin Hendrickson. You have a new brother. Your mother's beautiful."

I doubt that any of this would be very important to a book about a seminary experience were it not for a question I have never been able to answer satisfactorily: What were the psychological implications of my fluid escape from home at fourteen? The decision to enter the seminary came between the fall of 1957 and the spring of 1958, which was the approximate time of my mother's pregnancy. Was it just coincidence?

I doubt it. Is it possible that nine years after an apparent and actual night of family death, now thirteen, now scared

and inexplicably insomniac, confronted with terrors of aban-
donment and not understanding them, I should have completed a long-simmering decision to enter a school for the
priesthood, because seminary and religious life suddenly
begin to represent to an eighth-grade boy an antiseptic and
asexual sanctuary—a haven, a womb, for conflicts too large
and jumbled to solve, conflicts about birth, death, intercourse? Is that it? It sounds right, and sometimes it also
sounds a little like a late-night TV movie. In a post-Freudian
psychiatry-worshiping world, it is easy enough to conclude
that one winter night in 1948 drew a kind of string through
the center of my life, and not only mine. That what went on
in an Illinois farmhouse can be said to be a kind of summa-
tion of an entire family history. That that one night continues
to touch and shape things seemingly not in the least related
to it. Maybe—and maybe not. The more psychology and theory I read about Oedipal periods and other things, the more
irrelevant books seem, the more impatient I grow. The theory seems too reductionist, too easy.

But what is not reductionist or easy, what can never be
cheap or gaudy or fantastic or even improbable, is my mother's own incredibly heroic role. That is not a TV movie. My
father may be right: perhaps not he nor any other of us could
have been so brave. It was a tragedy no one planned, except
God, and He must have had His reasons. Perhaps only my
mother was strong enough and spiritual enough to say yes.

That engraved night may have to do with why I suffer
longer and seemingly deeper bouts against confidence than a
lot of my writing friends suffer—or why, in the first place, I
got into a business that demands product and a kind of nakedness and steady testing on deadline. I have no idea how
much, if any, afterbirth and fluid and blood I may have seen
that night, but I do know that bright red colors on women
have always repelled me.

Also, I should say that it is not a little ironic to me that my
baby brother Mark, now in his twenties, a skilled pilot, the
infant I gladly would have had die had it come to any choice
between him and my mother, is today my closest sibling and
one of my best friends.

What are not accounted for here, I know, are two essentially unknowable words—"grace" and "vocation." Who is to

say all this wasn't in the mysterious plans of a mysterious God, that death will have its own hour no matter what, and that what a dizzying snowy night in 1948 adds up to is but a silvery flashing tincture of an Unfathomable Self, and that one day, on the other side of here, we may all be given to know why it happened. Or again, who is to say, as Carl Jung once wondered, that the longing for a Maker is not a *passion* welling up from our darkest instinctual selves, and that therefore I felt pulled by the grace of a vocation in spite of everything, not because of it.

In any case I had gotten in. I was on the river and would not be getting off again for some while. Around the country, in Louisville and Birmingham and northeast Philly, others were getting in, too, each with his own story and set of contradictions. Bob Herzog had spent that summer in Florida. Eric Carroll, another of my future classmates, had worked with Father Gabriel at the parish fiesta in El Modena, California. Joe Hoffman was pitching hay on the family farm in northern Illinois. I didn't know these names yet. But soon I'd know them. And some other things, too.

PART TWO

YEARS OF AWE

When a youth desires to enter the profession among the Arunta and Ilpirra tribes, three courses are open to him. The simplest and least-esteemed method is to seek initiation from members of the craft. The candidate is taken to a secluded spot where he is sworn to secrecy.

—E. O. James,
The Nature and Function
of Priesthood

August 29, 1958

Used to be, eight or nine years ago, you could get a city bus out to Calhoun's grocery, then flag down somebody in a pickup who'd fisheye your suitcase and say, Sure, I'm going that way, hop in, bud. The buses don't go out to Calhoun's anymore, and for that matter neither does very much else. Cars traveling south on the Alabama side of the river these days are usually pulling a speedboat and headed for that big reservoir they built down at Eufaula, and instead of going via Calhoun's, they take the 431 bypass, which swims them through a four-lane glimmer of burger joints and Shoe Cities out into the red clay countryside.

But if you are an unconventional southbound traveler, and if you wish to see that onetime church school they used to have out there at Holy Trinity, you can still go the old way, out Seale Road to Guerry Preuett Highway, past the Mo-Jo Recap Tires and the tin-roofed filling stations and the Fort Mitchell Trading Post ("Weigh Your Fish Free").

THEY PICKED us up that afternoon in Columbus, Georgia, in two battered buses and an old green flatbed truck. Outside the train depot were two scrawny palms. Across the street I saw a building with a sign on its roof that announced: DR. MOFFETT'S TEETHING POWDERS. A billiards parlor stood on one corner, neon glittering through the noon heat like broken glass.

Two trains, one from Chicago, one from New York, had converged on the depot fifteen minutes before. The train I was on had started out at five-ten the afternoon before. My parents had driven Marty and me to the station in Chicago, and on the way our car overheated. My father got out to look while my mother exhorted him through the window that we'd be late. I was in the back seat, hoping we'd be late and not hoping it, too. I looked ready to make my First Communion. I had been scrubbed and talc-ed for three days. We already had sent my trunk Railway Express.

Inside the Chicago depot (all I can see is a great blurred brown room with huge clocks overhead) boys had begun coming up to Marty and clapping him on the back. "This is my little brother," he'd said more or less rotely, and just as rotely I had stuck out my hand. (My mother had said we must do this.) My mother came down to the platform, and at the last second I had brushed her lips with a kiss. She was crying, pulling at my jacket, forking her fingers through my cowlick. I had gotten on the train and found a seat on the opposite side of the car and stared out the window. My mother, I knew, would be waving from the other side. The train jerked into light.

Sometime that night, on his way to the club car with a gang of his classmates, Marty stopped at my seat to ask if I was having a good time. I was propped with a pillow against the cooled glass. Maybe we were in southern Illinois; maybe we had passed into Tennessee. Before I could answer he was down the aisle with his friends. Later I took out my rosary beads and stuck them beneath the pillow. I didn't say the beads, just held them there. Near midnight I got up and walked the length of the train. In the lounge cars I saw some sailors playing cards and smoking. I went back to my seat. The car was dark. Father Walter, who was accompanying us on the trip south, was snoring at the head of the car. I stared out the window at some blurred porches lit with yellow bulbs, at the red clanging dots of crossings. I fell asleep.

That was about twelve hours ago. Now it was middle afternoon in Georgia and I was peering out a bus window. My brother was on one of the seminary buses that had come to get us, but I couldn't see him. All I could see was the wide, leafy streets of a sultry town. We went past old brick warehouses and mills humped along the riverbank. We rumbled across a crumbling bridge. We came up through a stark and brittle brightness, into Phenix City, Alabama. We went past metallic-roofed washaterias and asbestos-shingled Baptist churches and a bait shop and some tar-papered shacks that seemed just propped there, on cinderblock and sand. We went past a school where a band was bleating drills on the lawn. We went past some dirt ballfields and a pecan grove and a creek and a general store and another wider field where stooped figures were picking white balls off vines and dropping them into gunnysacks tied at their waists. The field seemed on fire. And all the while the bus and my stomach going up and down, whining with low excitement, the heat dazzling and shimmering up from the straight black macadam that was so black and shiny and tar-soaked it looked white.

We passed more fields and some stands of high pine and rolling red ground. A voice somewhere behind my right ear yelled, "There's Red Level." I saw barns and someone on a tractor waving. (It was Brother Franklin, once a gunner's mate on a destroyer in the Pacific.) I saw what looked to be a massive figure of Christ nailed to a cross on a hill sloping back from the highway. (It was Calvary; soon I would be taking after-supper walks up there.)

The bus shuddered to a stop, turned right. We rode up a narrow blacktop lined with cedars. (Over the next two years one of my regular work details would be trimming these trees from precarious scaffolding.) At the top of the lane, inside a circle of hedge, was a white cement statue of Saint Joseph, and, just beyond, a handsome white wooden building, long and narrow. Mounted on the roof was a simple white cross. It was the chapel, and it stood that day as it stands in my imagination now: in perfect symmetry to the mowed lawns and edged walks and weeded rose gardens and the eight or nine other fleeced wooden buildings flowing off from either side.

I climbed off the bus and was assaulted by a smell I have never quite smelled again in exactly the same way, as often as I've been back: dried pine needles and fermenting silage and new-cut hay and probably just the terrible holiness of the place.

None of us there that day knew it yet, but within forty-eight hours three-quarters of the school—priests, brothers, seminarians—would be down on our backs: the Asiatic flu would have hit with a vengeance, as if plotted by Protestants. I would be one of the first down and last up. At one point my temperature would top 102. The school would run on a skeletal crew during the ravage, with deputized infirmarians running meal trays and fresh rolls of jake paper and bottles of Pepto-Bismol.

Getting sick early at least meant I got a bed in the infirmary with a semiprivate bathroom and a waxy linoleum floor to trot to it on. For three days, when I wasn't trotting, I lay in a white hospital bed with a bed crank that wouldn't work, staring at a pastel ceiling, wishing anything I could be home in my own sweet bed. Father Killian, the kindly rector, came by several times to visit me and sit on the edge of the bed and say he had written my folks assuring them everything was under control, that school would shortly commence. Father Killian, I would discover, was the school's most prayerful man. He had snowy hair and rooted for the Yankees and once, back East, had managed an A&P grocery. Now he was a saint. He was called by his boys the Great White Father. "Put on the mind and heart of Christ, boys," Father Killian liked to say, pushing up, with his thumb and forefinger, the pink pale glasses that seemed always to be sliding down his nose. Such was the rector's state of prayerfulness that he was said to sneak over to the priests' private chapel behind the infirmary and pray in the dead of night, not turning on the lights for fear of being misunderstood by his confreres. Some days he was said to read his divine office twice, offering the second reading for the salvation of fallen priests. But I was aware of none of this at that moment. I knew only my own retching and loose stool. "Perhaps you should look on all this as your initiation, Paul," Father Killian told me. It was a joke. Father Killian often told jokes that sucked eggs, I would find. "You're going to be crazy about it here, Paul, just as Marty is," he said, and this was no joke. It was the truth.

The Sacred
and the Profane

In the spring the rain ran in orange streams, flumes almost, down from the hill where the pool was, rutting our ball courts and the prefect's rose gardens, staining the cinderblock foundation of our old wooden dorm. We skipped crazily from building to building in those March and April monsoons. Sometimes it almost seemed as though we had moved outdoors. But we knew then home and summer couldn't be far off. Bob Herzog was X-ing off the days on a homemade calendar on the inside of his locker door. And Roger Recktenwald went around saying, "They can't stop summer." Roger would say it and laugh like a bandit. On rainless weekends we had movies outside on the lawn, *The Eddy Duchin Story,* or maybe a chaste thriller, or a Western with Alan Ladd, and then the nuns from the mission across the road came. Images flickered against the refectory wall while a yellow bulb under the pergola, where the water fountain was, drew moths and mayflies.

IF THE FIRST thing to get used to was bells and a schedule wound so tight you could almost hear it ticking, the second was living the Common Life, or the start of one. Suddenly, privacy didn't seem to exist, not even for bodily functions. "I was so out of it when I first went there I used to sneak out to the jakes to put on my deodorant," a Wall Street lawyer told me not long ago. I remember the feeling. I didn't want them

looking at my underarms, either. I suppose life at Holy Trinity wasn't as bad as living belowdecks on a battleship, bunks
stacked four high, sailors standing in line to brush their teeth
—but it nearly was. And besides, we were adolescents, grappling with sexual discovery, trying to compensate, though not
much on a conscious level, for the lack of females in our
environment. Many of us would increasingly learn about females on summer vacations, and we would also learn then
that when problems of relating to women have to be faced in
summer secret, it usually makes for lonely failures. But life
in an all-male society wasn't an asexual experience by any
means, and we were also learning that, though I suppose I
must really speak for myself here. I remember a priest telling
us in a talk one Recollection Day: "You must strive to develop
a love which is not so exclusive as to cut others out. You are
in the process of binding yourselves to a life of nonexclusive
love." I nodded, but I didn't really get it.

I was not precocious. I was nearly fifteen before I had my
first "nocturnal emission," as Father Benedict labeled it for
me the next morning in the box. Some eight hours before,
while all around me boys slept peacefully in ghostglow, this
rara avis had come winging over my bed. I simply didn't know
what it was. I thought I must be having some strange epileptic
attack. I tried to halt it, and that didn't work. I wondered, for
an absurd eternity of stop-time, if I should try waking Ray
Donnellan, who slept next to me, to tell him I thought I was
dying. I was on my back when the attack came, arms akimbo,
half-asleep, letting mildly dirty thoughts wash over me like
warm surf. Then it started. The next morning, in the box,
Father Benedict, whose week it was to hear confessions before Mass, said, with the slightest curl of incredulity in his
voice: "You haven't committed a sin, son. You've had a nocturnal emission." (Full of remorse and willing to accept mortal sin, I had described the baker's glaze that had jumped
from me and icked up my pajamas.)

That afternoon we had a work period after school, and I
remember going into vivid accounts of the night before with
my pal Bob Herzog. Father Constantine, the prefect of discipline, had assigned us to the rose gardens, a prestigious duty
for freshmen, and as Hertz and I hoed clumps of dried manure into a nutrient powder, he told me what *he* knew about

sex. "A wife can never refuse her husband, never, and a husband can never refuse his wife, never, and if either of them does, it's an automatic mortal sin," Hertz said with absolute authority. For days his "nevers" tolled in me like bells.

Bells. The Voice of God refused to stop calling. The first bell came at five-thirty, and the last one tucked us over to retiring prayers at nine o'clock, and in between, I've counted up, were nearly four dozen others, from electric bells to hand bells, announcing the start of class and the end of class, the commencement of study hall and the termination of study hall, the five-minute warning bell for Benediction, the signal to start scraping dishes in the refectory—and so on, from first to last, rising to retiring, first year to last year of theology, lives tooled to fit a new die. This was my earliest impression of what was meant by the Common Life, and though in time I could gain more mature meanings, the idea of precise observance to a schedule never quite went away.

That first year I used to think we'd never get out of church and school. The other day I sat at the table in the dining room with a pocket calculator and figured out that we used to spend three and a half hours a day in prayer (from five-minute one-knee shots to seventy-five-minute sessions) and another eight and a half hours in a classroom or study hall. That left four hours in the normal sixteen-hour waking seminary day for everything else—eating, recreating, going between buildings, moving your bowels. You could hardly afford to be constipated. I remember kneeling before the Blessed Mother's altar some nights with the feeling that tomorrow was hopeless. There were books I hadn't yet cracked.

The paper strain was crushing, and this was a school almost nobody had ever heard of. In the North, home on vacation, you could never find another Catholic, let alone a Protestant, who had heard of the Missionary Servants of the Most Holy Trinity at Holy Trinity, Alabama. "Oh, is that like the Jesuits?" was the first thing someone asked after you had gotten off the unwieldy name. No, it wasn't like the Jesuits at all. For one thing, the tiny American missionary congregation we aspired to was dirt-poor, at least then. For another, it had fewer than two hundred ordained men in its entire organization (as compared with, say, thirty thousand Jesuits worldwide). The Trinitarians, as my order came to be popularly known, had been started about four decades before I showed up by a tubercular itinerant priest, Thomas Augustine Judge, who was both mystic and missionary. Holy Trinity was Father Judge's cell at the outback of Christianity.

One of the lesser mysteries to me is how a flyspeck on the Mystical Body, deep in Russell County, Alabama, with a minimal library and primitive labs, without museums or nearby concert halls or touring lecturers, could recruit so many certifiably bright students and budding scholars and then provide for them a climate to test strengths, to find intellectual muscles.

When I got there, Holy Trinity wasn't even accredited. But that fact didn't stop the learning. Nor the pressure. A decade before I got to see Paris for myself, I had her major thoroughfares and *arrondissements* and bridges and gardens laid out in my head and was trying to write stories set in them. The stories weren't any good, because I couldn't really see the gleam of lights in the wet boulevards, the wide red cafe awnings that bend around corners, the little old ladies who demand centimes for the uncomfortable green metal chairs in the Jardin du Luxembourg. I could only imagine these things, but the fact that I could imagine them at all, and that I owned a mental map of Paris ten years before I got there, is owed in large measure to a priest-professor who was convinced that if you were going to study French, you had to have a love affair going with the world's most beautiful city —even if you lived chastely behind seminary walls. Father Benedict got to sail for Paris every summer to take courses at the Sorbonne. In the fall he would come back, a raging Francophile, and let us know how dreary and provincial we were. But he drilled the nuances of the language into us, and for that I'm still grateful. Today, his pupils dispersed, *monpère* ministers to a black parish in rural Mississippi. I can see a faded copy of *Bonjour Tristesse* above his pastor's chair in the parlor. I can see him slapping his ear and saying to somebody, "*Répétez. Répétez.*" Father Benedict never quite got over —and for that matter neither did we—the timorous seminarian who took one look at the phrase *pupitre grisé* (gray desk) and shot out "Greasy poopeetree." Instant legend.

The seminary was so focused, and the schedule so skewed, in the direction of books and prayer, it was hard sometimes to remember you were a teenager. There seemed little time for being a boy. Saturday afternoon was free (unless you were on jug), and so was Sunday afternoon after Vespers. Sunday night, following Benediction, the paper chase began all over again. There was little flexibility in the schedule and none in the course load: you took what they assigned you. It was a thirteen-year grid to ordination: algebra to the *Aeneid* to Aquinas. Every afternoon we had a 60-minute study period, every evening a 90-minute study period. In those sometimes desperate 150 minutes we were expected to get everything ready for the next day's classes. I can recall one seminarian crying himself to sleep before exams one year. Eventually I would know a boy lying in a bed in the infirmary during exam time, a psychotic grin on his face, announcing to any passer-by, "My arches have fallen, my arches have fallen." Who knows: maybe they would have caved in at home.

I have wondered, in the years since, if the toughness of it did not develop an inner toughness and resilient strength—and at the same time develop a certain pessimism and lack of compassion. The ability to focus swiftly, to maximize minimal work times, is something the seminary gave me, even if I had to learn the skill out of terror. Along with the ability to focus fast, to beat sixty minutes out of an hour, to be self-disciplined and largely self-starting, came, I see now, a too-early identification with adult roles, a too-ripe need for reward. Almost from the first we were trained to look for essentials and to work for perfection, and while the former is a valuable skill, the latter usually wreaks unhappiness. The rigidity of our environment reinforced what I was terribly good at— hiding my true feelings—and retarded the spontaneity I so badly needed. And yet all that sounds too slick and judgmental. Much of my own control and neurotic need for perfection I had picked up handily on my own long before I ever set foot behind a seminary gate.

The priest who presided over the schedule, made it run like a Swiss movement, was Father Constantine Doole, Prefect of Discipline, a.k.a. the Bayonne Bomber, the Frog, and sometimes, with particular nastiness, the Nigger Frog. Father Constantine had a wide, flat nose and a jaw going early to jowls. He had a habit—a tic, almost—of inserting a "huh?" at the end of his sentences whenever he was annoyed. The mannerism must have begun as a nervous punctuation mark, but by the time I came along it had honed itself into a nifty rhetorical device. There was never any comeback to one of those insistent huhs, no possible excuse. You blew it, gent. He was an incessant smoker and sucked in like a furnace cigarettes held between two upright fingers. He spoke deeply and sonorously. He was the man who loved consonants. Broom was "broom-uh," mop was "mop-uh," gig was "gig-uh." One of his beloved words was gent. "Okay, gents-uh," he'd say, and you knew there was no way the rest could be good. But there were other sides to him, too. On Recollection Sundays, when it was his turn to preach, I remember Father Constantine standing before us with a handkerchief folded into a small triangle in his right hand. As he talked, he dabbed at the perspiration gathering on his upper lip. He was nervous and vulnerable during those talks, a prefect out of role, and the talks were quite good, actually.

I have never been quite able to decide whether there was something naturally repressive about Father Constantine or whether circumstance and the vow of obedience had pressed on him a role he never really wanted. The latter may be closer to the truth, and the truth also may converge near the middle. It was Father Constantine's job to bend the twig double. But I never saw him break it. In the Rule of St. Benedict (which my religious congregation didn't follow but which would apply in some respects) it is written of the monastery disciplinarian: "In administering correction, he should act prudently and not go to excess, lest in seeking too eagerly to scrape off the rust, he break the vessel. Let him keep his own frailty ever before his eyes and remember that the bruised reed must not be broken." Father Constantine didn't use a switch; he did it all with his grimaces and his huhs.

And yet there were occasions when he seemed more anxious to be free of the yoke than we were. I remember him chaperoning a dozen of us on a trip in town one night. We were winners of an in-house college football pool. He didn't wear the collar, and far from being a damper on a rare evening, he seemed almost like a giddy sophomore. At the restaurant he didn't offer to buy us drinks, but at the movie he bought rounds and rounds of popcorn.

After lights out some nights that first year, he would come

back in and announce an impromptu party. These forty-five-minute parties amounted to little more than a case of soda and some cookies and free talk sitting around in our pajamas, but we felt like lottery winners. Once, I remember, he brought in a radio and we got to stay up and listen to a heavyweight fight.

Mostly I saw him as enforcer. What he could not abide, I think, was someone attempting to get away with something under his nose. The issue was control, and he maintained it with gigs. Any priest in the school could give gigs, but Father Constantine was the prime giver. Profanity, of course, nearly always garnered gigs. A "hell" or "damn" might be good for a single gig while a "shit" or "suck" might mean an automatic three. Suck was our ace curse. It was an adjective, a noun, an imperative. We hissed it out—"What the suck was that?"—aware it was foul, though not quite as foul as that other word. The Prefect of Discipline hated suck and every so often went on a tear to stamp it out. Some evenings during colloquy he would come lightly into the room in his crepe soles, stand over by the door. He'd position himself with his hands folded behind him, tucked up inside his cincture belt. He'd flip the cincture upward, another nervous tic, I think. He'd reach out with the tip of his shoe to straighten a corner of the rug. "Hello, mister," he'd say amiably, nodding at the boy nearest him. After five or ten minutes we would become desensitized to his presence, and in a while someone invariably would let fly a suck. "Come over, mister," he'd say, and before you could move you knew you had three. On the way to Benediction, Father Constantine might lurk in the hall, trying to get you with the ashes from his cigarette. Generally, you were glad to get his ashes. It was a sign he liked you. It was his own benediction. I got a lot of hot ashes down my back, though not in the beginning.

The gig list was posted every Saturday after lunch. It sealed fates, announced dooms. You would look for your name and the number opposite it, stroked in blue in Father Constantine's large, bold, neat hand, and if the number was a three or more you reported to his office in work clothes in forty-five minutes. The rest of the school had the afternoon off; you had a swing blade at the swamp. Jug was over at five o'clock. You had erased your three gigs, and a new week's sheets had begun. Some seminarians got so deeply in the jug hole they never got out. Others had done something so unspeakable the prefect dispensed with giving them numbers altogether, simply wrote "indefinite jug" after their name. This, I think, was how the nasty name Nigger Frog came about. I'm not really sure now why we thought of him as a frog, although it may have had to do with his way of speaking. But also he taught biology, and the high point of every year's lab sessions was dissection of amphibians: there may have been some dismembering fantasies on board. In biology class Father Constantine took a week to explain the facts of life in a grave, detailed, scientific voice, broken by a few witticisms. He explained them in minute detail, assuming, I think (and rightly), that many of us knew nothing. He drew pictures on the board, passed around slides, used "penis" and "vagina" like religious terms.

Father Constantine's three high school dormitories stood in a row under one roof. At one far end were the jakes, and at the other far end were the prefects' offices and living quarters. In between were the rec rooms. The building—long, low-slung, red-roofed, caving in the middle—was homemade, built from timber cut up on the hill. The freshman-sophomore dorm, where I lived, consisted of a vast open room where four rows of iron cots and bunks, spaced at about four-foot intervals, marched off to the woods, or at least the jakes. In between the beds were wooden folding chairs, one chair per boy. Along the walls were our lockers, homemade jobs cut from plywood. Every so often, but always on Saturday, crews of seminarians came along under the prefect's direction and swabbed the dorms down. Strands of mop string would catch on nails on the floor and encrust there. After the mopping, the mops were hung out back on racks where they dripped gouges into the red soil. On my way up to our outdoor ball court after inspection, I'd get a whiff of those mops and gag. Once Father Constantine saw me. "Don't do it here, gent-uh," he said.

Slowly I began to venture from my timidity. Eventually I got on to reading books under the covers. I'd be humped up with my flashlight and copy of *Rebecca* and pretty soon I would feel a tap. "Come out, mister," Father Constantine would say. "Three, mister. See me in the morning." He'd confiscate the book, too. Father Constantine nearly always doubled back after lights out, so the thing to do was try to wait forty-five minutes before going beneath the covers. This was hard to do, given how dead on our feet most of us were by nine-thirty every night. Some nights the prefect must have set his alarm for midnight, because you'd see this dim black form and a glowing red dot flowing horizontally through your sleep.

If you were lucky, the prefect had assigned you to a bed under a window ledge or next to one of the dozen posts that ran from the floor up to the rafters. This gave you a fraction more privacy, a sense of definition to the room's vastness. Some students brought throw rugs from home and put them between their bed and chair; that was about the extent to which you were allowed to customize. I got assigned to a bed next to a post rutted with initials. A few months later I was moved against the wall next to a radiator. On a trip in town I bought a three-dollar crystal radio and an ear plug. In March I tuned in the NCAA basketball finals, giving periodic updates to the beds around me. The radiator made a terrific antenna. Hissing and clanking at my ear, it was hot water bottle and aromatic Muzak.

I remember a seminarian a year ahead of me, from Ohio, who was something of an electronic genius, and one night after supper I sat in the pergola watching him tap a homemade telephone into a line directly below Father Constantine's window. He had rigged up the phone over in the ham radio shop, I believe, stuck it in a glass box, and was now proceeding to dial the folks back in Ohio, charging the calls, if I've got this right, to people who lived up the road. I was in my first year and incredulous. The guy has flipped, I figured. The place has cracked him. Actually he had just gotten more brazen. Later I heard he had been tapping into lines all over school for weeks. They caught him and threw him out, though by then they had other things to pin on him, including the murder of a frog during free time in the biology lab (hot wires) and buying a bottle of Chianti at a restaurant on one of our free days in town. One day he was there among us with his dopey smile and loopy walk and the next he was gone. Before the prefect put out the lights that night he told us the phone wizard had ulcers and had to be sent home.

Maybe he did have ulcers. He had great speed, Frankie did, but no control. Most of us were just the opposite—lousy speed, emotional overcontrol.

"Benedicamus Domino," the class president would call out every morning when we awoke. *"Deo gratias,"* the rest of us groggily answered. There was no talking but this. It was still the Major Silence. We washed, dressed, filed over to chapel by five forty-five. "Let us place ourselves in the presence of God," Father Constantine would say from his pew behind us. "Let us make acts of humility." The light on these cold, black, predawn mornings could seem like ether. The world was a tuning fork *yeng*ing in my brain: *Et in unum Dominum Jesum Christum filium Dei unigenitum.*

Today's meditation is on penance, and the prefect already has read to us from the founder's words. "The Church learned from Jesus Christ the truth the world hates. The world has never accepted the lesson of penance, the world never will; and this, really, my dear children, is the reason, practically the entire reason, of the opposition of the world to Christ and His Church. The Lord speaks of a strait and narrow way to the Kingdom of Heaven, and no matter where we look, on all sides, we see a cross. My dear children, remember we are sinners and we are the children of sinners and in sin did our mothers beget us."

Thawing, or starting to, during Mass. Washed daylight bleeding in through tawny windows. Knees full of needle ache; any day now the bones will rip through. Five minutes, ten minutes, fifteen minutes. Probing for a new spot on the board. After breakfast, in the dorm, waiting for bed inspection, we'll pull up our pants legs to examine one another's red ridges and bumps. I'll have Osgood-Schlatter knee disease before I get out of here.

Shifting forward on my elbows to take the cramp out of my back. Ah, better. In two more minutes, a new cramp, a new deadlock of muscle. The way you break the clamp is to lurch forward. The pain must be offered up for the poor souls in purgatory. A prayer comes: "O my Jesus, raised upon the cross between earth and sky, like the good thief at Thy side, let me say to Thee, Lord, remember me." This is nothing, I

know, compared with eternal damnation. The book in my
pew describes what that is like. Saint Theresa of Avila, mystic
nun, had a vision of hell. It is a place, she writes, "where
devils tear the flesh with red-hot pincers."

After Mass, breakfast. You could always smell the coffee as
soon as you hit the sidewalk outside chapel. We sat ten to a
table in the refectory, and every morning there were exactly
twenty pieces of toast on two serving plates. There was never
enough toast, which in time spawned an expression. We
would come in, take our places, spy an empty seat, shrug,
then silently mouth before the prefect had intoned grace:
"More toast." Someone had left. We thought it was terribly
funny, but what it really was, I think, was survival response.

Our two cooks were the Abbey girls, Miss Elsa and Miss
Julie. Miss Julie was the softer and plumper of the two and
looked almost grandmotherly. Her sister, Miss Elsa, looked
and talked like a top kick on a Russian women's road crew.
When either of them was angry there was seminary hell to
pay. "Get your buns off the counter!" Miss Elsa would command the waiters, and you hopped to it. What she meant was:
Get over to the counter and pick up the platters of brown-
and-serve rolls. We got these pasty buns at every meal but
breakfast. I always wondered if Miss Elsa wasn't trying to get
off a small pun with that line. Probably not. Actually, I
thought buns meant testicles.

"What are you digging for, boy, gold?" Miss Elsa once
roared across the refectory at me in front of the other waiters
as I blithely scratched my crotch and waited for the troops to
come over from the chapel. (That was *one* good thing about
being a waiter: you got out of chapel early.) The Abbey sisters
may have been a trifle hard on wretched puckies at seven
o'clock in the morning, but there is no doubt they knew how
to feed one hundred ravenous seminarians and not take the
place to financial ruin. I haven't any idea why Miss Elsa and
Miss Julie should have given up whatever life they had in
Wisconsin to come to the boonies of Alabama to put in seven
grinding days a week in a seminary kitchen. They lived down
below the refectory, in one of the guest houses. They had no
social life that I ever saw, save maybe an occasional evening
visit from a charitable priest. They were at their posts before

daylight, and until after seven in the evening, though I think they did get home in the afternoon for a nap. Every day they did the same thing—cook tubs of eggs, make stacks of toast, put out pitchers of milk. The pitchers were aluminum, and in time became as battered as old football helmets; the waiters would fill the pitchers from huge milk cans brought up from the farm. There was never any scarcity of milk. Our eggs, however, were usually watered and sometimes powdered. But we were glad to get them in any form. What we were not so glad to get were the pieces of beige crud that sometimes showed up in the eggs. We swore these tiny cinders were the Abbeys' makeup.

Nearly everything about my new life seemed different. The way moisture beaded on the iced tea pitchers. The way late afternoon in study hall felt, your body freshly cleansed, the roses climbing by the window and the fragrance of crape myrtle bushes drifting in, the air so concentrated and still and mysterious.

There was a communal joy to supper. Since we had neither dice nor coin, we used our fingers and a primitive form of craps to settle disputes over extra food. A few high rollers were famous for betting a week's, even a month's desserts on a single choose. "I bet a guy a year's desserts once, won, and the next day he left," insists a friend of mine named Butch Evans, who has never been hampered by his hyperbole. Choosing worked thusly: the guy across from you took evens, you took odds, or vice versa, and on a count of three both of you threw out one or two fingers. If the number of fingers totaled up an even number, and you had evens, you won. There were only so many combinations, and there were boys whose reflexes were so quick they could change their decision in midthrow, having anticipated my choice. A junior named Carl Seeba, from Dothan, Alabama, a slow-talking, fast-thinking Southern boy, had me all but convinced he was reading my mind. Usually the prefects allowed choosing, even participated on occasion. Choosing settled a) who got the ball after it had gone out of bounds; b) what records were going on the hi-fi in the rec room; c) whom the last piece of toast on the plate went to.

Local black men and women worked in the kitchen and in the seminary laundry and helped out with the farming. The going rate for hired black help in the early fifties in Russell County, Alabama, was two dollars a day—twelve dollars on a six-day week. The seminary, the best employer for miles around, paid the Blue Cross of its black employees, and additionally the help had "toting" privileges: at night we would see them going down the lane, single file, glass jars of succotash or beets or mashed potatoes on their heads. Eventually the blacks were making forty dollars a week, a princely sum.

These Negroes of Holy Trinity fascinated me. We had Negroes in Illinois, but they didn't sway down the lane with jars of leftovers balanced on their wrapped heads. Sometimes, going across the cotton fields on hikes to the Chattahoochee, we would come on their houses and churches. Some of the houses had painted gourds hanging in the doorways. The gourds were to ward off evil spirits, I was told. Some Negroes owned their patch of land (through most of the forties, Russell County land could still be had at ten dollars an acre), although most, I think, were farming on the share. Their places of worship, like their homes, seemed just stuck there, in the middle of nowhere; sometimes you couldn't even find a lane leading to them. I remember standing outside a black church in a wide field once, listening to the clapping and strange high sounds pouring out from inside: "What do you think of Jesus? He's all right. He's all right." Their worship was no more foreign than mine, though I couldn't see that.

Two prominent Russell County Negroes worked at the seminary. One was Andy Flute, who had a mule and a wagon with wooden sides. Andy would come to get our garbage. Once he had worked in the Birmingham coal mines. The legend about him was that he had outlived a crop of hag wives. Nobody knew for sure how old he was; I heard ninety. The other prominent Holy Trinity Negro was Esau. Esau had a son, Junior, who worked around the place, too, but Junior got into some kind of trouble and had to be let go. His pa was devoted to the seminary. Once Esau had worked the riverboats plying the Chattahoochee. He first came to Holy Trinity as an odd jobber, and by the time I arrived a decade later he was the school's Man Friday. One brutal December day Esau backed up to a fire outside one of the garages. He had been fooling with some machinery and had come over to warm himself. His hands were wet with kerosene and so he wiped them on his trousers. His pants ignited and both of his legs were severely burned. They carted him into town, where the doctors at the hospital wrapped him like a mummy but didn't give him a tetanus. The burns got infected and Esau died. On the way home from a Jayvee basketball game a few days later, a dozen of us went to his wake. The funeral parlor was a shack somewhere in the bowels of Phenix City, and we pretty much clattered in, unthinking. I saw Esau on a dais amid pots of cheap flowers. The casket sat behind a scarlet curtain, which was to be drawn, I suppose, when the wailing got out of hand. The room seemed no bigger than a couple of walk-in closets. After a while the funeral director went over and started a scratchy record. I tried to say a prayer for Esau, but it wouldn't come. I felt like an infidel.

Although Miss Elsa and Miss Julie have long departed, a few of the blacks I knew from my seminary years still work at Holy Trinity, tending the few priests and brothers who live there. I stopped in to see them on a visit in the spring of 1981. Corrine was in the kitchen, still humming to herself. She got embarrassed when I asked what the tune was. "I make them up, Brother," she said. She kept calling me "Brother," though I had said when we half-hugged, half-clasped that I had long ago departed. She said she couldn't recollect exactly, but she thought she'd been working for the priests and brothers for thirty-five years. Lela Mae, her bony sister, was in the next room ironing, and I wandered over to say hello. I wondered how many thousands of clerical shirts and altar cloths and table napkins and boys' underwear Lela Mae had ironed and folded in her time. We talked for a few minutes, and then she told me she was hurting bad inside because just the previous week another sister's son had shot himself and some of his family in a nearby town. "The son didn't die; the kids did," she said quietly.

She kept ironing. Then she said, "Little bit ago I said to Brother Michael, 'Brother Mike, you're about the only one left around this old place from the old days.' And Brother Mike, he said, 'Not exactly, Lela.' And I said, 'What do you mean?' And he said, 'Well, there's me and you and Corrine and Paul Anthony still in the family.'" Paul Anthony is Corrine's and Lela Mae's brother, and he also works at Holy

Trinity. The sisters, I believe, named him after one of the order's earliest priests.

The next morning, in a cold March drizzle, I skipped over puddles in the sidewalk, just as I used to do, to the chapel, where an eight o'clock school Mass for the local black children was going on. The priest saying the Mass was Father Walter, my old seminary recruiter from eighth grade. Father Walter has had several assignments in the intervening years; in the middle seventies he became pastor of the small parish that survives at Holy Trinity. I went in and took a back pew. Despite the rain, the chapel smelled woody and good, like a summer attic. I looked up at the old lanternlike lights that have hung down from the ceiling since 1928, when the place was built, and it was easy to remember the quiet that also hung down on limp black spring nights in the fifties when I was in my pew in the front row. Father Judge, the founder, used to tell his earliest associates that Holy Trinity was their Bethlehem; two generations later, when I came along, the chapel was still a boy's Nazareth to take along, even if he didn't know it just then, even if he should one day stop wholeheartedly believing in Nazareths.

In the pews in front of me this day sat kids in sweat shirts and leather school jackets. One jacket had SWEATMAN lettered on its back. In the sanctuary, on the floor, a small stereo played gospel music. Father Walter read the gospel and then closed the book. He went over and shut off the record player. He began his homily. "The deep mysteries of the pain and suffering of Jesus have a connection with our own lives," he said as the kids squirmed in their pews and a redbird warbled outside the window. "Try to hang on to in your heart the reality of God. Whether you want to believe, buy it, is entirely up to you. There is so much of God for you to take. Even our biggest ideas of God are so small."

In the afternoon the sun came out, steaming the place, and I hiked down to the Chattahoochee. I wasn't sure I'd find my way. I went along past Father Judge's first cabin, an old whitewashed slave shack that the founder converted into his first chapel, with a kind of hut off the side where the priest heard confessions and slept fitfully, then rose in the middle of the night to pray and write more letters. (They've jacked up the cabin now and put it on a stone slab and made it into a historical site.) I went along past the spot where the sisters' first motherhouse, and later, the priests' novitiate, used to stand, both of them destroyed by flames three decades apart. (A sturdy brick retreat house, functional and entirely bland, is on the spot now.) I found the little grotto to the Blessed Mother which Father Judge and two brothers built by hand in 1917, carrying stones from the nearby creeks, mixing their own crude mortars. The grotto still stands, back from a bone-white lane, into a thicket. Finally, I found the sloping swath down through the pines that had been cut years before by the power company. The path led me to the Chattahoochee.

The day was still wet from the rains; rich green ferns glistened at my feet. It was cool beneath the huge pines, and their browned-out needles, fragrant as a humidor, made a soft matting beneath my shoes. I felt bowered, protected. As I got close to the river I began hunting for the Spanish fort that Brother Franklin had discovered in 1956, after reading newspaper accounts of the supposed ruins of a stockade built by seventeenth-century conquistadors from what is now known as Florida, intent on protecting the northern fringes of their tropical empire. The fort was supposed to be somewhere near the seminary property, and after long hunting, Brother Franklin located it. The site is now a registered national historic landmark; for two and a half centuries, until the day in 1956 when Brother Franklin found it, the fort had been lost. Records and a description of it had resided in archives in Seville, Spain, since 1679. When I was in the novitiate we used to hike down to the fort on free afternoons and dig on the perimeters of the official excavations, coming away with shards of pottery and glass, thinking ourselves wildly rich.

As I got close to the river I began searching for the fort. I couldn't find it. I thought it was near Snake Creek, but perhaps my memory was deceiving me. After a while I gave up, feeling disconsolate, and went to sit on the river's edge. The Chattahoochee was as torpid and muddy as I remembered; Spanish moss wound like gray cotton candy through the trees lining its shore. I sat on the bank, hoping a barge or a pleasure boat or a Spanish armada might come by. None did, but the river itself was enough. There is a poem about the Chattahoochee I've discovered that I like very much. It's by a Southern bard named Frank L. Stanton, and it closes, just as surely as if it had Holy Trinity, Alabama, in mind: "The grieving Chattahoochee/Dream-weaving Chattahoochee/And whatever be its secret still it holds—enfolds it fast."

In a while I got up and hiked back, perspiring as I climbed the gradual inclines to the highway. I took a different route this time and crossed a railroad track sitting high on a white sandy roadbed. The track disappeared into a thicket of trees. I remembered how I used to fantasize about hopping freights to Florida, but in all the hikes I ever made to the river with my classmates I don't believe I ever saw a train on that track.

When I got out to Guerry Preuett Highway I decided to stop in at the old seminary post office to see if Sister Basil still worked there. Several years ago Sister Basil celebrated her fiftieth anniversary in religious life; forty-seven of those fifty years were spent at Holy Trinity, most of them in the campus post office. The Holy Trinity post office, still operational, is a doll-sized building with a green roof and white siding. In its day, when the seminary was at full enrollment, the facility operated as a second-class post office. It eventually slipped to a third-class designation and is now just a branch of the station over in Cottonton, from whence it came half a century ago. The local farmers and blacks still pick up their mail at the little shingled building, and Sister Mary Basil, once of the East Coast, is their sorter and stamp seller and postmistress and community newspaper all in one. She's still there. Mostly, she just sits all day and waits. It is her apostolate.

She was about to lock up as I walked in; it was the feast of the Annunciation (March 25), and she told me that the priests and brothers and sisters of the community were planning to renew their religious vows at an early-evening liturgy. The nun stood behind her wire cage in her fine old religious garb, framed by mail sacks and "Wanted" posters and a row of rubber stamps on hooks along the hall and also a falling, lovely afternoon light.

On one side of the room I could see a gas stove, a refrigerator, some files, a vault. Behind her I could see a small black desk with a blotter and a vase on it. A single white flower emerged from the vase; I couldn't quite tell if it was artificial. Most of the room, I was willing to bet, contained the original items the government had put there in 1923. Sunlight filtered through the screen dividing us. Sister Basil's fist was stuck up into the slack of her face. It was a strong face, almost masculine, not exactly a hawk's, but far from a lovebird's. She still had the Brooklyn accent, and she hadn't lost the cheek, despite half a century in Southern mission fields. I reached through and shook hands.

"How old are you?"

"Think I'm telling you?"

I looked at the framed certificate on the wall behind her; I could just make out the signature of Harry S. Truman.

"It's my commission," she said, pulling her head toward the wall, not turning. "Got it when I became official postmistress in fifty-one. I tell people it's my sheepskin."

"Think that's really his signature?"

"I don't know and I don't care if it isn't. I don't care who signed it."

I said I had been over to see Roger Recktenwald's sister, Audrey, the night before and that we had had a nice talk about her brother.

I said I guessed I'd better let her close up.

"So how's your folks? Your dad still a pilot?"

"He retired a while ago."

"Too bad. I aim to die on this job."

Hardship

<hr />

Things speak indelibly of their time. The whiff of ammonia mixed with radiator heat will never fail, I suppose, to arouse in me longings for Christmas at Holy Trinity. Christmas was the one time of year they left the heat on all day in the dorms. It was such a rare blessed event. Heat was part of Christmas, as much as tinsel or carols or the big gaudy tin star over the life-size stable scene down by the gym. Heat meant Christmas, and vice versa. The heat would mix with the ammonia fumes coming off the wooden floor, a deodorized Turkish bath.

HOLY TRINITY, Alabama, is a hard place in the 1950s, and not the least of it is that the congregation has no money. By the time I arrive, four decades after the founding, there is some effort at bookkeeping. The energetic Trinitarian who holds the purse, who runs the farm, who collects the tuition payments (such as they are), who wangles new cars and prize bulls and cast-off clothes and reject lumber, sometimes getting these things for little more than a corny gag and his blessing, is Father Norbert Sharon, seminary Procurator. Father Norbert, who walks very fast and springs on the balls of his feet and has the irrepressible good humor of the Fuller Brush Man, had come south to be a missionary in 1948. Now, in the late fifties, he is begging for God. To say that he has a business sense, that he enjoys handling money, putting it to

87

the Lord's uses, is like saying Ted Williams saw something white and hit it with a stick.

Father Norbert is originally from Iowa, where his daddy once had seven farms and also one of the first motorcars in the state. Father Norbert's daddy also had the Midwest Lumber Company, whose phone number was 5050: WE TREAT YOU FAIR. As Holy Trinity Procurator, Father Norbert, his daddy's son, has a jillion holy schemes. Once he gets the Baptist mayor of Phenix City, Mr. A. A. Thompson, to donate a hay rake. Mr. Thompson, a deacon at the Baptist church, has the Columbus Motor Works across the river in Georgia. The hay rake has come in on a trade or a repossession, but anyway there it is one day sitting out front of the dealership as Father Norbert drives by in a seminary car. The next thing anybody knows the seminary has a new Case hay rake. Back at school Father Norbert says: "Mr. Thompson asked me about the Pope; I got the rake."

Another time, pressed for dough, Father Norbert comes up with a scheme called the Dixie Box. The Dixie Box is a small cardboard carton containing a cotton boll, a magnolia leaf, some Spanish moss, a piece of sugar cane, a pinecone. These are then assembled and packaged and sold up North by the thousands to schoolkids through the Catholic Student Mission Crusade. The boxes go for two dollars a throw. No one, not even Norbie, knows how much moola comes in from this brainchild.

Seminary cars: It seems there is a syndicate of true believers up North, in Detroit, who are enamored of the good honest work of these impecunious Trinitarians toiling to erect the Southern Cross. The syndicate is headed by a man who has all kinds of Motor City connections. Every other season or so, a couple of the missionary brothers from Holy Trinity fly up to Michigan to pick up one of last year's solid-colored models. The syndicate even comes up with a free truck or two. This would seem quite enough, except that one connection leading quite naturally to another, "twelve non-Catholic friends on the board of directors of the Ford Farm Implement Company," as Father Norbert describes them, also wish to help. The next thing anybody knows, Holy Trinity, Alabama, is an official experimental farm for the Ford Company, which means all kinds of expensive equipment can be shipped down, written off by the good people at Ford and put to needy use by the friar-farmers of Russell County. Pretty soon a railroad car is standing on a siding over at Fort Mitchell, and in the car are a tractor with a front-end loader, a hay baler, an automatic posthole digger, a silage cutter, and —biggest catch of all—an Allis-Chalmers HD6 bulldozer powerful enough to change the topography of southeast Alabama. Additionally the seminary gets hooked up with Auburn University on an experimental basis, and V. O. Deloney, the county agent, also comes by to advise on aluminum ear tags and hoof nippers and Screwworm Smear No. 62, not to mention the precise mixture of nitrate, sulfate, and potash for this sandy loam.

The farm Father Norbert manages never quite manages to pay its own way or laden the refectory tables to the extent some benefactors would like to think it does. Nonetheless, it is a vital part of the Holy Trinity mystique. There is about the farm a kind of Trappist purity, and perhaps the least proof of this is that the soldiers who man the mess halls over at Fort Benning are only too delighted to pay premium prices for the seminary's eggs and milk. Father Norbert is delighted to charge, and the school's 1,000 layers are apparently delighted to lay, coming up with 1,600 eggs weekly. What Fort Benning doesn't want, the Goo-Goo Restaurant and St. Francis Hospital and the Big Apple Super Market in town do.

Goobers. Every fall, two or three weeks after school begins, Father Norbert's peanuts are ready for harvest. The seminarians are the harvesters. One hundred boys, bare to the waist, spend all day in sweltering fields out by Red Level, stooping, shaking, rolling vines. From the road the dust cloud looks like an atom bomb explosion. The boys have T-shirts tied around their noses; their forearms swell with sweat and grime and rag-itch. The work consists of an almost continuous stoop, and lasts all day for three or four burning days. Lunch is usually served outdoors from the backs of flatbed trucks. You earn a Dixie cup of ice water only after you've been up one row and down another.

In all, twenty acres are harvested, and every year there is the small air of holiday. At first. Father Norbert walks up and down the rows in khaki pants and a black shirt and straw hat. He has a walking stick and he cries with nearly unbearable enthusiasm: "Hup-ho, hup-ho, let's go." Ray McCormick, from Gulfport, Mississippi, is working one year beside a new seminarian from Illinois. "Afternoon, Father Norbert, afternoon," McCormick says, nodding, smiling, as the priest passes by overhead. After he is up the row a few feet McCormick says, "The mother. I'd like to pitchfork him." But the gripers you will always have with you. Eventually the crossbars of goobers are loaded on the seminary trucks and tied with ropes and covered with canvas and driven to market in Eufaula, three tons of profit groaning down Guerry Preuett. The coolies go back to translations of Caesar and the Pythagorean theorem.

Perhaps Father Norbert's greatest legacy at Holy Trinity is Norbertville, which is a clot of five-room cementblock houses for the Negroes across the road at St. Peter Claver Mission. The village gets started after one of Esau Hartman's kids is bitten by a rat in his sleep. The child awakes one morning and there is blood on his ankles and on the coarse blanket at his feet. "I love kids and I hate rats," Father Norbert says, setting off. The houses cost only $800 and are built with Number 3 lumber and reject doors, but they are sanitary and sturdy and have real floors. The Negroes are grateful to the point of tears. So that it does not seem totally like charity, Father Norbert asks each family to contribute three dollars a week from its earnings toward the village. In the sixties some people in and out of the order will cry "colonialism" at the thought of a village built by and named after the white employer in the straw hat across the road. But that is hindsight and probably taking pure intention out of context.

Seasonally, Father Norbert feels it his obligation to get on a train and personally visit some of the seminary's Northern benefactors. He has a clergy pass on the Illinois Central, and he gets off at various stops—St. Louis, Chicago, Decatur—blessing at each stop the various visions of the Lord's munificence, stuffing, in his small black overnighter and pants of his clerical suit as he goes, the checks and odd tens and twenties and fifties and even hundreds that, before a trip is over, may add up to three or four thousand dollars in ready cash. Father Norbert promises to return soon to the good homes of Webster Groves and Winnetka. "It got to where I was raising fifty thousand a year on my own," he says years later.

"I figure when it's all added up I have personally accounted for something over two million." Lest all this sound venal and be misinterpreted, let it be said quickly that the Order and the seminary can use every penny of the holy dough, at least in the period we are talking of here, and that Father Norbert cares not a fig about money in and of itself. He is not after any cushy life-style of his own. (He is so tight he squeaks, his confreres say of him, and there is no particular humor in their voices.) What Father Norbert and a few others in the Order care about is the game of getting money, building piles of it on the Lord's monopoly board. Except religious fundraising is much more than this, too. Father Norbert knows, as a few others in the community know, that God financially helps those who help themselves, and that if the Order is to survive in the years and decades ahead, it must continue to acquire sound financial base. Father Norbert feels that a person in religious life can be creative with money and still keep avarice, like the devil, down. Good stewardship, if you wish a Biblical context. Father Norbert knows about wealth addiction.

Before he comes to Holy Trinity as official Procurator, there is no standardized program of tuition or housing fees. Things are a mess. Father Norbert sets up a tuition program, sending out monthly statements to boys' parents. As it is, the total costs of sending a boy to the seminary are almost a joke: $360 per year, which breaks down to $1.33 per day. This is all Father Norbert asks. And even that can be waived. "No boy who seems to be an acceptable candidate is ever refused admission because his family hasn't a big bank roll to back him up," it says in one of the Order's recruiting booklets. Every month the motherhouse outside Washington sends down two thousand dollars to Father Norbert, and from this, plus the tuition payments, plus his visits to Northern benefactors, plus his schemes, the priest must make ends meet. Father Norbert is the first to admit he doesn't know everything about money (his brother Jack is a Chicago stockbroker and really knows something about it), but on the other hand he does know the essential truth of a saying he is fond of quoting to his confreres: A one-eyed man is king in the land of the blind.

•

Boys' schools are alive with Gothic stories, and ours was no exception. Old boys used to tell about the seminarian who stole up to the hill one moonless night, poised himself at the edge of the diving board, sprang, and jackknifed into concrete. He lived, although as a hopeless vegetable.

The Great Rat Epidemic struck in the spring of my freshman year. Glistening foot-long rodents were devouring Brother Michael's chicken yard, the foundations of the chapel, our lockers, our minds. After lights out and the dorm was still, we'd hear them grinding away like beavers on our plywood lockers. They'd go for the locker doors, the shelves, and in the morning we'd see miniature pyramids of sawdust. Some mornings we'd wake, pull a handkerchief from the pants draped over the chair beside our beds, and find a filigree of holes: they were mad for mucus.

Leo Wilson's dad came down from Syracuse on a visit. Mr. Wilson was in the exterminating business, and he had just the thing for these impious marauders: Compound 1080, a sodium fluoracetate, odorless, tasteless, so toxic it would kill you within seconds of touching your tongue. (The exact number of seconds became an item of hot debate at meals.) Father Constantine directed upperclassmen to pull the lockers away from the baseboards and draw them into semicircles: Conestoga wagons against savages. The fiendish black powder was mixed with water and set out in inviting bowls along the walls. Father Constantine said that anybody who went back there wouldn't live to tell about it, but that if he did somehow survive he'd be on a work detail the rest of his seminary life. The warning worked: nobody got close, except the rats, and they were sorry. One morning we rose to find a huge salivating beast jumping at the foot of Jim Sullivan's bed. The poison hadn't quite finished him off yet (maybe it had only brushed his paw), and so the thing twitched in front of us, then flopped like a Mexican jumping bean. Sully, still weak from an appendectomy, struggled for his locker to get his camera: he knew this was a historic moment. Pete Krebs, a junior, came in on his way to the jakes, saw the rat twitching, ran outside, got a two-by-four, came back in, and clubbed it to death. The cross was not our only sword; even Christ got mad at the money-changers on the temple steps. It was still Major Silence, but we applauded Krebs anyway. In a week the Rat Plague of '59 was over and the lockers went back against the baseboards. Several nights later, after lights out, a boy crawled across the dorm on his belly, got under the bed of a classmate. His hand came up from the deep, slimed across the kid's pillow. A scream took off through the dark, climbing like a high sneeze.

Rats plagued my first year; so did "uppers." Once, when things in the dorm bordered on mutiny, Brother Michael and Brother Franklin, both of whom had muscles like full moons, came over to rattle a few heads. Brother Michael was in charge of the chicken yard. He had come south in the forties, from Division and Western streets in Chicago. When I knew him he was a fierce-looking three-hundred-pounder in his late twenties. He had one eye and one arm. (His other eye and arm were lost to a dynamite explosion while blowing out tree stumps down by Lonesome Duck Lake.) When I was a freshman and assigned to Brother Mike's dung-cleaning crew in the chicken yards, I remember watching him swoop up fat hens destined for the Sunday table, stick their squawking irreligious heads in his armpit, pin them there with his sweaty stump, giggle, then wring off their necks with a delighted little jerk of his good hand. Brother Michael had a high, squealy, almost girlish laugh. You wouldn't have wanted to make lengthy speeches when he was riled. His pal, Brother Frank, an old sailor, had a face that looked like leather dried in the sun. They were a formidable pair, ideal for quelling a band of uppity juniors and seniors. Brother Michael: "So this one afternoon, Frank and I go over to the dorms to see if we can be of some help, and here's this *punk*, a junior, standing in front of the door to the attic where they keep all the mattresses and spare beds. He tells me I can't go up. He's standing in my way. I pick him up and heave him across the room. He lands on the opposite wall and folds up and slides toward the baseboard. We go upstairs and here are six juniors working over this poor first-year kid. They have his hands and feet intertwined in the coils of a bedspring, crucifixion style. Well, we take care of that little problem. No more problem." High, squealy laugh.

The furnace that heated my dorm was in the bowels of the old high school classroom building, adjacent to us across a cracked walk. In its earlier life the building was an army barracks and had been dismantled and trucked over to Holy Trinity from Tuskegee Institute in Tuskegee, Alabama. The building had a hulking furnace in its basement, crucial to our warmth. The furnace room looked like a set from *The Hairy Ape*. The coal was kept outside in a three-sided cinderblock bunker and was wheelbarrowed into the furnace room every afternoon before rosary. When I got to the novitiate the novices themselves had to stoke the furnace for morning heat. My classmate Roger Recktenwald now admits he used to set the alarm at four-thirty, fumble for it, take his shoe from under the bed, then bang on the pipes for the next twenty or thirty minutes while he tried to go back to sleep with the other side of his brain. Then he'd get up.

Since I couldn't remember how the furnace worked, I asked Roger to explain it. "The process was that at about nine o'clock at night you'd stoke that mother up good, then bank her, then lay some heavy raw coal on top of the live coals and cover the whole thing with a much finer coal, damn near smothering it, so that it would burn slowly through the night. This was putting it to bed. Then at about four-thirty in the morning, or whenever you got down there [Roger is chuckling here on my tape recorder], you would shake it down, stoke it again, and try to build a fast head of pressure. Technically you were supposed to get all the water out of the pipes, crack the valves, and let cold water seep back in as the fire began to roar. But this was not half as dramatic as cutting the valve off altogether and stoking that son of a bitch white hot and then opening the valves all the way so that a stream of cold water hit red-hot pipes and the heat went coursing through the pipes with a hellacious clang and bang, waking the rest of you mothers up and obviously taking the risk of blowing the system wide open." Several times, I recall, the system did blow, and once it blew all the way. We didn't have heat in the dorms or the chapel for two weeks while new parts were shipped from New York. There was hell to pay— on all sides.

Before we were forced to learn the finer points of stoking a furnace, the missionary brothers who lived at Holy Trinity did it for us. There were about half a dozen missionary brothers assigned to the minor seminary, and they were not in

training to be priests. They were manual and clerical work-
ers, most of them in their middle twenties, who lived the
three vows of poverty, chastity, and obedience, plus a life of
obscurity. They got to wear the religious habit and sleep in
the faculty wing and eat in the priests' dining room, but they
weren't priests, or intending ever to become priests, and few
bones, at least then, were made about their subservient status.
Later, in the sixties, some of them would tell the priests to fix
their own damn leaky toilets. Termites and ants are colonial
beings, and so, too, are the men of religious life, though not
nearly so much as they once were. Once there was a division
of labor and a seeming predestination of roles that an individual seemed to have little chance of changing.

After a while you could almost guess which brother had
furnace duty that week by the quality of morning heat. Some
mornings there was only a trickle of warmth, and you knew
then that Brother Henry O'Sullivan had overslept. Brother
Henry was in charge of the town shopping; he was also our
self-appointed sports expert. Every day during the week he
got to put on his black suit and drive into town for provisions.
If you had a doctor's appointment you got to ride in with
him, and since he was usually gone all day, you also got to eat
with him at the Goo-Goo Restaurant. Sometimes Brother
Henry would pick up socks or underwear at Metcalf's for the
students. (You'd get permission for the purchase, and the
prefect would then hand the town shopper a note, and
the amount would be checked off against your running account.) Every afternoon Brother Henry came back to school
with a laden car. We thought his job a racket, and so probably
did Brother Henry. He had a lantern jaw and scuffed his
black penny loafers with immense cool. He gave you the
strong impression that someday he was going to make the
cover of *Time* magazine.

Brother Henry liked my brother a lot, because Marty had
a set shot from sixty or seventy feet out that no basketball
coach in his right mind would ever use at a critical point in a
game. Brother Henry was always working on Marty to perfect his bomb, and in time Marty nearly did. "They'll remember you, Hendrickson," he used to say. Once, at the Bibb City
Tournament, Marty came off the bench, paused at just over
the half-court stripe, and fired the bomb. I hid my face with

my hands, even as the ball streaked through the net, rippling the cords. We were behind, and after that we went ahead. After that I figured Brother Henry knew an awful lot about life, even if he was a lousy furnace man. I figured that if he ever left religious life he'd probably end up in the general manager's office of a pro basketball franchise. He did leave religious life, and for a long time I never heard what became of him. Somebody said Brother Henry had married into wealth, and that sounded right. I made a call the other night and found out he tends bar in Florida. He's happily married. And still wears black penny loafers. And can buy and sell you on sports trivia.

Father Constantine's three dorms were connected to each other by heavy wooden doors fitted with tightly wound springs. The juniors, who slept one dorm over, and the seniors, whose dorm was on the other side of the juniors, nightly came pounding through with huge airs of superiority. The idea was to stiff-arm the door on a dead run so that it slammed back against the frame with a terrific bang. Once, when a virulent flu had nearly the whole school down, a junior named Marquis, who was one of maybe a dozen spared the plague, came through our dorm with his usual hauteur. He was woefully short for such a seemingly superior attitude. He always wore spit-shined shoes and had reddish hair that curled on pipestem apple-white arms and legs. His sidekick was Roger Skifton, roughly the same height, and together they were the local Gestapo. "Sawed-off piece of sharkbait," my pal Bertin Glennon once called Marquis, which was as apt a description as anyone had come up with. Actually, I got along fine with Marquis; not only was he a classmate of my brother's, he had once lived in the same town we did. On this particular day, during the flu ravage, with nearly the whole freshman-sophomore dorm down, all Marquis could see as he pranced through was pale forms in no mood to fight. What he didn't see was an especially fat and loathsome sophomore struggling to get to his feet on the other side of the room. Marquis bounced on down the dorm, greeting the sickies with a loud "Suffer!" He hit the door at the jakes, surveyed the stalls like a reigning monarch, slung his towel over a ledge, and occupied the first hopper in the first row. The hoppers, as I've said previously, didn't have doors. Marquis was on the throne for maybe ten seconds when a galloping-sick body, diarrheal unto death, came rounding the corner, ripped down his pajamas, and plopped atop him. It was the fat, loathsome sophomore. "No, no, no," we heard a muffled voice screaming.

Despite all, Marquis made it. He is Father Clif now, working with juvenile delinquents in Orange County, California. On the Saturday I rode with him, we hit three detention facilities; Father Clif said a Mass and preached a sermon at each. He had a tuft of goatee. He was still woefully short and walked with the old high, kicky bounce. The shoes had their same gloss. The first place we hit was the Joplin Ranch for Boys, high in cool green hills overlooking a taco factory and a polluted greater L.A. We walked through a concrete block dorm, past boys reclined on cots that were made up with gray blankets. There were wooden shelves and lockers beside the beds. "Look familiar?" Father Clif said. "Holy Trinity," I said. "This one's built better," he said. In a while I watched him set up for Mass in a tiny, musty wooden chapel that the boys had built themselves. The priest positioned the paten on the altar cloth, then placed an unconsecrated host on the plate. He took a small plastic bottle from his shirt pocket and poured out wine into makeshift cruets. "For all the time I've been doing this work I know of maybe one kid who has really gone straight," he said. "And maybe six hundred of them go through Juvenile Hall in a month. There's a lot of frustration. What I try to share is that there's another way, another feeling."

In a while the kids began to drift in, in prison denim. "Hey, Father Clif, I heard your car got stuck in the mud," said one boy, maybe fifteen, who was in for stealing cars. Father Clif shot the kid a grin. "Sit down, you," he commanded. Mass began and the priest seemed to lose himself in it. It was a warm spring Saturday afternoon in 1980, and I couldn't help thinking that somewhere down below, cool California people were smoking dope and making love and sitting in sushi bars and being utterly fascinated by their bodies. At his sermon Father Clif surveyed his flock. "What people are looking for, I think, is something inside that will make them less lonely, less scared. But the only things that happen quick that I know of are popcorn and McDonald's."

•

It's a small marvel to me that more of us didn't crack from the strains. One of the brightest people I have ever known, in or out of a seminary, ended up, in the final week of his final year, looking like a mirror ready to shatter. I found him pacing, five steps over, five steps back. The prefects had told him to stay in his room. So he paced. We were older by then and had moved from dorms to rooms, and one of our commandments was: Thou Shalt Not Enter Another Seminarian's Room. So I stood in the door and tried to hold a conversation. This seminarian and I had worked together on the school paper and yearbook. We had palled around occasionally in the summer in my dad's olive-drab helmet-humped 1959 Rambler American, going out to Rockford, Illinois, to visit some Trinitarian sisters; calling on prospective seminarians as a volunteer summer project; thinking ourselves at the ripe noonday of our vocation.

So here he was on the other side of the river Styx. There were only a few days left before school was out, and while he paced, the faculty was over in a room in the cloister deciding which boys would be asked back the following year. My friend didn't make it. He may have been one of the two or three brightest students in the history of the school, and they voted him out.

A while ago I looked him up. In the intervening years, half of his stomach had been cut out. We had lived in the same city, Washington, for nearly a decade, both of us dimly aware the other was there and never bothering to find out. One February Saturday I called him up and there he was: same voice, same corkscrew humor. He was married now, had kids, lived in the suburbs, attended church (his wife is a charismatic Christian), spent weekends teaching his son how to count cards in poker and beat electronic computer games. We arranged to meet for lunch, but it got called off. We didn't see each other for another eight months, as it turned out.

Then one autumn afternoon I sat talking with him in the dreary coffee shop of the building in downtown Washington where he works as a planner and speechwriter and occasional lobbyist for one of the country's most powerful corporations. What he really is, I think, is a resident brain trust. He said they had never really found a niche for him at the company, and I knew instantly it was because he was too smart to be held to any one job and too contemptuous of, and probably naive for, corporate star wars to make it to top management. He was as fast and perceptive and funny as he ever was, able to peel back in a second to the core of anything I wanted to bring up. What I wanted to bring up—and I was trying to find a way to do it—was the faculty's rejection of him in the last week of a brilliant minor seminary career. He must have read my thoughts. "They wouldn't let me go on, you know," he said. "Their tests, plus that visit to a psychiatrist we all had to undergo, said I was psychologically unfit for the life. They said I might crack later on from the pressures. I have to think I proved them wrong, because after I got out I was taking a full load in college and was supporting myself by working for a senator on Capitol Hill. But anyway, it was God's will."

This last he sort of tacked on, and so I said, "It was their interpretation of God's will."

"You've got a point there, of course."

The next morning, before I could find my way to my writing desk, he was on the phone. He was at his office downtown and had looked up a story about the seminary I had published a month or two before in the *New York Times*. He sounded excited. "I think you're discovering that you've never left," he said. "You're still there. I don't have to search my memory for it, either. It's just there."

I couldn't get rid of him. That afternoon he called me again. He had another thought, which became four or five thoughts. I've had this experience with some others. At first they don't wish to talk. Have nothing to say. And then once you open the trunk you can hardly get it shut again.

The public evidence of our classic liberal arts schooling would come later, when the brightest of us would enter places like Harvard Law and Johns Hopkins Medical, coming out of these schools with distinction, while the rest of us, a tier or two below, would find ourselves gliding through Rockhurst or Rutgers or Penn State. When I was in graduate school in English at Penn State and it came time to demonstrate a foreign language proficiency in order to get the degree, I simply presented myself one afternoon at the little building by the library that housed the Latin department and asked to be given a test. The chairman didn't like my implied arrogance but told me to show up the next morning at ten. I did and he handed me a lengthy passage from Cicero. He said I could use my Latin dictionary in translating it. That made it like monkey work. I finished the passage in about an hour and a half. That afternoon he called me at home. "Where did you go to school?" he said. "I was in the seminary," I said haughtily. "Had six years of the stuff." He offered me a job teaching low-level courses, but I had other fish to fry.

The most unlikely seminary scholar I knew has his Ph.D. in Russian from Cornell. After the paper pressures of the seminary, his doctorate was mostly a snap, he said. Somebody else I know worked on the law review at NYU, then clerked for a justice of the Supreme Court. Somebody else got ordained, became a widely known scholar of moral theology, left the priesthood, edited the world's first bioethics encyclopedia. And on it goes, an impressive list (maybe legacy is the better word), most of us, I suspect, having discovered in our own lesser or greater ways that we were brighter individuals than we were generally given to know inside the walls. As with some other things, we had to leave to learn that.

Christic Figures

———

They were more than teachers, these two dozen men who watched over us and prepared us for the future. They were Christ figures in religious gowns and Mission Crosses, and they dominated our lives. I think we feared and loathed and cared for them in a richer way than any of us knew. If we, in the years since, have known a Diaspora, so, I think, have they. Several are dead now. One went to South America to be a missionary and ended up falling in love with a nun. One is a recovering alcoholic who works in a ward in Ohio where he once was a patient. Another has made his way back from the ledge of nervous breakdown. One is married to a black woman and has two small children. Several are out on the missions, a couple still teach, and at least one other strikes me with the same awe and impenetrability as he did when I was sixteen and taking third-year Latin and he was chalking lines from Cicero onto the board.

HIS NAME was Vincent Fitzpatrick, and he was our animus, a man whose shadow side we seldom saw, to use the terms of Carl Jung. There was an aura, spiritual and intellectual, about him. Part of the aura, I think, came from his aloofness. One could not imagine Father Vincent hugging someone at a sixties guitar Mass. And because he never took the top job at the seminary, but stayed number two, he didn't have to make the key decisions that would have brought him off the mountain. Perhaps he instinctively knew he wasn't any good at making decisions. Or maybe he liked the air up there, which is to say he was aware, I think, of his own legend, maybe even subtly promoted it. There wasn't anything cold in his distance, just a height you couldn't scale. I doubt if even his fellow priests felt they could scale it. His subjects were Greek and Latin, and he ate them for breakfast, lunch, and supper. He had a way of instilling terror when you didn't have your translations prepared. As his voice grew quieter his anger mounted. A thumb raised to furrow the back of his head, as if in stony disbelief, was an immediate cue for coming passion. He was terrific at making you feel guilty, as if you had personally injured him with your stupidity or unpreparedness. "I guess I'll have to give you gentlemen the Dutch Rub," he'd say, and you felt you could hear feathers crashing in the next room. Like some great savage football coach, a Lombardi of Latin books, he worked essentially on negative emotion—anger, fear, guilt, grief, recrimination. The results were often awesome. As with Lombardi, his cardinal virtues were hard work and second effort. His true gift, I think, was driving us to things we never knew we could do. It was all of it together, his talent and ego and self-sacrifice, pushing him forward, into our lives.

His face was craggy enough to be on Mount Rushmore; we used to joke he was born a thousand years before Christ. (Actually he was only in his early forties when a lot of us knew him.) His hands perpetually shook, whether he was saying Mass or lecturing in a classroom or spooning soup. (Especially when he was spooning soup.) His walk was a creaky jerk, usually hurried, from side to side; we used to say he'd been run over in a chariot race. We called him the Old Roman and Zuggie, after zeugma, a Greek figure of speech. He had only an M.A. in the classics, but we felt he was smart enough to write shelves of texts. (We did find his name footnoted in several, as I recall.) Although I realize he was teaching, and shining, only at the level of prep school and junior college, I still believe he could have held his own on a university faculty. I looked up his master's thesis once. It's on a fourteenth-century scholar of Saint Augustine named Bartholomaeus of Urbino and is dissertation-length. Other priests on the faculty had their doctorates, but Vincent Fitzpatrick was our symbol of academic excellence. I think all of us craved to please him, and I wonder if even now he can decide whether what happened at the seminary was a hemorrhage or a natural evolution. After he told me my translations had pizazz, I walked around on air. I wasn't sure what pizazz was. It was the way he said it.

He was notorious for pop quizzes, "quickies" he had run off crookedly on a duplicator in the faculty mailroom. We'd see him coming down the hall, briefcase in one hand, the loathed, purplish, wet, and curiously sweet-smelling tests in the other, and panic would set in. "I have something here FOR you," he'd say, coming through the door. For some reason he emphasized his prepositions. Maybe it was a private joke. Once, during a quickie that he was administering to another class, a dog began barking outside the window. Father Vincent creaked over to the window, studied the rude beast. *"Tacē,"* he said. It is Latin for "Silence." In the imperative. The dog shut up. Whimpered and quit. Somedays the Old Roman would creak through the door and the first word out of his mouth would not be English. "Uh, *nonne juvabit . . . ?"* he'd begin, and you knew then he had arbitrarily decided to conduct the class in what he refused to think of as a "dead language."

He may have had a genuine renaissance mind. I remember him telling me once how he admired the ancients for being able to express their world view in literature and the arts, for that is chiefly what they had, while today's best thinkers work out their ideas in the realm of science. He was always tinkering with some new idea himself down in the shop or in the biology lab. He kept plastic bottles in the lab filled with mysterious potions and would wander in at odd hours to inspect them. I felt sure he was on the verge of a major breakthrough, even though his experiments were there when I came and when I left. He was practically a master carpenter; he was a silk screener; he was a photographer and developer. He directed us in Greek tragedies on the stage; he coached us in varsity sports. There, too, he exercised his skill at withholding praise, at keeping the carrot just out of reach. In intramural softball games he liked to pitch: that was the star's position. I remember watching him round the bases in olive-drab canvas low-cuts and high-water Army pants and a fatigue hat. He looked ridiculous. No one would have told him.

Once, he came down off the mountain. Right in front of

us the animus melted to anima. Father Lawrence Brediger, one of the Order's most revered priests, a man who had spent his priestly life paralyzed from the shoulders down, died suddenly in Washington. Father Vincent happened to have Mass on the main altar the next morning. After the gospel he turned and faced us. It was six forty-five, and all we could think of was sleep. He started to talk about Father Lawrence, got out a few sentences, cracked on a word, audibly swallowed a sob. He started again, stopped. He started again. He stood staring for several more minutes at his waxy wrinkled fingers, clasped before him, then turned to the altar and finished his Mass. At breakfast we practically whispered about it. Two hours later, in Latin class, he was the Tiger again. That was the name a generation of seminarians ahead of us had given him. He called on me that day to translate, and I wasn't prepared. That was how you said it: "I'm not prepared, Father." He was disgusted. I felt as though I had chinked the *Pietà*.

He had first gone south himself in the twenties, an urban kid out of New Jersey. One way to reach Holy Trinity back then was to sail on an intracoastal steamer from New York down to Savannah, then come across Georgia by train. To a fourteen-year-old Jersey boy on the lip of the Depression, the several-day journey must have seemed as glorious as rounding the horn of Africa. I have an idealized image of a fresh-faced, already serious youth with knickers and a wool cap and a cardboard suitcase. The boy is standing on the bow of a packet one day in 1929, waving madly as the boat pulls out of New York harbor. The boy is bent on the full adventure of himself, but of course it is more than adventure that propels him toward this rude, anonymous place in Alabama. Something transcendent is mixed in. Fitz, as they called him, got down to Alabama in time to know Father Judge, or at least see him, in the last four years of the founder's itinerant life, when tubercular lungs and an obsessed vision had all but consumed him.

After his own ordination, in the early forties, Father Vincent didn't know plans had been laid to send him back to Alabama to become a teacher. Like everyone else, he had come to be a missionary, a saver. Father Thomas, then the head of the order, made Father Vincent his temporary sec-

retary, and one day, at the congregation's headquarters outside Washington, while the newly ordained priest stood on a
table fixing a blind, Father Thomas flipped an envelope toward Fitzpatrick. In the envelope was an application to the
Catholic University of America's graduate school. The community needed a classics man for its minor seminary and
Father Vincent was it. He taught in the minor seminary during the year, worked on his own degree every summer back
East. The life of a classicist soon enough fitted, and so did a
ministry to kids and junior collegians at Holy Trinity.

I saw him down at Holy Trinity several summers ago, on a
swamp-hot August weekend in 1980. My seminary's first-ever
attempt at a gathering of its far-flung departed was not a
raging success. For one thing the weekend was poorly
planned and promoted. They sent out about five hundred
letters, using an old computer list of names; scores came back
stamped Address Unknown. Still, there were enough of us
there, if you counted some wives and babies, to fill about half
the chapel. Two other of my classmates whom I hadn't seen
in years showed up. Joe Hoffman came down from northern
Illinois, where he runs the family manufacturing business,
and Joe Appollo came down from Meadville, Pennsylvania,
where he runs a mental health facility. Joe Appollo hadn't
heard about the reunion, and when I called him at the last
minute to ask if he was coming, he about leaped through the
wire. "Hell, yes, I'll be there," he said. "When is the damn
thing?" Joe hadn't changed much in all the years. In the
seminary he used to have a locker full of sport shirts (he had
an uncle in the business), and at the reunion he showed up
in a shirt with an alligator on it. In a lot of ways Joe was cool
when the rest of us were clods. The summer that I turned
sixteen my father got me a pass on his airline and I flew over
to visit Joe in New Jersey. He introduced me to a girl he was
sort of dating on the sly. She must have thought I was a mute.
In the last year that Joe and I were together we went around
whispering to one another in the halls, "G.L." It was code for
"Get laid."

Father Vincent, along with two others of my old teachers,
drove down to the reunion from the North, fifteen hours
straight, three aging clerics in a sedan; the next day they
would turn around and drive straight back: all had commit-

ments in the East. On Saturday afternoon, in 100-degree Alabama heat, we wound in awkward procession from Mary's shrine up to the chapel. It was the first rosary I had partici-pated in since I had left the seminary, and I don't think I was alone. At the chapel Father Vincent got up to speak. In the intervening years he has spent his time as a giver of retreats, as a Novice Master, as a confessor, as a font, I think, of spirituality for the priests and brothers still left in his reli-gious community. This day he had on a short-sleeve clerical shirt and slightly belled black slacks with a big cuff. I kept wondering if his sister had picked them out the last time he was home and he had shrugged and said okay. He was only slightly bulkier. The face was no more ancient than it had ever been. He spoke the way he used to lecture in a class-room, with one hand crooked stonily at his hip, as if posing for a sculpture. His voice was liquid, passionate, full of trem-ble. But this time there seemed less willful distance, less mountain.

"I am personally overwhelmed at the significance of our being here together," he said. He said it didn't matter to him that there were only forty or so of us present, and that he would have been happy to come "had there been only one." He said that lately in his own life he had been struggling to understand the passage of history and the meaning of change. "I think of that beautiful motherhouse of the sisters' across the road that disappeared at the beginning of 1930, burned to the ground. And years later, the men's novitiate, built on the same spot, burned to the ground, too. What was the meaning of that?" He said he had been listening carefully to our various stories that day—where we'd been, whom we'd married, how many kids we had, our jobs. "And what I'm hearing are the values that *did* take root. There are spiritual values that grew up here at Holy Trinity and did *not* die. There was something beautiful that went out of Holy Trinity. It was you. It was you." Then he said, so softly it was easy to miss, "Forgive us if we missed you. But you see, we were sorry for your departure." I didn't get that right away, but I think he was expressing his own regret and maybe a small apology for all that had flowed on between us, for some misunder-standings and wrecked dreams.

That night Father Vincent and several others from the

Order drove into town to the Ramada Inn, where most of us were staying. He sat among us at a row of pulled-together tables in the bar and wore an open-necked white sport shirt. He fiddled with a drink. For all the bartender knew, he was just some old coot who had turned up on a Saturday night in a wheezy cocktail lounge to share a drink with some younger friends. The next morning, back at Holy Trinity, shortly before he left for the North, I asked him if he still kept up his Latin. We were sitting at a wobbly card table, and he was trying to cut through a hot dog with a plastic knife. The wiener skidded on a paper plate below trembling fingers. He fixed me with that heh-heh little smile that always had a way of cracking him open, like bone-china splintered, and at the same time parking you and your impertinence in the bleachers. "Just can't turn off the lights some nights without dipping into a little Horace, Hendrickson," he said.

If Father Vincent was our animus, Father Brendan was our anima, although he wasn't motherly and the softness in him was deceptive. He could be willful, like anyone else; it was just that he knew, I think, how to live between the spaces and so get along with almost anyone. In a way he was one of us, down to his awkward body and absurdly baby face. For several years he had served as an assistant prefect of discipline in the dorms. I think what he really wanted to do was play Ping-Pong all day in the rec room.

He was hopelessly, comically disorganized. He was a sort of religious hippie, attached to almost nothing material. Like Holly Golightly in *Breakfast at Tiffany's*, he could have kept a card on his door that said: TRAVELING. Except he probably would have lost the card. His room looked like Pearl Harbor after the attack. I can't swear to this, but I believe he kept his clothes, those he could find, in a plastic trash liner. I'd go in to see him about something and he would make an effort to clear space. Usually I just sat on something—a moldy play-script, a box of yellowing correspondence (he was famous for getting out Christmas cards the following July), piles of theme papers. There were stacks of partially marked papers everywhere. He always got the papers back to us, but there was never any telling when. At least once we got them after the term ran out—hell, after the year ran out. It became a running gag, passing him in the hall, to ask, "Father, about those papers?" "Oh, I'll just go and get them," he'd say. Then he'd dissolve into something that was halfway between a sneer at you and a mock of himself. He had that look down like a hat trick. He was full of squeak and sneer and the theological self-mock.

I always wondered where he slept because his bed—a cot, almost—was also buried under books and papers. Maybe he raked it on the floor every night, or maybe he climbed in with everything, or maybe he didn't go to bed at all, but stayed up reading William Faulkner and T. S. Eliot and Flannery O'Connor. I had heard of Faulkner, but I had no possible conception a novel could be read in terms of symphonic structure. Father Brendan's English classes opened windows like that. He was our audio-visual multimedia lightbox, illuminating Shakespeare, Agnes De Mille ballets, recordings of *John Brown's Body*. He taught us how to scan poetry, undulating us through endless iambs and anapests. He is still the only man I've ever met who can make clear what James Joyce's Epiphany and T. S. Eliot's objective correlative are about. After I had left the seminary and was faking my way through American lit seminars, I remember wanting to call the motherhouse, find Father Brendan's whereabouts, and beg him to explain those terms to me just once more. It was in his high school English classes that I first plotted my own future: I was going to be the Order's Writer-Priest, or Priest-Writer, never mind that I could barely pass his weekly grammar quizzes. Once I wrote a short story for him and titled it "The Reluctant Timepiece." I remember the title, though not the story, because I stole it. I also remember Father Brendan letting me know with masterly kindness and understatement that it wasn't any good. Later, in college, when I was editing the yearbook and writing impassioned purple forewords and prefaces, he wrote in the margin of one of my manuscripts, "You don't have to say everything." Once, I recall, he and Father Shaun drove to Atlanta to see Bette Davis in a one-woman reading. The next morning in class he imitated her reading of Sandburg's poem *The Fog*, his slender, almost feminine fingers slipping over the lectern on "little cat feet." He practically *was* Bette Davis. Back then we considered him a raw genius. I'm not sure of that anymore, but I know something more important: he was incapable of being unkind, or seemed so, which could not be said of every priest in our midst. Even for the most leprous, disliked of seminarians, he had time. Perhaps he saw in each of us a little of his own awkwardness.

Some of his chaos must have been worked with mirrors, for I don't recall a curtain not rising on one of his play productions, even though backstage the cast had begun to run in ever-widening circles. The curtain would be going up and there was Father Brendan—in a T-shirt streaked with poster paint, a cigarette with an impossible ash hanging at the tip of two fingers—applying a last dab of makeup to somebody's face. "Get your places!" he'd shriek. For the length of the play he'd stand in the corner by the lights, mouthing every line to himself, miming nearly every gesture. By the end of the night he would have lined up on the ledge beside him several dozen spent cigarettes, tip to tip, like bedraggled toy soldiers. It was next to impossible to get him to come out for a bow, and when he did he would skulk out with acute hang-dog embarrassment. Part of his gift was that he always found a role for everyone, no matter what kind of horrible actor presented himself at the gym. In fact, one of Father Brendan's old tricks was not to write the script until after the number of volunteers for the play had been tallied. His homemade entertainments, as he liked to call them, with cribbed show music and specially adapted lyrics, were a maze of subplots, so that everyone could get on stage for a reasonable period. Some of the shows had corny names (*Yes, We Have No Bonanza*) and even cornier characters (Mean Marvin Mastoid; Snirk Sneath). But they all entertained.

Sometimes he would stage legitimate shows from Broadway, and then some of our families and people from the community would attend. Under Father Brendan we put on renditions of *A Man for All Seasons, Guys and Dolls, Damn Yankees, My Fair Lady.* He would go over and over our lines, blocking out movements and dance steps, showing us how to swagger, to bully, to preen, to talk Cockney—whatever the script called for. Picture gawky seminary boys trying to convince an audience that they could have danced all night and still have begged for more. Father Brendan always listened to our lines in rehearsal from the back of the gym, sweeping along the wall in his blousy habit and crazy long-legged gait, head down, smoking, nodding. He'd get to one end of the gym, turn, start back. Sometimes, when we hadn't worked on our lines or dance steps, he would flash with irritation. He'd look apologetic and we'd start over. He did it all: scavenged and sewed costumes; designed sets; painted scenery—usually at three o'clock the night before the show. There are any number of Brendan Smith chaos stories worth recounting, but one of my favorites has to do with painting some canvas. It seems that Father Norbert, who by then had become head of vocation recruitment, talked his colleague into doing a huge rendering of Trinity missionaries raising a cross on Southern mission fields. Father Brendan got down to the canvas on the last possible night, and when Father Norbert found him the next morning, he was curled by the side of his work, brushes in hand, job done, snoring like a babe. It was a great job, too.

In the case of *My Fair Lady*, he charmed Messrs. Lerner and Loewe into letting him put on the musical without royalty fees. I can see the two famous men of the theater in their New York offices getting a letter from some Catholic priest named Smith in some place called Holy Trinity, Alabama, who wants to know if he can stage their show with an all-male seminary cast *free of charge*. Father Brendan could work magic with female parts—putting wigs on boys, rouge, jewels, new walks. It isn't true he taped coffee cups under our dresses to affect breasts. I asked him. "No, the only allowance in that direction I recall is that when Father Vincent directed some of his Greek tragedies, he sometimes let the heroines tie towels around their chests." Father Brendan didn't need the cups; his productions had enough verisimilitude, which was a word he was constantly trying to explain in the classroom. Part of the reason he liked doing plays so much, I'm certain, was that dramatics could afford a large number of adolescents a particular kind of maturing experience. But the rest of it, I'd be willing to bet, was that these hokey, sometimes surprisingly adroit performances gave their creator a lampshade and cane he wouldn't otherwise have had. In another life he might have been a lot of things, among them a clown in a circus. But fate or God or something in between led him to the religious life. Though he had nearly a critic's knowledge of theater (he grew up in Brooklyn, near enough to Broadway), and though he had the crush of the pure movie-goer (he could name you bit players in a 1946 Republic two-reeler), he didn't in the least seem worldly or secular. If any-thing he seemed out of it, more than a lot of the faculty, and we thought it our constant duty to clue him in about real life. He was out of it, in a way; he was the priest with the Nutty Putty body, only it was stretched over a glowing rod of prin-ciple. We knew that, I suppose, but only viscerally. I've visited him several times these last few years, and I recognize now how much he loved the seminary and how badly it hurt when the place died, even though he knew it had to die. In the seminary and in seminarians he had found a true apostolate. Even on his three weeks of vacation every summer he would organize trips to Radio City and Rockaway Beach with the New York-area students: he couldn't wait until September to see them again. If there are grim absurdities in all our lives, the abiding one in his is that, like a cowboy when westering was over, his way of life had closed up before he did.

Although in a sense he carries on. He lives now in a large stone house in northeast Philadelphia with seven or eight young men who are students at nearby La Salle College and who are thinking of becoming Trinitarian priests. As it hap-pens, the house isn't far from old St. Vincent's seminary on Chelten Avenue in Germantown, where, at the end of the last century, young, already tubercular Tom Judge of South Boston studied for the Vincentian priesthood, hitching the seminary mule to a wagon on Saturdays and riding to the Reading Terminal for green groceries. I stopped by to see the founder's mother seminary once. St. Vincent's is a somber old place, wood and gray stone, with a high wall out front and green wicker under overhanging eaves at the back. In-side, removed from the din of the street, I found a white-topped priest who told me once he saw "Judgie." He saw him in 1930, three years before Judge died. "He was a controver-sial man, a controversial man," the old Vincentian told me. "He had a higher calling, you might say. The Lord wanted him to found you boys."

Father Brendan, with his boys, lives a couple of city bus rides from where Father Judge studied. Father Brendan's place nowadays isn't exactly a seminary, and it's galaxies from the kind of life I used to know (female friends drop by for supper; the guys go out at night with the cars), but still the place functions as a house of formation for young men seriously contemplating the religious life. There is common prayer in the morning, and there is an afternoon liturgy when classes are done. From the street it looks about like any other house in the neighborhood. You wouldn't know that a makeshift chapel and a rough-hewn Southern Cross with burlap wrapped at its base are in a room upstairs. You wouldn't know that Brendan Smith, the composer of unfinished symphonies who resides in the house, makes it a point to spend a part of nearly every morning sharing coffee and talk with some retarded people who live in the neighborhood.

Some things don't change much. The first time I went to see him was on a nasty day in January. Father Brendan was in the kitchen trying to get a fire lighted on the stove. It was a Sunday and he wanted to make pancakes for the guys. (He had invited me to "brunch.") The house was a mess, the kitchen a disaster. Things had a sort of Naugahyde, dirty-shag-rug, three-legged feel. My old English teacher kept peering at the stove, then approaching it as stealthily as a burglar. All the while he asked about my family (his computer memory came up with each of their names), told me about his brother Bud (a diocesan pastor in Brooklyn), brought up a movie he'd just read about in the New York Times Arts & Leisure section. (Now, as then, he reads about film and theater much more than he ever attends; the vow of poverty has never allowed that many admissions.) He wore a baggy flannel shirt with two buttons missing. One cuff of his pants had snagged and turned itself inside out. He had put on a good deal of weight, and the face that was always fifteen years old had now caught up to, even overtaken, its more than five decades. But it still cavorted like rubber.

He got the fire lighted at last but didn't have anything with which to grease the skillet. He tried butter—and burned it brown. The fire was now roaring hot. His cigarette, suspended at the tip of his index and middle fingers, had grown a precarious ash; the ash began to drop into the skillet. "Quit laughing," he sneered at me, sounding just like Mean Marvin Mastoid or Snirk Sneath. He poured out a pancake. Perversely, the batter spread in all directions—it looked like an ink blot test. Just then, as if somebody had blocked it out, one of the La Salle students showed up. His name is Kevin, and he sort of hung in the doorway wagging his head.

"Would you like me to try, Bren?" he sighed.

"Here. I didn't become a priest to make pancakes," my old teacher snarled, shoving the bowl at Kevin, tromping off to save brunch and dignity.

At our reunion at Holy Trinity in 1980, Father Brendan preached at the closing Mass. He had to follow Father Vincent, who had stirred us the afternoon before. He spoke, without fire and above the squalls of babies, in that reasoned, calming voice that used to come from the back of a gym or the front of a classroom whenever its owner was trying to lead us to another room where new ideas waited. His idea that Sunday morning went to the mark like a dart, though of course its tip was made of rubber. As he spoke he rocked, as was ever his wont.

"Last night, at the Ramada Inn, when some of us were gathered and talking about where this reunion, or homecoming, or get-together, might lead us, someone said, 'Well, I don't know if I'm ready for anything religious right now. I came because I wanted to see some old friends again. Couldn't we let it go at that?' Personally I think I *could* let it go at that, because lately I find myself questioning a lot of things that pass under the umbrella word of 'religious' and instead finding myself accepting more things that fall under the word 'faith,' that word that echoes through today's reading from Wisdom. In that first reading the writer is speaking to a chosen people who are currently in exile, in Egypt, and he is reminding them that one time before, when they were in bondage, the Lord released them, the Lord showed His favor to them, and one can almost feel the way they might have started gloating and posing again: 'Yes, we are God's favorite ones, and therefore we go on under a charmed cloud that protects us.' But I think the message here this morning is to realize that when Christ comes, there are no favorites, that Jews and Egyptians will have to travel together, and that what really matters then is how much you are being good, doing good, helping others to do good. I think what the writer is trying to tell us is that a people may one day be chagrined to hear, not for the first time, but maybe more emphatically than ever before, that so many of their rituals, regulations, and rules were really worthless because their hearts had never melted and they never became compassionate people, and that is all that really matters to their Father."

He went back to the Mass. Toward the end he faced us, and, with the barest smile on Snirk Sneath's face, said, "Father, it is good for us to be here. It is better for us to move on."

Father Columban didn't make it to our reunion, though I suspect he might have if he had had any say. He was dead by then. Father Columban taught mathematics, a subject I despised. He was grossly overweight, and he was Germanic in a community of Irish-American priests. To boot he was an ugly and inelegant man, unpleasant to be in a small room with, and he surely knew it. He once told a colleague without apparent self-pity that there was little use in his trying to lose weight: after he got down one hundred pounds he'd still have the same face. That face, usually sweaty, was pocked and pale as milk. It was crowned with reddish-orange hair that looked coarse as mop string and was wrung straight back. The rear of his head was a series of ledges that defied seminary barbers (who were seminarians with one or two lessons and then a warm body in the chair; basically everybody got a bowl job). Father Columban's sausage-link fingers were yellowed with nicotine from the filterless cigarettes he smoked in chains. Sometimes his mouth held in the smoke like a vise clamp, and other times his mouth jiggled a cig along his lips with a soft sucking noise. He had a cough that sounded consumptive, and which once unleashed might stutter on, like ack-ack fire from a machine gun, for the next four or five minutes. We'd study the ceiling or the initials carved in our desks during those attacks. And yet, for such inelegance, this priest had a curious gift: on roller skates, in the old gym, a couple of years before I came, he was said to glide wondrously over a floor slick with banana oil: a Humphrey Pennyworth on air, mocking the laws of physics. Maybe this odd grace was proof of a sort that his heart was as big as his body. All we saw was the body.

His nickname was Moo Moo, and there were students ahead of and behind me who could make me quiver with laughter with their burlesques of his Brooklynese and his stomach-out walk. (His spine seemed merely along for the ride.) One of my periodic duty assignments, before I got semipermanent duty in the rose gardens, was sorting clothes in the little laundry behind the refectory. Once I found a pair of Moo Moo's boxer shorts; they looked like tenting. Three of us climbed inside them.

Moo Moo's favorite expression was "All right, fine." Those three words punctuated nearly every sentence, preceded and followed every algebraic equation demonstrated on the board. He also liked to say, "This much we know," the "this" coming out as "dis," with his hands, palms out, madly shoveling air at his sides—like a tuna with its flippers. Halfway through a class my eyes would start to burn from the salt his body was putting out. Invariably before a class was done he would be provoked to hurling erasers and huge chunks of railroad chalk at the dimwitted. He'd ask me an easy question, I'd say something dumb, and the next thing I knew a missile was sailing at my head. He had deadly aim, and so you had little choice but to shield yourself with the top of your desk, which was on hinges. This would agitate him even more. The chalk would explode off the desktop and Moo Moo would utter a small profanity. But that was usually the end of it. He was only frustrated.

Before Father Gavin joined the faculty, Father Columban was saddled with teaching college chemistry. I don't think he ever knew much about it. The chem lab was on the second floor of the old high school building, and more than once I remember hearing what could only be Moo Moo's lungs bellowing overhead: "Hit the dirt! Hit the dirt!" An experiment had gone wrong. In a sense Moo Moo himself was all pyrotechnics. His excesses were so completely up front, it was easy to misread him. I think I see now he was one of the fairest men we had. A priest told me not long ago that Father Columban almost never voted to toss someone out. But who knew it? What we knew was the sound of his bulk hitting the dirt. It sounded like a thunderclap.

He was also the moderator of seminary publications, and since I edited the school paper, and later on, the yearbook, we often found ourselves working alongside each other. I don't think I was ever comfortable in his presence (it did not occur to me to wonder what he thought of mine), although I learned to be grateful for his sense of improvisation and his ability to get things done. In my last days in the minor seminary, out of time and imagination, I began to despair of finishing the yearbook. As the deadline approached and the book wasn't even nearly done, I began to feel a queer lightness in the back of my head. I got so wrought over the fear of failing that I ended up going to the infirmary for a week. Nobody quite knew what was wrong with me, although I think the doctor who came out from town to examine me probably guessed an attack of nerves. Father Columban went down to the Prep Room and took off his habit and whipped the book into shape. When it came out, on time, I got the credit.

He died a few years back. After all those years in the seminary, over a decade and a half, they had rewarded him with a mission in Kentucky. He loved it, and then he got cancer of the bowel. It was an inelegant way to go; maybe he figured God is a humorist. He entered the Cleveland Clinic for cancer surgery. The doctors there didn't have to tell him he was dying. He came to the major seminary to convalesce. At first he was able to say Mass and turn up some evenings in the rec room to look at TV. In his last months, encased in pain, shrunken, an old beached whale, he moved through the halls in a wheelchair. Finally he didn't leave his room. People who were there say Father Columban didn't complain much. And then one morning he was dead.

Father Brendan had suggested it was better to move on. I kept moving on, finding old friends, seining feelings, hoping thereby to discover my own feelings, and three weeks after our 1980 Holy Trinity reunion found myself in Cleveland, Ohio, where I hunted up another Christ figure and role model, Barnabas French. Father Barnabas hadn't come to our Alabama get-together and I suppose I couldn't help wondering if at least part of the reason was that he had become an alcoholic in the intervening years. But he had licked it, too, and I had heard some stories about that. I also heard he was counseling men in the same ward where he was once confined as a patient.

Father Barnabas was our proud artiste in the seminary,

and it is hard for me to think about him for very long without hearing somewhere in my head that breathing, hypnotic line of plainsong church music known as Gregorian chant. Barney French took a bunch of adolescents with lots of neck and squeakbox voices and turned them into a respectable *schola cantorum*. I sang second tenor and later first bass for him and over the years came to see a complex man at firing range.

He seemed to me then to be a man living on the edge of rage, or at least perpetual indignation. I had no real idea why. Sometimes he would step over the edge. I can recall his slamming books and storming off beet-red from choir rehearsal. We would be practicing late at night for an upcoming feast—maybe Easter midnight Mass—and something would go wrong. It was as if we had committed on purpose our four-part-harmony blunderings of *Terra Tremuit*. He would go off and we would be left there. Then somebody would get the lights, and we'd walk the darkened halls in embarrassed silence to bed. But, on the other hand, when things went right you felt you were in Barney French's private club. He could make the chapel float, pulse, with those skinny arms, that clicking head in tune to its own inner rhymes. He really did believe, I think, that singing can be twice praying.

Because he was unathletic and not in very good health, and maybe because his widowed mother visited more often than did some of our own parents, it was easy to think of him as a pantywaist. I think he knew it. He once told me his lifelong curse was trying to catch a ball; in a male society he couldn't do what everyone else seemed to do naturally. "Once I caught one," he said. "It stopped the game. Father Stephen came over and shook my hand." To compensate for his haplessness, he burlesqued it. Every year, on Thanksgiving morning, the students played the faculty in what was called the Turkey Bowl. The contest was usually softball (though once I remember volleyball and another time a football game that was touch in name only) and was supposed to show good-natured family rivalry. Usually it was played out to mock hatreds that weren't so mock. For a few hours every Thanksgiving morning it was open season on frustrations—theirs and ours. What we tried to do was dance with our taunts and jeers just this side of outright disrespect. By the time we got back up to the dorms and were taking a shower, the joke was over. The faculty was back in habit. And so had we better be. Father Barnabas couldn't hit a lick with a softball bat, but he got up there in his rolled pants and Tiger T-shirt—they were the Tigers, we were the Cobras—and fumbled around while the pitcher fanned him with three straight pitches.

We called him, behind his back, the Kidney, because he had only one. (The other, diseased, had been removed.) Some mornings he would show up to say his Mass with a lower lip that was inexplicably empurpled; this was good for a rash of abuse. He was always carefully groomed and smelled of after-shave and wore clothes under his habit that conveyed a sense of taste and style the others didn't have. On feast days he would come to chapel with French cuffs shooting from his sleeves. There would be a high gloss on his black penny loafers and on his fingernails. I remember his fingers: they were freckled and elegant, with tips as flat as spatulas. I wondered whether they had gotten this way from years of playing a piano or whether he had been magically accommodated from birth, the better to suction up keyboards. In his youth, in Syracuse, Father Barnabas had played in a jazz combo, and this, combined with his stylish dress, set him apart in my estimation, gave him a gleam of worldliness that wasn't exactly anticlerical but suggested secular haunts all the same. I like to think now that if he hadn't become a priest he would have one day subbed for Bobby Short at the Cafe Carlyle. As it was, he had studied music at Pius X School of Liturgical Music at Manhattanville College, an institute devoted to Gregorian authenticity. This made him a star. Except in the classroom, that is. He taught religion and chant, and we gave a damn about neither of them as academic subjects. What precious study time we had went to readying our thirty lines of Greek and Latin for the Old Roman. I think Father Barnabas's classes were kissed off by every student in the school; he must have felt a terrible inferiority among his colleagues. Some days I would sit in the back of his class and snore, and he let me get away with it.

Because I had taken piano in grammar school and could still play tolerably well, I sometimes got to plink out chords for him on the organ in chapel while he worked out front with the choir. I became a sort of pet. One evening in my second year at Holy Trinity, he came up to my desk in study hall and asked me to step outside with him. He was the monitor of study hall that night, and I figured he wanted to see me in connection with choir rehearsal. Outside in the dark he lit a cigarette. A red point glowed at intervals in front of me. At length he said, "Paul, I'd like to help you in some way with your skin problem. I was standing in there a while ago watching you pick your face till it started bleeding. I'll bet you didn't even know you were doing it." I was embarrassed down through the soles of my shoes, but I think he felt worse. Father Barnabas was no good at confronting on a one-to-one basis, and the orb we dwelt in hardly encouraged assertive behavior. But he said it, and I think I could see then a kind of ballsiness that was easy to overlook because of his dandy, though not dainty, exterior. A week later a small package showed up on the chair beside my bed in the dorm. In it were bars of facial soap and tubes of ointment. I knew who sent them.

I hadn't seen him in years. I decided to call blind one morning from Chicago, where I had gone to interview a classmate. I told him I was working on a book. Father Barnabas said he knew that. He sounded doubtful about my coming: there was a lot of work; he wasn't sure of his schedule. We talked for a while longer and finally he said come ahead, though he didn't say it with any enthusiasm. "I wouldn't want to be part of anything that would sully the congregation's name," he said.

On the flight over to Cleveland I sat studying a faded newspaper photograph. I had torn the picture from the December 23, 1959, edition of the Columbus (Georgia) *Ledger-Enquirer*. It was a four-panel picture and carried a lengthy caption. It said: "Students at Holy Trinity, Alabama, are shown making preparations for Christmas. At left, two students of St. Joseph's Preparatory School who are gathering bows of holly to be used in making green wreaths are Danny McCormick, left, and Pat Ryan. Seated in the front row with Father Barnabas in the choir practice session is William C. Siarny. The trio shown putting up the Nativity scene, left to right, Marty Hendrickson, Harry Evans, Antonio Rodriguez."

In all, fourteen boys and one priest were identified. Of the fourteen seminarians, one was to make it to priesthood. And the priest in the picture had become an alcoholic. I folded this piece of old newspaper and put it back in my jacket.

Father Barnabas and I met about eight o'clock in the evening in the parlor of the house where he lives with several other men in religious life. The house used to have a church next door to it, but only a bell tower and a vacant lot are there now. The house is on Euclid Avenue, east of Cleveland's downtown, in the heart of Hough, which is a ghetto not as famous as Watts, maybe, but easily as desperate. The riots came to Hough in 1966, and afterward a writer for *Time* said this: "Some sixty thousand Negroes are jammed into a two-square-mile warren of squat apartment houses and decaying mansions carved up into flats." Shortly before I went to visit Father Barnabas a nun had been robbed and raped. If crime is down there somewhat now, it may be because the crime vulture doesn't have so many bones to pick clean. I saw a lot of rubbly lots.

I rang the buzzer and was led to the airless parlor. About fifteen minutes later Father Barnabas walked in. He clacked lightly across the room in wooden clogs, opened a window with padlocks on it. The city night poured in, a kind of neon narcotic darkness. He sat down, lit a smoke, folded skinny arms across his chest, crossed his legs. I could see silky blue hose probably reaching to his cueball knees: class. His face looked as though he had just shaved and talc-ed it. He studied me with a nodding, bit-lip, half-amused, half-sardonic grin that was suddenly easy to recall. The smile always said: Okay, buster, what now? He still was no bigger around the waist than a bantamweight. Behind him was a shiny black Steinway grand. I made a reference to it. "I didn't want it at first," he said. "It was part of the past."

I fidgeted and said something about reassessing old heroes. It came out stupidly and patronizingly. He kept nodding and studying me and suppressing the bit-lip smile. "Gutsy, huh?" he said, echoing a word I had used. "Well, I was a perfectionist. You may recall that."

In a while, though, his talk began coming out in streams. He told me about his father, a precise and aloof man who had been a cabinetmaker. "When you kids knew me the idea of being 'the priest' was everything to me. Well, not now. The idea of community is everything. I think I could even be a missionary brother. I started out in another order as a lay brother. That was the Franciscans, and they had me scrubbing steps, making sixteen beds every morning. I was too proud. I didn't last long. A priest there told me, 'Listen, I don't think you're cut out for this life.' Since then I've learned a little about humility, about pain.

"There was a time a few years ago when I felt that the Pope had given up on me, the Church, God—you name it. I felt I was an immoral person. But I never drank as a priest. I drank as a human being. God didn't put that drink in my hand. And I never asked Him to take it out. God's will was always fine as long as it coincided with mine. I used to get even with people by drinking at them.

"A psychiatrist in Washington told me, 'Father, aren't your arms tired from holding up the weight of the world?' I blamed my parents, my superiors, the seminary, you kids. After the seminary closed, I used to go to this dry-out program in Washington, not because I wanted to, mind you, but because my superiors said I had to, and so I trotted along like a good little religious. I went for three years without really participating. Then one day I broke down in front of a beautiful lady. She had coiffed silver hair and an amazing interior beauty. I couldn't imagine her being a drinker—no, a drunk. 'Oh, yes, Father,' she said. 'I've had my romance with the bottle.' I loved the way she said that. Anyway, I just blubbered to pieces right in front of her. She handed me a box of tissues and told me to go to my room.

"One of the biggest demons I had to slay was this thing about perfect priest. 'Father doesn't take a drink. Oh, no, not Father, somebody else, maybe, but not Father.' You get ordained; people start coming up to you at your first Mass. 'Please say a prayer for me, will you, Father?' And you say, 'Okay, but you have to say one for me, too.' And they look at you queerly and say, 'But you don't need prayers, Father. You're a priest.' Oh, yeah? I need a carful of them."

He talked about his ordination and his first years in the seminary (he had been ordained with Father Brendan, in 1954, and afterward came immediately to the seminary) and how anger and frustration slowly found their way to drink. It was mostly beer at first; later, anything he could get his hands on. Eventually he knew the kind of cravings that drive men to other men's medicine cabinets in the middle of the day for cough syrup or mouthwash. For a time, when he was up in Canada drying out, the head of the Order, Father Stephen, sent him letters saying the Order still loved him, *he* still loved him. "I'd read those letters from Steve and throw them on the floor. I'd pick them up and read them another five or six times and throw them on the floor." In 1976 he came to Cleveland, to a hospital treatment center, where they made him "wear those stupid pajamas that never fit anybody." And now the recovered alky priest, proud no more, witnesses his life and counsels men on the same floor where he once was confined as a patient. A priest, courier of God, has come all the way around, made his way all the way back. What you see is the humility. "Men come into my office and say, 'Is there really a God? Will you help me to pray, Father?' Dammit, I feel alive."

Before I left Cleveland I had an encounter that seemed to throw me out of sync. I almost took to my bed over it. At Father Barnabas's insistence, I decided to call up a priest named Father Emmet Sawyer, whom I had seen just three weeks earlier that summer, at the Holy Trinity reunion. Father Sawyer is a crusty, argumentative, reformed alcoholic who is also a minor legend in my old religious Order. He goes all the way back to the founder's time. I never knew him well when I was a seminarian, but at the Holy Trinity reunion I had gone up and reintroduced myself and said I was writing a book, and he had said, wagging a finger, "A writer shouldn't write things he'll be ashamed of later." He wasn't combative, just resolute. I had already published several mildly controversial stories about the seminary in the *Washington Post* and the *New York Times,* and I figured this was what he referred to.

I hadn't told any of this to Father Barnabas, probably trying to deny my mild worry. Anyway, at Father Barnabas's urging, I called Father Sawyer. He came straightaway to the point in a gravelly voice: "I think your attitude stinks. I've read some of the things you've already written about us, and I think they're garbage. I want you to know exactly how I feel, and if you still wish to talk to me you can meet me

tomorrow morning at nine o'clock in my office at the hospital.
Now good night. And, oh, yes: God bless you." He hung up
in my ear. I stared dumbly at the receiver.

The next morning I was at the hospital a half-hour early. I
hadn't slept well overnight and by now was defensive and a
little indignant and probably self-righteous. I guessed that
Father Sawyer would come in, yell at me some more, I'd take
it, or most of it, and then the two of us could—I hoped—get
down to some talk about the Order's early days. About nine-
fifteen he came in. He looked shaky and pallid. He motioned
for me to follow him. Instead of leading me to his own office
and closing the door, he led me into Father Barnabas's office.
Father Barnabas sensed trouble immediately, but he was
caught: Father Sawyer was senior to him in the priesthood,
and to boot Sawyer was Barnabas's counselor in the recovery
from alcoholism. "I think I can vouch for this character, Father Sawyer," Father Barnabas said quickly, trying to smooth
things over and sound cheery and at once his old deflecting,
sarcastic self. "We talked for a couple of hours last evening at
the rectory. Besides, he's my old second tenor."

It didn't work. Father Sawyer seemed not to hear. He
seemed frail as parchment. "Sit down!" he said, and immediately I sat: a priest had given a command. A sickly retro-
grade feeling came over me. I had been a very bad boy. "This
will take maybe two minutes," he said. "I tried to avoid you
in Alabama, thinking you might get that idea, but you weren't
smart enough. Maybe Father Vincent or Father Brendan or
some other of your mentors thinks you're on the level, but
I'm on to you. You're trying to dredge up muck and get us
to cooperate. You wanted me to tell you something about the
founder. Well, I'll tell you something about Father Judge, all
right. If he were in this room, God rest him, he'd tell you to
your teeth that you are nothing but a piece of bastard wit. I
don't intend to disgrace the good name of our founder or of
our community by spending another minute in here with
you."

He rose and lurched forward and sent spittle all over me.
For an instant I thought he was going to topple into my lap.
He didn't mean to spray me and I didn't duck. It was a
ridiculous punishment.

I tried to stand up and say something, but he had already

turned his back. "I'll leave it to you, Father Barnabas, to show the gentleman out," he said over his shoulder. From the rear he looked like a tired, bent old man. I felt sorry for him but far worse for myself.

Father Barnabas tried to smooth it over. He felt terrible. He walked me to the elevator, pushed the button. "Look, Paul, write the guy a letter," he whispered, avoiding eye contact. "He'll come around." I wanted to write the guy a letter, although not at all the kind Father Barnabas had in mind. At the Cleveland airport I called my wife. I was practically in tears. "Something awful has happened," I said. For days a spittle-spraying accuser haunted my reveries, although in time I could almost elevate this ghost, or at least its message.

Knifing

I remember a group march to a boy's locker one night.
We were in search of sheets we thought he had urinated
on. The soiled bedding was found stuffed in a pillowcase
under some dirty laundry. It was held aloft triumphantly, a scarlet letter, only the letter was yellow and
had a stench. Afterward we went over to Benediction
and chorused through great cathartic bars of *Salve Regina.*

IN THE SOUL of each of us is anarchy, even or especially in the
souls of reputedly pious seminary boys. Seven times I went
away to the seminary before I was through with it, or it with
me, and sometimes what I think I remember best is the meanness. Uncharitableness, the prefects called it; knifing, we
called it. In several senses we had traded one family for another, not always for the purest motives, and if the seminary
became an acceptable escape for many of us for too many
years, too often it was a poor substitute for even the poorest
of home lives. But we couldn't see that then, and there is no
sense now in trying to assign blame, mount recriminations.

If the refectory, where we slammed down our food like
packs of dogs, was a survival of the fastest, in a different way
so were our rec rooms and the pergola, where we often spent
our thirty minutes of evening colloquy before Benediction.
Out there the ground could go scarlet with somebody's
blood.

You never quite knew when it was going to be your turn, and in a way the cool arbitrariness of it reminds me of Shirley Jackson's famous short story "The Lottery." The flow of abuse would somehow get turned in your direction. Maybe something you said at supper, maybe something someone else said but which had its intended or accidental slant toward your life, your looks, your "build." Destroying someone's build was a prime form of entertainment.

As in any closed male group, from professional ball teams to prison cellblocks, the place was rife with code names and esoteric speech. Almost none of it travels in translation. Generally, the names we thought up for one another were more an expression of puerile wit than outright cruelty. But sometimes the line got blurred. After a time, even if at first it had been a nasty name, the name became the person and the person the name, and then it was never so much an opprobrium as a small compliment to be called Hocker (if you spat a lot) or Digger (if you scratched your crotch a lot) or Bangi (if you had "plunger" lips) or Zero (if you didn't count) or Horsehead (if you had one) or Mole (if there was a furry brown patch on your cheek) or Jap (if you had slanty eyes) or Flush (if you were a turd) or Hatchet Face (if that's what your face reminded someone of). Hatchet Face, in fact, was the name owned by one of the ace bequeathers of nicknames. He was the tough, wiry son of an immigrant Italian steelworker in Birmingham. In the hallways, on the way to chapel, no one was quicker at zapping you with a name or a "cut" than Hatchet Face. A certain mystique grew up around those seminarians who could flick their savageries on and off in the last few minutes of freedom every night. In those closing minutes, between the end of study hall and the start of spiritual reading and retiring prayers, Hatchet Face was our school champ.

A name or an expression would spawn, live for a couple of weeks, perish. The priests could never keep up with it. *Poulailler* means chicken coop in French; to us it meant "nigger heaven." *Quasee,* as in Quasimodo, was an all-purpose adjective or noun for anybody you didn't like. For a time at table we were going through the entire animal kingdom, coming up with alliterative names for testicles: hamster hondies, beaver bogongees. As with any boys' school we had dozens of

names for testicles: the pills, the *cojones,* hockey pucks, the
biscuits, the ganangees.

What you wanted to resist at all cost in the knifing game, as
I was unable to resist in the beginning, was showing you
couldn't take it, because this only dumped wood alcohol on
open flame. Then they'd never leave you alone. They'd be
delighted to drive you out. Several times that first year I
remember going off to the jakes to cry because I had been
knifed by the group. I'd take a seat on a hopper and let the
waterworks burst. Except for Boy Scouts, I had no experience
in an all-male society, and this wasn't Boy Scouts. Even after
I knew you were supposed to show you liked it, or at least
could swat it off like flies, I couldn't help getting puffy and
red-faced every time my turn came up. It made no sense my
own classmates—Bertin, Roger, Hertz—would want to hurt
me this way.

For some of our teachers we reserved the cruelest cuts, and
this was true in Father Benedict's case. Father Benedict's subjects were French and geometry (although he was bright
enough to have taught us anything). We considered him an
inflexible man, in everything from his golf swing to his blocky
walk to his convictions about "backsliding" seminarians. Behind his back we called him the Clank. Or the Slush. This was
because he spoke from the side of his mouth, slamming down
on the words, as if his jaw were a small-game trap. Occasionally he sprayed water when he spoke. In the pulpit, I remember, he preached with his head locked at a forty-five-degree
angle away from us. In the classroom he lectured with his
head turned slightly to the board, good side out. He must
have had some kind of hearing problem, for he was always
cupping his hand to his ear and squinting at us for the answer. He held his thick, muscular hands as if they were full
of wet paint. Seated at the teacher's desk, he would take off
his nearly rimless glasses, bring the stems together, hook
them on his index finger, set them swinging, sigh, then repeat
the question. "Sophomores grow tall but not up," he would
say, and I got good at parodying this and slobbering water.

He sowed himself a putting green down below the refectory, and on weekends we'd see him out there tending it
lovingly. Up and down that little napkin of clipped grass he'd
go, his trousers rolled. He pushed an old clanky hand mower,

and his pale arms protruded from his T-shirt like fireplace logs. Sometimes, when he was in a good mood, he'd invite us to shag the balls he drove down the lawn toward Guerry Preuett Highway. His swing was rigid, but he could power the ball.

I haven't seen Father Benedict in two decades and find myself thinking of him just now with an odd antipathy. If I were in the rec room and had an audience, I could be tempted into a Slush routine. I write this knowing full well that when I had flunked geometry two quarters out of three, when some of the faculty were down on me for being a malcontent, Father Benedict gave me a 75 for the final quarter, just enough to lift me over the top with a passing average for the year. It was a gift outright, and I didn't thank him. A classmate of mine ·named Harry Gerken has told me he needed an 80 from the Slush that final quarter. He had less pride than I did. He went in and begged for the grade. And got it. I got a letter from Harry the other morning (he is a town manager in New Jersey, divorced, father of two girls), and he said: "Is it unique to the seminary experience that most of us, and most of our teachers, were/are masters at the put-down? I don't recall that my service experience was comparable in this aspect; yet that was a society of males. I'd like to suggest that it was simply because of innocent youth, but I'm not sure."

Several years ago I decided to look up a student from the seminary who had come in for a lot of group abuse. Bob was a year ahead of me and was bright in his studies, but there seemed about him a klutziness and sloppiness that invariably made him ripe for the knife. I located him in Ohio. That is where he left the Order. He was finishing a doctorate in clinical psychology, writing a dissertation on left-brain, right-brain functioning.

He picked me up outside my hotel in his unwashed Chevy Nova, which didn't have shocks and was swimming in White Castle hamburger wrappers, and we then jarred through several thousand potholes back to his apartment. He had on rubber galoshes and a stadium coat with mottled fur on the hood. There was a tangle of beard on his jaw, and something from a previous meal—breakfast, maybe—had lodged on the knee of his gabardine pants. All of it fitted, as did the elaborate, convoluted explanations and the pained gestures once we had gotten back to his place and he had begun to warm to my visit. (Like others he was wary at first; he would have been content, he said, to let it all keep sleeping.)

But there were also in him this day a softness and pensiveness and reflectiveness that I guess were there all along, but that we couldn't see very well back then, or maybe didn't let ourselves see. Now these interior things were larger, fuller, easily overtopping the things we used to mock. The two of us sat around that dreary January afternoon, with sullen light coming through the window, talking and laughing about our "seminary pants" (they had to stop at your ankle and have plenty of bag to be the genuine article), about how egg-headed and out of it we mostly were, and then finally I said, "But why do you think we could be so mean? Remember?"

He said he remembered, all right, and that maybe it was nothing more than just good old scapegoating. "Maybe you felt lousy about something. Maybe a priest had just made you feel stupid in class. So to feel better you got somebody else afterward. It's like those bumper stickers you sometimes see on the back of big trucks: I May Be Slow but I'm Ahead of You." But he said he also wondered if it had to do with the absence of women in our environment, with the absence of a feminine, softening influence. Then he leaned forward from his quasi-lotus crouch on the sofa and said, "Do you remember the nickname Si?" He pronounced it like Sigh. I said I dimly recalled it. "Do you know what it stood for?" he said. I shook my head in a no. I said I thought Si was an abbreviated name of a student we despised, a short, pasty boy with pants up around his nose. "Well, it stood for Snot Inspector. It wasn't my name, but once, in one of Father Vincent's Latin classes, I used the word 'sigh' in a translation. And the class starts to snicker. And Father Vincent, who always wanted to be in on our little secrets, came over to my desk and said, 'Oh, is that what they call you—Sigh? What does it mean? Huh? You won't tell me? Okay, Sigh, I guess we better get on.'

"Well, the class is roaring now. And I began to get this terrible panicky feeling. Here I was, nineteen years old, wearing a cassock, in the college department, having reached the point where I thought my peers were respecting me for what

I was, and now I'm going to get stuck with Snot Inspector— just because I accidentally say the code word in translation? I didn't know what I'd do.

"That night I tried to talk to Pat Day about it. Pat was my roommate that year, and we were really good friends, but he had been one of the guys laughing loudest that morning. I said I couldn't go back to where I'd been, I just couldn't. I started to cry. I tried not to, but I couldn't help myself. Pat said he had no idea it bothered me that much."

Most of us had no idea, I suppose. Looking back now I see that for some of us getting cut by the group was the only means of acceptance. This was the ugly sycophantic side of it.

In my first two years, which were the worst for knifing, there was a Hispanic seminarian named Ramon in my class, and somewhere along the line Ramon must have decided that the way to win favor was by calling himself Spic in front of the class opinion molders. He was a slight—almost frail— boy, with tawny skin and a fastidiousness about it. I can re- member two things about him: he had a great devotion to the Blessed Mother; and every afternoon at four o'clock he pad- ded to the jakes with a collection of ointments and powders.

After a time Ramon took to inciting mock riots on himself. "Hey," he'd call across the dorm in a hyped-up Latin whine, "I dare you to call a race riot." Somebody would shrug and yell "Race riot!" and go back to whatever he was doing, and then three or four of us would belt down the dorm to Ra- mon's bed and pound on him. "Ave Maria," he'd yelp happily between peals of pain. Later, a miffed lover, petulant, he'd get out his beads or one of his holy cards or a plastic lumines- cent Mary. A while ago I saw a cartoon which suddenly brought him back to mind. A kid named Harold is saying to his mother, "Mom, please don't call me Harold anymore. All the guys call me Bugs the Creep." By the time he left, Ramon was fully one of us. He had insinuated himself brilliantly in the only way he knew.

There were a few key individuals in every class whose turn for the knife it never seemed to be. They were the Lords of the Flies. They held the conch. They knew from the first you must knife before you are knifed. Such first-strike capability was lost on me in the beginning, and it nearly drove me out.

The Fly Lord of my class was not only fast and very funny, he was Germanic and physically imposing and had a temper nearly as quick as his wit. Almost from the start he assumed a canny unannounced control of our free-period time, of our five-minute breaks between classes out on the concrete deck of the old high school building. I can see his red pumpkin face out there; I can hear his shuddering raucous laugh, taking Bob Lloyd apart, taking *me* apart. He called me Bone. And Pretzel. And Stick. And Board. And Beanpole. But the pièce de résistance was Pirate's Dream: supposedly, I had a "sunken chest." The name strikes me as laughably harmless now (and not a bad joke, either), but back then I wasn't laughing. For a time the Fly Lord would come up to me on the walk with a pair of crossed hands flapping toward my chest. His hands were bats and they were winging toward my "cave." I was supposed to yuk along with everybody else. Once, in a pickup game in the gym, I called him a "kraut," and before I could shield myself he smacked me to the floor with one clean open-palmed shot. He didn't use his fists. No one came to my rescue; no one would have taken him on. I think he would have been terrible at taking the knife himself, but we never found out.

Just as there were a select few whose turn it almost never was, so there were also a select few whose turn it almost always was, and my guess is they had gotten it before they came. Like DNA molecules, the dynamics and mysterious forces of group taunting had followed them into their new home and rearranged themselves in different clusters. Maybe these individuals liked it this way, I don't know. But I do know that even our teachers could be masters of the knife when they wanted to. After all, they had come from the same mill we were in.

Why did it feel so good to get someone? Nastiness, once you get the hang of it, can be quite pleasant, of course. Maybe we were just bored. And much of it, I suppose, was just the unthinking ways of barbarous kids, except that these particular kids were living life under a glass dome of perfection. There is something in psychology called reaction formation, in which a socially unacceptable feeling is turned into its opposite, but this, I think, was the inverse: charitable feelings could invariably turn to little group savageries. I would call it the phenomenon of unexpected behavior, and knifing in the pergola wasn't the only place it reared its ugly head. Once, I recall, the phenomenon occurred at a passion play.

That Easter all of us were bused into town to see a touring Oberammergau production of the death and passion of Jesus. We weren't crazy about going, but on the other hand it *was* an evening off the property. Inexplicably, halfway through the first act, with nothing but respectful silence all around us, we found ourselves stuffing handkerchiefs in our mouths, trying to stifle laughter. I will swear to this: Some of my best friends were down on the floor of that auditorium, between the seats, holding their breath and bellies, making weird drowning noises. It was like farting-power in church; it unleashed some wild, exotic contagion. None of us could resist it. Each nail driven into the ripped flesh of the Saviour brought more tears of hilarity streaming down our faces. The acting was awful, but it was deeper than this. On the bus home, and for days afterward, we looked at one another and wondered: Did that really happen?

Finding the Founder

———

The rural Deep South was an unlikely place for a four-teen-year-old Northern boy to take up studies for the Catholic priesthood. On the other hand, it had been an even more unlikely spot for a tubercular Vincentian priest named Thomas Judge to found a new American missionary congregation. In the twenties, when Father Judge started his group, Russell County, Alabama, had kudzu and hard-shell Baptists, mainly. De Soto had passed through in 1540 with twelve priests and four friars; it may have been the last time Catholics made recorded history. But poets find their poems and mystics find their Bethlehems. Thomas Judge found his Holy Trinity. Like Brigham Young, this is where the mystic, itinerant priest must have said: Here, we'll build it here. He didn't have two dimes to rub together. But he thirsted for souls; God would provide. He was reckless for God. If this work is of God, he liked to say, it will go on. If it is not, let it perish immediately. "Depression is a blessed state," he told his little band of missionaries. They didn't know what he meant. But the work grew, the work went on, providentially, almost miraculously, rippling outward. In 1929 ecclesiastical approval from Rome came. And by 1958, when I arrived with a suitcase in my freckled paw, the Missionary Servants of the Most Holy Trinity had missions and parishes in fourteen states across the Southland. The Vatican had recently sent an official Decree of Praise. The congregation had grown improbably from a cell at the outback of the faith to 114 priests, 49 missionary brothers, and 161 seminar-ians, 2 of whom were Marty and Paul Hendrickson of

Illinois. Father Judge is gone now, but you can still find
people who knew him. There are still people who will
tell you what the founder's fire was like.

IN THE SHANK of the new century, 1928, lean Tom Benson is
eagle-beaked, impetuous, sprung from Niagara University.
Spectacled, he wears black fedoras. Ascetic, he has a lecher's
smile. A smooth white knob hums in his left ear: he is deaf,
or mostly so, the result of childhood diphtheria. Some days
Tom Benson's world is like a great seamless bubble; some
nights he lies in bed mooning up at the moon. Benson knows
this upon graduation from college: He won't go down to Wall
Street and take a job in those hot walking canyons of bore-
dom. He wants adventure, maybe a religious adventure, although he doesn't yet think of himself as a religious person.
One day, shortly before leaving Niagara University, he tells
these things to a priest. He says he has been thinking of
joining up with an Order, a missionary outfit. He doesn't
want the Jesuits or Franciscans, any of the older, more estab-
lished Orders. No, he wants a group just starting out, one
that might seize on his talents for writing and oratory. The
priest tells him of a Vincentian, a man named Judge, working
down South, in a place called Holy Trinity. This Judge has
recently founded two missionary communities, one for men,
one for women, and is looking to sign up associates from the
North.

Letters are exchanged; a meeting is set. The meeting takes
place one weekend on Judge's next trip north, in a parlor in
a Victorian house in Stirling, New Jersey, looking down on a
sea-green expanse of wood and swamp. Young Tom Benson
is led into the room. Thomas Judge is waiting for him. The
founder has on a coarse woolen clerical shirt and Ground
Gripper Surgical Shoes and a small pair of steel spectacles he
otherwise keeps in a blue velvet case inside his shirt pocket.
In Judge's pants pocket is a rosary with a large black cross
and small brown beads. In his hands is a worn leatherbound
copy of the Spiritual Maxims of Saint Vincent. "I think he
must have been studying me to see how much I loved God
that day," says Tom Benson now. "That's what he'd always
ask you right off: 'How much do you love God?' "

A month later Tom Benson leaves for Alabama. It is September 1928. When Benson takes the habit he also takes a new name—Brother Joachim. He has thrown off the world. He is dead to it. Christ has called a man.

Now Father Joachim Benson is old. Fifty years have passed, and Tom Judge is long dead, and Tom Benson's own days are like glides in dream time, what certain aboriginal tribes of central Australia call the Alcheringa. Within six months of the founder's death, in 1933, Joachim Benson began work on a lyrical book called *The Judgments of Father Judge*. The work was published by a major New York company and had a modest sale. Now Father Joachim would like to get another book about the founder done, but it is hard to focus, time is running out. On an April morning in 1980 he sits slack and pale beneath a lamp in a bedroom at Holy Trinity. After half a century as a missionary he has come back here, to Bethlehem, where he first threw off the world. His skull looms in the light; it seems blue as bird egg. He wears a wildly flowered shirt locked at the throat, a pair of beltless polyester pants. The pants don't fit him so well any longer, so he has flipped them double at the waist; the effect is that of a truss.

A wet cough comes from deep inside. I glance around. The room is a jumble of books, posters, wadded tissues, vials of medicine, folded-over issues of *Saturday Review* and *Variety*. (Despite his spiritual life he has always had a show biz and literary strain in him.) A passport sits on a table beside him. He is going to Germany this summer, he says, to the Passion Play at Oberammergau, though something in his tone belies the statement. Last week he told a doctor he was planning a trip to Puerto Rico, the mission land Tom Judge opened in the twenties. "You're not going anywhere near Puerto Rico," the doctor answered. "Oh, not today, of course," Benson said.

"He . . . ee," Father Joachim wheezes, trying to summon for me the mystic and missionary and fool for the world who so altered his life that Saturday in New Jersey so long ago. Father Joachim's mind still darts, and his voice has a strange charged quality, not unlike the founder's, some people say. Once this voice crackled from pulpits and into radio microphones. As Father Joachim talks now, a veined right hand flutters toward the arm of his chair. He rests a finger beside his nose and smiles, as if he were going to say *abracadabra* and then vanish to the prayer closet where Tom Judge is waiting for him. He begins to speak:

Father Judge could take whatever you were talking about and get it back on the spiritual. I could never make sense of the man at first. I remember writing him a long letter asking what I might do for him in Alabama as a Missionary Servant. He wrote back: "You will study the wounds of Christ. The Word made flesh." That meant nothing to me. That was on too lofty a plain. I had a degree, I was a college graduate. But he had sparks of faith. He wrote me another letter: "The Holy Ghost is busy with you. Why not yield to His sweet impulses?" His conversation was full of riddles like that. Once he was riding horseback to a mountainside village in Puerto Rico. He loved Puerto Rico, you know. Anyway, he suddenly barked: "I'm thinking of the Blessed Mother. She had these riding experiences. Over the hills of Judea."

He would get up in the morning, first thing he'd say, *Benedicamus Domino*. I couldn't understand it, getting up in the middle of the night, practically, and then thanking the Lord for the privilege. He worked many nights late. I had a room down here, he had a room over there; they're all torn down now. He'd say to me, "Good night, Brother Joachim, I'll call you in the morning." And he'd call me in the morning, all right. He'd get me up at four o'clock to pray with him. He was charmed by those morning hours, subdued, solemn. He had a kerosene lantern, and he'd carry it along the walks with him to chapel, a watchman in the night. He'd set the lamp on the choir rail above us. A faint glow reached down into the pews where we sat, huddling against the frost. I considered it all very mysterious. It might have been happening in the catacombs.

He'd come home from a trip in the North, and I'd carry his bags to his room. "Peace be to this house," he'd say when we entered a room. That meant nothing to me. "Peace be to this house!" he'd say again, louder this time. Then he'd turn around. "Say something, Brother Joachim!" You see, he was so deeply spiritual that he thought other people must be this way, too. With Father Judge you would say prayers when you passed a cemetery, prayers when you got into a car, prayers when you

got out of a car, the rosary on a train, rosary in the car.
You never knew when the rosary was going to stop, but
you knew it was going to start. You'd better be ready.

I remember the first time we drove over to the other
side of the property. We always called it the Other Side.
I was driving. Often I drove him. Sometimes I would
take a long time to go a short distance because I knew he
was tutoring me. Father Judge had this way of getting to
you, teaching you something. I was very much careered
by him, although I didn't know it then.

One day we had just turned off the main road when
he said without warning, "Out of the depths I have cried
to Thee, O Lord!" I glanced over at him. I didn't know
if he was sick or what. He was staring straight ahead. I
had to say something, so I said, "O Lord, hear my voice."
"Let your ears be attentive to the voice of my supplica-
tion," he barked. I thought perhaps if I drove a little
faster it might take his mind off it. I had never heard the
De Profundis before. I didn't know it was a prayer. If you
and I were driving to the other side we wouldn't suddenly start praying the *De Profundis*. The man confused
me. He bewildered me. His mind was always in heaven.
It took me the longest time to figure him out. And by
then he was dead.

He couldn't drive a car, or I never saw him drive a car,
at any rate. But he was always telling me how to drive a
car. Once we were coming down from Gadsden after a
funeral. The roads were a terrible dust. He said, "I command you to drive this car thirty miles an hour, not
twenty-nine, not thirty-one." We got to Phenix City; I got
out and said, "Here, you take it." He said, "Get back in
here, Brother!" He hated self-will. He'd step on it every
chance he got. Once he gave me a homily on how to eat
a pork chop. We were having dinner in the refectory and
he got up and came down to my table. "That's not the
way to cut a pork chop, Brother," he said. I said, "Well,
then, how do you cut a pork chop?" So he took my knife
and fork and taught me. There was no special way to do
it, of course, but to him there was.

He despised selfishness, somebody ungenerous with
himself. We were constantly in conflict. Like Saint Paul,
I saw through a glass darkly as one who did not believe.
I persecuted him. He had very little pity on me. He'd
say, "You're Christopher Columbus, aren't you? You

think you've just discovered us. You think you know it
all. You're a big shot. You think we've nothing to do all
day but listen to your fiddle-faddle." He had the impa-
tience of a saint. He was like a prism flashing contradiction. He used to pray for the "sign of contradiction." The
sign of persecution. He wanted that. Once, when the
sisters were starting up their hospital in Gadsden, Alabama, somebody told him that Holy Name of Jesus Hospital was a turnoff name for the South, that the place
would never get any patients. He said he'd rather have a
failure in Jesus' name than success in another. He could
shut you right up like that.

He wasn't proud, though. He felt he was meek, miserable, forever making mistakes. Like Saint Don Bosco,
he wanted souls. "Give me souls," he would say. "Take
everything else from me, but give me souls." He didn't
have college degrees; he had simplicity. He used to sign
his letters to his Vincentian superiors in the North, "In
Saint Vincent, Your Unworthy Son." He was always on
the move; he could never stay home. He was a gypsy. He
was always off to "the work." He said he hoped we would
always be poor, because then he would know where to
find us—on our knees. He said he wanted no "waste
products" in his priesthood. There weren't many, either.
He used to tell us wild things. Once, I heard he went to
the baths in Boston, took off his clothes and just went in.
Those were the children of God in there. He probably
started telling them about the Lord, asking them how
much they loved Jesus.

He would sign up absolutely anybody to come down
here as a seminarian. Let the child of Jesus do what he
can to save souls, he would say. I wrote him once in the
North. He had put me in charge of the place by then.
"Don't send anybody else down here!" I said. "We have-
n't any money." He writes back: "Don't you forget,
Brother Joachim, that anybody who comes to the cenacle
in *Nomine Domini* comes! Don't you forget whom He
might send us. Don't you forget: Whoever comes, we
must live up to *His* expectations!" You see, he could get
you like that, turn it on you.

He loved the farm. He loved going on walks to the
farm. He loved nature; he was a child of nature. He
loved every atom and every star. We always had chickens
down here. They drove me crazy. He was always plan-

ning ways to make money from chickens laying eggs. He had no mercy on a white leghorn that couldn't produce dozens of eggs. Chickens also had to do the will of God and they must be made to know it. If not, off with their heads. We had a mule. Well, that mule was the only one of us that could look him straight in the eye and get away with it. He had absolutely no influence on that mule. He actually pampered it, if you want to know.

Archbishop Curley of Baltimore once attacked him on the front page of the *Catholic Review*. I think it was 1932, December 1932. Father Judge had been trying to sell bonds in Baltimore city to keep us afloat. We were going broke. Once the bishop had been a great friend, a patron, of Father Judge. Not now. "We are sure he has visions of being able to meet his obligations," the bishop said in an insulting front-page open letter to the people of his city. "However, we do not want to see our people banking on visions." Well. A copy of that paper was put in every mailbox of every religious house of studies at Catholic University in Washington. I was living then in Washington and was trying to get a degree at the university. Imagine us walking into class after something like that. Curley thought he was right, I suppose, and eventually the letter helped our cause. But at the time it didn't help. I was furious. I asked Father Judge what we were going to do about it. I wanted to sit right down and write the archbishop a letter and tell him to go to hell about forty times. Father Judge said no, Brother Joachim, we haven't time for that. It got so bad we had to leave Catholic University for a time. Nobody would teach us. Nobody would take us in; everything stopped. We had friends among the Carmelites, though. I went to see the superior of the Carmelite house on the feast of Saint Thérèse, the Little Flower. I took him a rose. I swear to this. Stupid, I'm very stupid. But it all worked out in the end. You see, I know so much of this early history that the others never knew that I have been accused of making it up. I don't have the brains to make up stuff like this. There was too much Divine guidance in Father Judge's work, there were too many people who tried to stop him. He had the trials of a saint. People said he was a fanatic, but crackpots aren't tested like that. He wrote a letter once to Father Hayden, an old Vincentian friend who had sent him one hundred dollars at Holy Trinity.

"Others have given me nothing but knocks and criticism; but you have been true to me, you have given me something else," he wrote.

Here, take a look at this. It's a copy of a letter Father Judge once got from some roughnecks in Phenix City. They signed it, "The Rough Boys of P.C." I love this letter. "Dear Priest, We the patriotic citizens of this beautiful Southern town take a decided stand. Your parochial school isn't wanted here at all, especially taught by your Yankee women. We have heard enough about your convents, jails is a better name for them, we think." You see, this is what he was up against. But the man had a sense of humor about such things. He wrote to the Bishop of Mobile and referred to Holy Trinity as "this backwoods resort of misunderstanding and prejudice." Resort, ha.

I have no idea why he should have come to me in a flash after he died. I think I must have had a special illumination to understand him. He died on November 23, 1933, in Providence Hospital in Washington, D.C. I hadn't seen him in nine months. Actually, we had had a fight, a terrible row. It was a misunderstanding, too much to go into now. He had told me over the phone: "You have been disobedient, Brother Joachim. Now you go home until you learn to obey!" I got my back up. I went home to Albany. But I returned, of course. The Holy Ghost was busy with me. I was yielding to His sweet impulses. Father Judge was dying in a hospital on Capitol Hill. I and four other guys, all dead now, drove down to the hospital one afternoon to see him. Somebody got the bright idea I might upset him, so they went up to his room and I stayed in the car and wept. Got very despondent but said nothing. I never got to see him. Things were so upset in the Community at that time. There was no money. There was the real fear of extinction, that Rome would suppress us. Father Judge didn't know whom he could trust in the end. He had no one to turn to. He died alone. He died convinced he was a failure. He had just three priests in his community. His death finished off three straight years of loss: the loss of Mother Boniface, who ran the sisters' community he had founded; the fire at the sisters' motherhouse; the hurricane that destroyed a piece of our property in Puerto Rico; a drought that killed all the crops at Holy Trinity. He had gotten his "sign of contradiction," all right.

After he died I went to see his nurse. I made her tell me absolutely everything he had said, every breath he took, in those last hours. His poor lungs had given out. She said that if he was permitted to walk a little, it was three times across the room in honor of the Holy Trinity, seven times in honor of the Seven Gifts of the Holy Ghost. A Carmelite nun sent him a little chaplet of the Child Jesus. He touched it as through a fog. Through the night he inquired of the time and then once, suddenly, rose up and said, as if an audience were before him: "The chalices are flashing in Rome."

His last letter, the day before he died, was on the feast of Blessed John Gabriel Perboyre, Vincentian martyr to China. That's the letter where he said, "Remember, we must get the child for Jesus."

Escape

———

Three or four times a year we'd get a day in town. Town glimmered in our imaginations for weeks. They'd cart us in on the seminary's old green buses, drop us off opposite Holy Family Catholic Church in Columbus, Georgia, and we'd then scatter like quail to the movies (the prefect would have posted the night before what was permissible to see), to sporting-goods stores, to barbershops and shoeshine parlors, to the twenty-five-cent photo booth in the back of Davison's Department Store (where we slung arms around one another and froze the moment in sepia), to Morrison's Cafeteria and the Goo-Goo Restaurant and the Black Angus (it was out on Victory Drive—you had to take a cab), but most especially to the Krystal, a long and narrow oasis on Twelfth, where we hunched at the counter on red leatherette stools in a tarnished yellow gleam and gobbled fifteen-cent hamburgers. Freedom was delirious. That night, riding home through the Alabama blackness, somebody would start singing about "Brudder Gum" or "I Got a Girl in Every Port," the tune humming, like the tires, against asphalt and soft snoring.

THE POOL was always open by early March. Brother Senan had painted a South Seas mural on a cinderblock wall up there, and you could lie on your scrap of sand and dream you were in Tahiti, wherever that was. In reality the pool was a concrete hole that it was impossible to keep the slime off. They had dug it in the twenties, after the old Federal Road was relocated and put out in front of the school. Eventually they manicured the pool—took down the Rube Goldberg diving platform and put in an aluminum board—but it was still a homemade eyesore.

On spring Saturdays you couldn't get close. We'd climb atop one another's back and start "chicken fights," class against class, brother against brother. There was something deeper than we knew in all that splashing and grappling, I think. I can still remember the specific and pleasant sensation of knocking into people, trying to wrestle them into the water. There was something visually sexual about it. That afternoon, in the showers, with twenty minutes left until we were due in chapel for the rosary, several of us might grab another boy, get him down on the floor, and proceed to give him a "red belly," our variation of the time-honored prep school depants. In a red belly the victim was spread-eagled on his back. We would begin smacking his tightened stomach into a hot rash with our open palms.

If the pool was an escape, the gym was a larger one, at least for me. Released from inspection on a rainy Saturday, I would tear down with a slicker over my trunks and jersey, skip across puddles in the cracked walk, leap under the wooden overhang at the door, suck for my breath, go inside that musty barn of a place, shed the slicker, choose for sides, and play nonstop, cross-court, all-out basketball until the bell rang at five o'clock.

We had fierce intramural games and even fiercer games with the local Baptist boys from Columbus and Phenix City and Fort Mitchell. Once I scored ten points against Mount Olive Baptist, an all-Negro school. That night I was a small celebrity in the refectory. In my freshman year a 225-pound seminarian from Vicksburg, Mississippi, named Will Booth was our certified varsity hero—a stoic, gentle force beneath enemy boards, flicking off rebounds, setting up the fast break to Dick Ohrt and Eddie Murphy and Butch Evans. We'd scream our fool heads off every time they ran out onto the court. Basketball was what we had to show the world we weren't such "fairies." Every March we played in the Bibb City Tournament, against college-ranked talent. The priest/coach would sit on the bench in his religious habit or Roman collar while we were up in the stands in our black suits, screaming. We had the oddest cheers, sprinkled with Greek and Latin. We never won at Bibb City, but we made it to the final four several times. Teams who played against us went away with new respect.

Once, during a warm-up before a game in a spanking-new gym in Phenix City, Will Booth went up to dunk the ball and tore the rim right out of a shiny glass backboard. Ripped it down the way you'd pop the top off a Fresca. Shards of glass flying in a million directions, seminarians scrambling out of the stands for souvenirs, referees looking dumbly at one another, then shrugging and heading home to supper. (Will, feeling plumb awful, goes over to the sidelines and sticks his head in his hands.)

Our own gym was a onetime roller rink from Fort Benning, Georgia. They had converted it into a gymnasium by putting slats of wood atop a cement floor. By the time I arrived the floor was nearly lethal from too many moppings with banana oil. There were also any number of dead spots in the floor, and you did your best to dribble around them during games so that the ball would come back up. We used to get the damnedest looks from opposing teams who unwittingly dribbled into one of those dead zones. In the wintertime the gym was as cold as a meat locker, and they tried to take the chill off by lighting the half-dozen "salamander" heaters that stood along each wall. The heaters were lit with diesel fuel and coal oil and turned everything around them sooty. They smelled foul. By May every year the gym was like a tropical aviary. Pigeons would defecate from the rafters.

The pool was an escape. The gym was an escape. Christmas was one of the *great* escapes. Father Constantine must have understood that the only way to lick our homesickness was by slaughtering us with activities and a sudden freedom from routine. School would let out about the nineteenth of December, and then we'd spend the next few days rubbing and polishing the place (cleanliness was next to godliness and the Saviour Himself was coming), waxing floors, shining candlesticks until they glowed like ads for Brasso. When the cleaning was done we'd begin the decorating. Crews of boys would forage in the woods for trees and branches for the wreath making. Platoons of wreath makers would assemble in the garages behind the refectory. Scores of wreaths were made. Stable scenes—gaudy visions of plywood and cellophane and aluminum foil—began to show up on the lawns. But it was in the dorms that the real spectaculars arose. For those two weeks Father Constantine let us turn our sleeping quarters into jungles of pine ropes and bamboo and fir. We'd stencil every window with snowflakes. We'd drag in floor-to-ceiling trees, propping them with rocks in Number 10 cans. About five o'clock on Christmas Eve all work would halt; the Feast was nigh. After Midnight Mass and a two o'clock breakfast in the refectory (real bacon, rashers of it), we'd tear off to the rec rooms, where the packages and cards that Father Constantine had been hoarding for weeks now lay. The rec room looked like a United Parcel depot. Invariably there was a seminarian or two who didn't have a pile of packages waiting for him, but Father Constantine always managed to come up with stray gifts hastily wrapped.

After the package bazaar we were free for the next fifteen hours. You could even go off on a hike in the middle of the night, if you were that nuts. I wasn't. I was crazy enough to go down to the gym and play mad games of one-on-one basketball with my pal Bertin Glennon until dawn, both of us wrapped in stocking caps and warm-up suits, our breath frosting in front of us, the ball making eerie solitary pounds against the night. We had the place, obviously, to ourselves. Afterward, Bertin and I came up to the dorms and steamed ourselves raw for an hour in the showers.

I had basketball bad, and who knows exactly why—sublimation, *machismo*, a latency? At thirty-eight, I'm not exactly Rabbit Angstrom, but there are times when I still sneak down to a gym at a noon hour and fire at a bucket for thirty minutes, nonstop. I stand out there in my socks feeling ridiculous and glorious. In my sophomore year, as a jayvee star, I averaged sixteen points a game. I have pointed this out to my wife many times.

New Year's Eve meant a Holy Hour from eleven to midnight. Handshakes and greetings on the step outside afterward, followed by coffee and doughnuts in the refectory. That night there would be a movie. January 3 meant death day. The bells were back. The schedule was back. The Frog was back. Then the days blurred until spring.

The biggest escape of all was a free day in town. When we finally got in there you might say we were easy to spot: knots of buzz-headed black-suited boys in skinny ties and white shirts and high-gloss shoes. (Buffing up the night before was part of town ritual.)

Town was never tawdry Phenix City, Alabama, but Columbus, shining on the Georgia shore. Columbus was much bigger than Phenix City and had a real downtown, and, besides, Phenix City was a tainted town. In the early fifties the place had been a hellhole of gambling and prostitution, a little Newport, Kentucky, much of its vice serving the fifty thousand soldiers stationed at nearby Fort Benning, Georgia. In 1957, the year before I went south for the first time, the Associated Press came to look over Phenix City. A lyrical reporter filed this story: "Three years ago this town of twenty-eight thousand across the Chattahoochee River from Columbus, Georgia, appeared completely rotten. You name it, Phenix City had it—and it was easy to find. Dames were available by the dozens—and they weren't exactly ladies. You could go to cock fights, view bedraggled stripteasers, get your head bashed or be rolled for your money by B-girls." Phenix City's fleshpots were mostly scoured clean by the time I arrived in Alabama, not that I would have known a B-girl had she been wearing a neon sign.

Columbus, with its string of honky-tonks and pawn shops and Army-Navy stores, with its rebel flags flying off every other license plate, wasn't exactly Vatican City, or Paris, either, even if Edwin Booth had once played Hamlet at the Springer Opera House. What art and beauty my teenage senses could connect to consisted of Cousin Al on the radio; huge white mansions fragrant with camellias and dogwood; the Goo-Goo, which, true enough, was a queer name for a restaurant (it had a yellow duck on the roof), but the place did serve awfully good food.

In the late 1950s a fourteen-year-old Northern boy was exotically surprised, though not quite shocked, to find that public buildings in Columbus had separate restroom facilities, side by side, for blacks and whites. I remember the drinking fountains at the Columbus airport. They were identical except for the signs. One said: White Only. The other said: Colored Only. I didn't know it, but I had arrived in the last hours of an era.

●

You can jet down to Georgia today and see a broad-based integration and a restoration of historic areas—and also the plasticizing of America. The North has come South, and not all of it is good. The town's graceful old homes still stand, though in diminishing number. (The parking lot of the Sheraton Ralston motor hotel butts up against the back side of one fading mansion.) These days the barbershops aren't called tonsorial parlors, nor do old glossy black men with suspenders and foul-smelling cigars and two-tone shoes sit in them grinning at seminary boys getting their seventy-five-cent haircuts. The Goo-Goo is now a car wash. And when I called WDAK Radio to ask about Cousin Al, the lady at the switchboard told me that that great disc jockey of the Southern airwaves had lately passed away. Arteries had hardened, I believe she said. Heart had failed. The Cuz is gone, she said, sounding just terrible. So Columbus didn't wait, and for me to have expected anything else was arrogant and naive. Still . . .

On a visit to Columbus recently, I was knocking around down at the decrepit railway depot, trying doors, peering in windows, when I came on a retired agent for the Southern Railway (which amalgamated the Central of Georgia). He was sunning on a bench. We talked beneath a blistered tin roof. He had on a straw hat and a white open-necked summer sport shirt. It was still mid-March, though warm enough for Northern boys to think it summer. "I used to ride the Seminole down from Chicago," I said, hoping to engage him in a story. "The Seminole," he said, intoning it, as you might intone the word "Alaska." "She had reclining seat coaches and a sleeper with six roomettes and four double bedrooms and a diner with real silverware and niggers in white coats to wait on you. Helluva train."

Helluva town, too, at least for a kid with ten bucks in his pocket and eight hours of freedom. The heart of Columbus, when I stalked her, was Broadway, a wide boulevard with a center strip of green, a kind of symbol for the day's hopes. We'd go up and down Broad all day long, in and out of the five-and-dimes, the Army-surpluses, the pawnshops, looking for something we never quite found. Each of us had dough given us the night before by the prefect. (You'd line up outside Father Constantine's office, and he'd check the amount

you requested off your floating account; the ceiling was about
fifteen bucks.)

Early on the morning of a day in town we would gather
outside under the pergolas, waiting for Brother Loughlan
and Brother Anselm to come around the corner of the refectory in the buses. Just before we left, Father Constantine
would step aboard in his habit to bless us and warn us once
more to behave ourselves. He'd climb down, and the buses
would groan down the lane. Odd, but I can't recall that any
of us ever missed the bus back that night. The fear of reprisal
was too great, I guess. Though a few of us got into dirty
bookstores, or maybe talked to girls at a drugstore, this was
about the extent of our wildness. There was an Italian restaurant in Columbus run by a man who hated the Pope. It was
off limits.

Once, on the eve of a day in town, Father Constantine came
into chapel at the end of retiring prayers. There was a
"graphic documentary" playing at one of the theaters. It was
about aborigines in New Guinea. "Some of the people in the
movie don't wear clothes, gents," he said. "You can go, but I
expect proper behavior." I think every last one of us went to
see that movie. What I chiefly remember about it is a lot of
strange small bronze humans running around with tubes
over their erect genitals. We used to get movies in the seminary, too, though none of this variety. (Except for the time
Written on the Wind somehow slipped through the gates. They
showed it in the refectory, and the sisters from across the
road came. Tires screeched, liquor bottles flew, the screen
grew hot with female flesh. About halfway through they cut
it off, and we all trooped to bed.)

As always, Father Constantine put out the lights after a day
in town. He'd go up and down the aisles reading his breviary
while we undressed. You never knew whether the lights were
going to go out immediately or whether he was going to say
something. It was the last mystery of the day. He'd stand in
the corner by the switch. "Good night, gents," he'd say. Darkness would drop down.

There were interior escapes, too.

Faculty meetings are witch covens held in creepy light. This
is when you get axed, voted out with the bean. A dread hangs

in the air on nights when the priests convene. There is a pall over supper, over study period, over spiritual reading, over the rubric of preparing for bed. Through the years, elaborate fantasies have grown up among us about faculty meetings, and one of the most sacredly held concerns the Vote. I have never attended a faculty meeting, of course, nor has any other seminarian, but each of us knows exactly what goes on down there: names solemnly intoned, a porcelain cup passed around into which each priest/witch must plunk either a white or a black bean. White means you stay, black means you go. (Piles of beans are set before each chair before the meeting: chips for a satanic poker game.) Only in the rarest instance may a man abstain from the bean. Whichever color tallies higher after a round determines destinies. Names of the dismissed are chalked on a board, and in the morning, when the news is out, there are trunks on the front step, seminarians weeping. . . .

Study hall. There is a faculty meeting tonight. Heads bent over books; there is the steady creak of ballpoints. Bugs ride in through thrown-up windows. A fluorescent communion of bodies lined row by row. In forty-five minutes the bell will ring, and then desks will slam and there will be a great sea-wash to chapel for retiring prayers and spiritual reading. The halls will be alive with talk then, desperate almost.

At eight twenty-five, Joe Troncale, Hatchet Face, rises casually from his desk. There is a bulge in his right front pants pocket. He goes out into the hall, asks permission of the monitor (a college man tonight) to go down to the bio lab to pick up some notes he left there earlier today. There aren't any notes. Hatchet Face is going to gas a bullfrog. He is mad to know how long the fat pulpy prize he caught this afternoon in a field below the pool will be able to last under direct application of toxic gas. The Tronc has selected tonight for his amphibicide because the priests are over on the other side, meeting behind a door marked: CLOÏSTER. None of us has ever been past that door, or at least down its dark sanctums, although nearly all of us have wandered around to the back of the building during free periods to sneak glances through a tile fence at the faculty meditation garden adjoining the priests' rec room. There is an ornate statue of Our Lady of Guadaloupe in the courtyard, executed by the Vatican Mosaic Works. Nothing very shocking is ever seen through the tiles, maybe a cleric in a sport shirt holding a highball. Still, it's a little like trying to peek on your parents' bedroom, coming on a nun with her headdress off. Shivers of guilt attend. No cleric with a highball will be glimpsed tonight, no nun with her headdress off. The bad seeds are being voted on with beans. Visions of this stoke Troncale's lust.

In the lab now, he flips on a light, closes the door. He takes a large clear beaker off a shelf, gets out his frog, tries to stuff it inside the bottle. He has to push a little, jam the damn frog. His hands are trembling; he gathers a film of sweat. He gets the frog inside the beaker at last, puts a lid on the glass, and leaves only the smallest opening for a nozzle. The nozzle he has in mind is connected to a thin black hose which is connected to a jet coming out of the wall behind him. Hatchet Face eases on the jet. There is sick delight on his face. A pleasant moist scent begins to perfume the air. Soon the frog begins to twitch. Then its eyes bug. The frog is on its back, heaving in huge, croaking sobs. And it is here, just as the deed is being consummated, that Vincent Fitzpatrick walks in. He has left the faculty meeting to check on an experiment.

"Wh-what are you doing?" the Old Roman says in that fierce, undulant voice he reserves for moments of special incredulity, inexplicability. His thumb arches for the back of his head.

Troncale keeps gassing. He is in a close encounter of the spiritual kind. The gas makes a soft hissing sound—a benign rattler, a hidden grenade.

"D-don't you know that's a highly volatile gas?"

"Yes, Father."

"Well, then, why don't you stop that?"

"But, Father, this frog's almost dead."

"Would you please turn off the gas! I insist you turn off the gas!"

The frog lives. Joe Troncale makes indefinite jug. He spends nearly every moment until school is out digging a trench for a pipe out to a running track. Some days he climbs in the trench he is digging and goes to sleep. His life of crime isn't over, either. The following year, on a free day in town, Hatchet Face and a classmate go to an Army-surplus store

and buy starter pistols. Back at the seminary, they sneak out
to the front gate one night after supper and wildly fire off
rounds of blanks. The starters are much more fun than cap
pistols, but, sadly, they're not real revolvers. What else might
be done with them? Ah, Troncale has bulbed with an idea:
the prefect's dog. That night, after lights out, he and his co-
conspirator sneak from their beds and coax Father Constantine's pooch down to the gym with cookies. Inside the gym
they lock the doors, turn off all the lights, begin firing the
starter pistols at the dog. The animal goes nearly berserk
trying to escape.

After he quits the seminary (he lasts nearly eight years and
is in vows) Joe Troncale gets a degree, then joins the Army.
Soon he becomes a conscientious objector: doesn't want to
kill, not even frogs. Eventually he gets discharged, gets a
doctorate in Russian, becomes a respected college professor
in Virginia. Married (to a woman raised Southern Baptist),
father of two girls, he occasionally amuses his family with old
seminary stories, standing in the middle of the floor after
supper and acting them out. Bearded, aquiline, eyes bulbed,
as if even now the nimble mind behind them is plotting some
new nefarious night deed, he says one evening to a visitor
from back beyond the moon: "I think we must have been
creating a seminary as we lived the other one. As survival.
There were so many damn rules. We wanted to do what we
wanted to do, and they weren't going to let us. But, say, don't
you know Father Vincent went back to that faculty meeting
and they roared?"

Lust at
the Hotel Atlantic

In June, a year wiser, another year of seminary under
our belts, we spiritual mariners would come back to our
home parishes with a certain sly status. We were the
parish's little priests, forbidden fruit not to be touched
by the town girls, who therefore eyed us with curiosity if
not quite lust. As a hedge against such touching, Father
Killian, the rector, would have sent home ahead of us a
list of summer do's and don'ts. Chief among the do's:
attendance at daily Mass. Chief among the don'ts: attendance at "mixed" parties.

PERHAPS my summers home weren't as awful as I now seem
to recall, although looking back I can see myself only as a
displaced person. Those three months from June to September were mostly something to be waited out until I could get
back to my real interests, my real friends, my real life. I got
by on occasional mail from Rosedale, Long Island, and Mil-
lington, New Jersey, and from boozy summer evenings in the
rectory with Father Sullivan, the assistant pastor, who poured
out tall glasses of bourbon and turned up his hi-fi and said it
was always like this for him, too.

I remember a rhyme some of us used to pen more or less
mockingly in the back of one another's yearbooks: "Don't

abuse your vacation, and you won't lose your vocation." I took it as literal truth.

One seminary summer, after my parents had gone north to our cottage in Wisconsin, leaving me at home with the cocker spaniel, the second car, and a refrigerator full of TV dinners, I drove into downtown Chicago and took a room, presumably for the night, at a cheap hotel on a side street near the old LaSalle railway depot. As I pulsed down the Congress Street Expressway into the Loop, I don't believe I was consciously working through why I wished to rent a room and what I might do once I got it. God knows, I doubt if I was capable of bringing a woman back to a room, though fantasies of that must have resided somewhere in my head. I was nineteen that summer and between my fifth and sixth years of seminary. I had never rented a room in a hotel before. Just the taking of a room on my own in a city the size of Chicago seemed its own tawdry thrill. Years later I would write a short story—I called it "Lust at the Hotel Atlantic"— about that night.

"I said you look scared as hell." She was tugging at his arm on the fringe of the crowd.

After they had freed themselves from the crowd they began to walk up the avenue. She just fell in alongside of him. He choked down his nervousness and began to tell her about his trip and the excitement of being on his own, and she said she had picked him for an out-of-towner, all right. He was careful not to mention the seminary but said instead he had finished his fifth year at Staunton, a military school in Virginia (he had looked it up once on the off-chance something like this could happen), and that he was thinking of going on to West Point in another year. She cut him off.

"Listen, if you've got a room here like you said, why don't we buy some beer and go up there and drink?"

I was working that summer at Mr. Carmody's printing factory. Mr. Carmody was an outstanding Catholic layman who had made room in his plant for an out-of-work seminarian. He even offered to drive me to the job every morning, drop me off each afternoon. When he dropped me off that Friday afternoon my lustful odyssey in nighttown had been formulated. I bathed, talc-ed, got into my mint-green shirt and skinny black tie and the checkered sports coat that my brother Marty had left behind a year earlier, after he had left the seminary and joined the Coast Guard. I couldn't do anything about my lawn-mower haircut. I fed the dog, locked the house. I pulled out of the driveway. Something important was about to happen.

He could scarcely believe his luck. She liked him. She was attracted to him. He remembered opening the door to the room a little while later with the feeling he had already done something terribly sinful. He raised the one small curtainless window and turned on the small rotating fan above the dresser. There were exposed pipes running the length of the ceiling, and these made the room look even narrower and more confining than it was. The place smelled vaguely of old wine, or maybe a combination of wine and urine. They opened the six-pack. The metallic taste of the beer combined with his nervousness to give him a heady feeling fast. He felt sick. He excused himself. He went down the hall and found the bathroom and tried to throw up. When he came back she was lying on the bed in her slip, a beer can resting on her flat belly. The white rubber clips that held up her stockings were just visible where her slip was hiked up. He felt excited and nauseous and resolute.

In the Loop I put my dad's Rambler in an all-night garage. I found a hotel. The building I chose was tall and narrow, darker than any other on that side street, with a vertical neon sign flashing, in red, the word "Atlantic." The desk clerk had the complexion of someone who has lived in Liverpool most of his life. He demanded eight dollars in advance. He slid a clunky skeleton key on a brass ring from behind his little grated window. I nearly lurched for it. I had reached the first gate of the Inferno. The room the key opened was oppressive and yellow, and after I had bounced several times on the bed, and congratulated myself on my daring, and put my toothbrush in the bathroom, I wondered what I should do next.

I came downstairs and stepped out into the humid early evening. Directly across the street was an appliance store with an accordion iron gate stretched across its front, a common enough sight in a city, although I had never seen such a sight. It startled me.

When he got back from the bathroom he remembered hesitating inside the door, stunned at seeing her like that with the beer can balanced on her belly and the white rubber clips showing

beneath her hiked-up slip. He went over to the bed and kissed
her on the mouth while a dizzy throbbing began in his temples.
She liked him. She was attracted to him. Her fingers were white
and his toes were cold and then she began pulling at his shirt.

Nothing remotely like this ever happened to me while I
studied for the priesthood, although, as I said at the outset, I
once wrote an (awful) short story, after I left, based on my
lustful and celibate seminary summers. The story was to be
part of a novel for Professor Knoepfle's creative writing class
at St. Louis University. I didn't finish the novel and the world
has not been poorer. I drafted "Lust at the Hotel Atlantic"
on yellow paper, and I still have it, as I still have my old
seminary steamer trunk, which is now antiqued green and
serves as a coffee table in the living room.

The real story of my hot white night in Chicago that summer, my ravenous prowl of the city, is that it was a bust. Guilt
and shame got me once more, although not until I had
gorged myself for several hours on dirty movies and dirty
magazines and Wimpy burgers. By ten o'clock I was speed-
ing, with an erection so prolonged my testicles ached. I paid
an admission to another soft-porn movie. Outside the theater
were gaudy cutouts of semi-naked women. I don't recall the
movie, but I remember coming out afterward onto South
State in gas-vapored light and smelling hot pizza from an
open stand. The light was like weak tea in a clear glass. Then
I went to a restaurant and took a table near the door and
watched a young woman at the bar fiercely arguing with a
man much older than she was. The woman got off her stool,
crushing her cigarette, cursing the man. She turned and
walked straight toward me, and for an instant I knew she was
going to sit down at my table. She was only going for the
door, but even after I realized that, it took me several minutes
to stop trembling.

It was too late to go over to St. Peter's church on Madison
and blurt out my sins in the dark of a box to a voice I didn't
know. The Franciscans who heard confessions there wouldn't
be back in their stalls until morning. I walked through pale
shadows back to the Atlantic. I waved to the desk clerk with
the Liverpudlian tan. I undressed, lay with the light on, my
heart pounding like Poe's telltale heart about to come

through the floorboards. I stared at the overhead pipes. I tried to fall asleep. Ruin and damnation would come to me; I was a sinner beyond saving. One day the police would find my crumpled body in a smashed car along the barricade of an expressway, and in the wallet of poor dead Paul Hendrickson would be an i.d. linking his squalid present to his Camelot past. Paul Hendrickson, the news accounts would say, had once studied for the priesthood.

Shortly after midnight I got up, dressed, rode the elevator to the empty lobby, walked straight up to the clerk. "Sir," I said, "I've just gotten word my mother is very ill. I'm going to have to leave. But please don't worry about refunding my money. Here's your key." I turned on my heel and walked out. The jerk was laughing at me, I knew.

By one o'clock I was back in my own dark silent suburban bed. On my way home I prayed fervidly for one thing: that I wouldn't get creamed by a drunk on the expressway. The next afternoon, in the Saturday box at my parish, came the real orgy—of remorse. The priest seemed somewhere between amused and shocked. I think he recognized my voice. "Are you sure you're praying to the Blessed Mother to overcome your problems with purity, son?" he asked. "You know you can always speak to the mother of Jesus." "Yes, Father," I murmured, grateful once again for the dark.

One of the problems with summer vacations was that I didn't have anyone to pal around with. My old friends from elementary school had gone on, just as I had, to new friendships and interests. They had also gone on to new secrets. I can still remember the pain of several disastrous Friday nights of trying to sit casually in the back of somebody's car on a tour of A&W root beer stands and Big Boy hamburger joints and miniature golf courses. The talk and the people in these places were achingly foreign. There were girls hanging on the arms of boys in harshly lit booths, in the dusky interiors of jalopies, and I think they picked up my virgin scent as a basset picks up a rabbit. I was trying to mount gaiety and cool, and I was only pathetically stiff and false. All my old friends had crossed to the other side of a lake I knew nothing about. I couldn't wait to get home from these outings, and I'm certain my friends couldn't wait to drop me off, having finally appeased their mothers, who were good Catholics, by taking out seminarian Paul. We'll do it again real soon, everybody lied. I felt like Father Frank Jr. at the disco. My clothes were wrong, my hair was wrong.

Maybe I would have had a better time on vacations if I had even once landed a decent job. Seminarians unfailingly got home later than anyone else so you took what you could get. One summer I caddied; after four hours of lugging a rich dentist's golf bag I'd have $3.75. Another summer I mowed lawns in a cemetery on the edge of Chicago, despising every swath of it. Someone in the Serra Club, a Catholic men's organization, had gotten me the job. My father knew I hated it, so at supper he'd try to get me talking about my day's adventure, hoping, I suppose, I would discover it wasn't really so bad after all. There wasn't a lot to tell. Every morning they would haul me and two dozen migrants from Mexico, each of us with a gas can and funnel and small red trimming mower, into a sea of tombstones. The cemetery must have been the circumference of London. I could not have found my way out of there if I had tried. They'd drop us off, come back at noon, and again at four-thirty. None of the Mexicans spoke English and I didn't know Spanish, so there we were, stranded amid acres of stone angels and crypts and gargoyled mausoleums trying to talk with our hands over the whine of mowers. Dillinger was supposedly buried somewhere in the place, and almost every day somebody with a camera drove up to ask where the gangster lay. I was the spokesman for the group. After a week or two the Mexicans discovered I was a seminarian. (I think the guy driving the wagon told them.) *"Oh, Pablo, padre,"* they'd call, and laugh and point and wave, and I'd call back, *"Oh, compañeros,"* pointing and waving and laughing.

The first several days on the job I don't think one or two of the migrants understood the theory of the internal combustion engine: that it needs gas. The mower would sputter to a stop, having run out of fuel, and then its driver would begin kicking at it and cursing furiously. *"%¢$&¢%$## máquina!"* the migrant would yell, pulling at the blasted *máquina's* starter cord. The first word sounded like *ching-gow.* I didn't know what it meant, but I figured something like "damn." I would walk over, say, "Excuse me" with my hands, pour some fuel into the tank, and a minute later walk off like a miracle worker, a loaves-and-fishes man from Galilee who, if pressed, could probably do a trick or two with lepers. We were all fast friends by the time I left. I could say *ching-gow* with the best of them. They'd howl and point and laugh at my use of this word. *"Pablo, padre, ching-gow."* I never did learn what it meant.

The job got aborted early in August when it turned out that the man I was riding to work with every day started getting "perverty" on me. His name was Wickey, or at least that was what was written on the back of the red bowling shirt he sometimes wore to work. Wickey also had wrap-around Jackie Kennedy sunglasses and smoked a foul fat rope of a cigar. His stomach leaked through a small hole in his bowling shirt. He wasn't married and spent an awful lot of time on weekends at the bowling alley. I knew from the first day he rolled into our driveway that something wasn't quite right, though my analytical powers were not such as to grasp the idea he could be interested in me. "Deviate," my father would later call him.

My mother, it turned out, had mistrusted Wickey from the start, but he had come highly recommended to us as a local Catholic layman from an adjoining parish. Besides, I had no other way to get to work. Wickey was on the year-round maintenance staff of the cemetery, and at first he was the perfect, if gabby, gentleman. Eventually it was small, creepy things in his talk. Then it was a squeeze on my knee one morning, then a pat on my behind when I got out of the car. Then it was a half-giggly account of how he had had a dream the night before of tying me to a tree with my clothes off. Then one day he said, "Say, Paul, did you ever wonder how many holes a man has in his body? Let's see, he's got two nostrils, two ear holes . . ." I told him I had never wondered and edged toward my door. I was ready to try to leap from the car.

It went on like this for about another week, and then one night at supper I blurted to my parents I couldn't stand this guy, he was a jerk, and I wasn't going to ride with him again. My father had been out of town on a flight when Wickey had first come for me, but my mother understood what I was now trying to get out. None of us had ever talked about homosexuality before, or at least the subject had not been raised in my presence. That night we called Wickey and said we wouldn't be needing a ride from him anymore. My parents stood behind me while I talked. My father wanted to get on the line.

I drove our second car for the rest of the week, then quit the job, though not before Wickey cornered me in the lunchroom and demanded to know what was wrong. Nothing, I lied. I spent the remaining weeks until school packing and repacking my seminary trunk, digging potatoes from the garden, mowing my own lawn. I never saw Wickey again. Back at school it made a good story at table.

Heresy Is Just
Truth Out of Proportion

Up past the pool was an old loggers' road that led to a sawmill, and near it was a gigantic dune of sawdust, off limits. Sometimes two or three of us sneaked up there to play King of the Mountain. Once, seated at the top of this forbidden yellow pyramid with Pat Ryan and Mike Scarbrough, weary, I cupped my hand into the still-warm shavings and sliced downward six or seven inches. Blue flame ignited in the sultry air and the fire seemed to curl and lick at my fingers. I drew back, both frightened and awed at what was down there.

NEARLY THE WHOLE time I was in, and for a long time after I left, I went through bouts of worry that the seminary had "turned" me into a latent homosexual, and that it was only a matter of weeks or months or years before "it" came roaring out. Amid a navy of worries this was easily the biggest boat. Usually my worries were seasonal, coming in the fall and lasting into winter, and for years after I was gone, when they still came at those times, I could never see the logic. I remember a woman named Margie whom I was dating in Michigan, when I worked at a paper there, confronting me once about homosexuality in the dark of her Grosse Pointe driveway. "Paul, are you worried for some reason you might be gay?" she said. I was out of the seminary eight years by then, had been married and separated, and was in the final stages of a prolonged and guilt-ridden divorce. I thought of myself nonetheless as something of a Detroit rake. Margie and I had been going out for several months, and her question, seemingly from nowhere, knocked me flat-footed. "Why, noooo!" I said, sounding, I imagine, a little like comedian Don Knotts in those man-on-the-street routines on the old Steve Allen TV show. (Allen to high-wire walker: "Are you nervous, sir?" High-pitched blurt: "Noooo!") How had she found out?

In the seminary my worry about catching homosexuality was the size of a Buick. There were times when I was sure I was fated. By my second year of studies an odd antithetical pattern had become apparent: in June, home for the summer for several weeks, I would discover that my fantasies and images about sex were reverting to the heterosexual. It was flooding relief if also constant torment for the confession box. *Hey, I'm no queer,* I'd tell myself like some punked-up street-corner eye-talian sharpie, practically ecstatic over my ability to get erections in the back of Chicago dirty bookstores as I stood in creepy light beside men three times my age. I'd be in the city all day, having told my folks I was meeting several of my classmates for a day at the museums or Comiskey Park. That night, drying dishes, my mother would say, "How was it?" "Fine," I'd say.

And yet, by fall, back at school for four or five weeks, I would start all over again to be both distressed and stoked with a secret joy to find myself physically stimulated, tingled, by certain seminarians. These tingles could come from the "accidental" brush of my arm up against another arm on a sofa in the rec room, from the sweaty entangle of arms and legs going up for rebounds on the gym floor, from the seeming special import invested in traded punches, or shared jokes, or bartered desserts, at table. Not that I was feeling these tingles from just any seminarian, and not that my brain was flooded purely with homophile images. We still talked an awful lot about girls. Generally my attention seemed directed toward a select three or four seminarians every year; my subconscious must have done the preselecting. Sometimes they were seminarians older than I, though more often they were younger boys who tended to the fair-skinned and slight-framed. By turns I could feel jealousy, ardor, anger, and protectiveness for them. The prefects knew about such hidden emotions in us, I believe, and watched us like cats from a perch. No one talked about it. And I could stop neither my feelings nor my shame.

It did not occur to me in those days that blond, slight boys might be a reasonable, if ersatz, substitution in a consciousness for blond, delicate girls, and that once the latter were wiped from a field of vision, it might stand to reason the former could evoke both emotional and esthetic responses, could seem both pleasing and arousing in a confounding way. I suppose in some fashion this explains the phenomenon of homosexuality in prisons and trenches, although in such places the imagination gets meaner. In the seminary I could seldom bring my fears out onto any kind of open ground, except occasionally in conference with my spiritual director, and then I think I was too confused about other things going on there between him and me to get any real assurance on my sanity. I was sure I was a "homo."

Almost literally were female images wiped from sight. I am not saying this was someone's diabolical intent. A day in town would provide a sudden field of vision, but this came only three or four times a year. And in the library every week we had *Time* and *Sports Illustrated,* although I also recall pictures excised from those magazines by an all-knowing scissors. Word of a "snatch" in the library would spread like grassfire, and before you could get over there to lean your elbows on the case and casually browse the week's issues, page 46 of *Time* had a window of air instead of lust in it. (It was only Sophia Loren in a two-piece bathing suit.) Then you might cool down by looking at the latest issue of *Vital Speeches* or maybe taking a thumb-through the Oxford English Dictionary.

One had books to find women in, and I was a ceaseless reader. For some reason the prefect let me keep James Michener's *Hawaii,* and I can remember to this moment my profound excitement over a passage in that novel about a ship captain reclined on his back while a plentitude of island girls worked on him at once. My imagination had not conjured such a thing.

It was implicitly given that someone caught in a "perverty" act would be gone by morning. The following sentiment is from a document privately published by the Province of St. Augustine of the Capuchin Fathers in Pittsburgh: "Of course the case may occur of a boy who commits a sin with a girl while home on vacation, and I should be inclined to think that psychologically this would be a greater deterrent to the advancement to the priesthood than the sin of sodomy, even though the latter is a graver transgression of God's laws from the theological standpoint." Odd sentiment, but then we were in an odd atmosphere. Last year, in a talk with one of my old seminary prefects, I brought up the subject of homosexuality. He told me it had officially been handed down to him from above that he was to boot out, on the first transgression, with no chance for excuse, any student caught in an overt homosexual act. (Later they would soften the policy.) "Sounds like a dumb rule," I said. "Couldn't be dumber," he said. Like all of us, he has come a far piece.

Between unequivocal perverty behavior and, say, the light fevered brush-up against somebody's arm on a divan lay a multitude of point-shaving. For me it was all disguise and point-shave and probing experiment. Things could be more than they seemed and look less. It was seeking without knowing, or at least acknowledging. It was whether and how and why. I have this image now of a fierce, humming sensuality among us, a blooded presence, while up above, where we wore our smiles, there were only our piety and camaraderie and bonhomie. Some will say that is too stark, and maybe it is. Most of the schoolmates I have discussed homosexuality with shrug it off. They can't remember. It isn't important.

And yet at least one boy, now man, from my time has related how he used to lie in bed in his parents' farmhouse in Arkansas those first five or six months after he left and contemplate his suicide. He had decided to put a shotgun in his mouth and pull the trigger with a string looped to his toe, if it came to that. He was blackly depressed about everything and some of it, he suspects now, lay in his sexual confusion. He can remember getting an erection nearly every time he got near a classmate with smooth features and a Florida tan. In time the depression went away. On the night I saw him he was finishing law school in New York, was an editor of his law review, was being courted by the best firms in the country. He was married and a Vietnam veteran. He said he was an atheist and then corrected himself and said he probably was an agnostic: he can't prove God doesn't exist. Almost immediately after he left he experienced a rejection of his faith—part repudiation, he suspects, part defense mechanism. "The whole Catholic thing is so far away," he said with a kind of dreaminess when I tried to press for something more.

One felt all sorts of odd things and didn't dare act on them. How in hell did you tell your confessor you felt aroused from touching someone's arm on a davenport and that you wished to do it again? That sounded stupid. Was it mortal or venial? We were subjects in a small, cramped moral universe of laws and careful controls. I said something like this a while ago to an old seminary friend named John O'Connell. "Aw, you took it too hard," he said. Maybe he's right. Come to think of it, a lot of that stuff was pretty comical. I remember a seminarian named Riggie, one dorm over. Riggie had a huge, creamy, red rear and could prove it on demand. "Hey, Riggie, moooon-shine," the juniors would softly chorus after Father Constantine had put out the lights and gone to his office. Then Riggie would sit up in bed, drop his pajamas, and turn his behind into a dozen cross-arcing flashlights. No one thought that was perverty. It was hilarious.

I now suspect that most of the "fruity" things going on among us were simply adolescent rite and passage. Was it more than this? Was some of it what clinicians call "transitory" homosexuality? I don't know; I am not a clinician. So far as I know, no one ever staged what is rudely but accurately known by boys as a "circle jerk." We were too old for that, and besides our sexuality was more hidden. There were nights when I recall lying awake and listening to the light cacophonic concert of creaking springs up and down the dorm. Then the room was still. I used this image on a priest friend a while ago. I told him I thought there was more masturbating going on than most of us knew. "Maybe you just heard people who were restless and couldn't get to sleep," he said.

It has been fully documented by now that many preadolescents and adolescents go through a phase of life when they are strongly attracted to their own sex and engage in an experimental homosexual activity. In most cases the attraction is not arresting, and they go on later to heterosexual relationships. There are blurred, special feelings that simply exist sometimes between males and other males, between females and other females, and I believe that if you have lived a significant portion of your adolescence in a boys' school composed of uppers and lowers, composed of heroes and goats, boys of beauty and boys of brawn, then it is nearly impossible not to have experienced at times something lingering and something far deeper and more quizzical than the word "friendship" suggests.

In my first few years I used to idolize Butch Evans. Butch was four years ahead of me and probably the best-liked student in the school. We used to say it was impossible for a parent or a guest to get on the seminary property without having Butch come up and say hello. I wanted to pass him my desserts, I wanted to fold his laundry during work periods, I wanted to get letters from him on vacation. (I did and saved them all; we were yukking over some of them a while ago.) At the same time I should say I have encountered a number of my old schoolmates who insist they never once, the whole time they were in, felt a physical stimulation, much less an erection, of the kind and source I am writing of here —and they can say it without sounding like Don Knotts parked in a Michigan driveway. But enough others, I think, were secretly fretting as much as I was about what they seemed to be "turning into." I asked Butch about it not long ago, and he said, dissolving into that boisterous cracker laugh of his, "Didn't you think it was funny when your best friends kept wanting to ride piggyback up at the pool?" There were times, in the rec room, when I could have asked somebody to dance—had I known how, had there been waltzes.

I think of all those mad vicious games of Ping-Pong in the rec room on Saturday afternoon or before evening Benediction—boys standing six and seven feet back from the table and slamming the balls till they cracked. ("Gents-uh, I told you about this, huh?" Father Constantine would say, his eyeballs dancing like William Buckley's.) We'd run over from supper, grab the paddles, and keep games going right up until the last thirty seconds before we were due in chapel. There was frenzy in those games, and I wonder what they signified. Passions got unleashed. Once my friend Moose

Gerken got so agitated by the Fly Lord of our class during a game that he threw down his paddle, picked up a heavy chair, and began screaming and cursing at the seminarian. The Fly Lord took off across those oiled floors with Moose in hot pursuit. The Fly Lord ran the class, but he knew when it was time to fold his tent for the night. I asked Gerken not long ago if he remembered this incident, and he looked at me as though I were deranged. I guess he remembered.

At its repressive worst, I suppose it could be said that the "system" led to some voyeurism, some morbid preoccupations, certain passive-aggressive dysfunctions. You could say our behavior was too imitative and conditioned by fear. Too often, I think, we were given to understand our sexuality as the enemy of chastity. The myth was that the body could be overcome. The body was for chastising. And while all of this may be true, more or less, it also is probably irrelevant, or at least diversionary: generalize and categorize and get yourself off the hook. No amount of amateur hindsight will explain how and why one hundred boys coped, dug in, got by. Got by? Most of us were nuts for the place. The school was strange in certain ways, yes, and it was also spiritual and mystical, deeply so. There was awe there. I never knew the former so much as I intuitively understood the latter. I know dozens of priests and brothers from my old religious community and from other communities in the Church who seem to me neither unhappy nor maladjusted. Some of these men, like Vincent Fitzpatrick, our animus, went right through the system, from age thirteen onward, just as we were trying to do a generation later. The point here, I believe, is not amateur clinical hindsight, but the skein of sexual memory. And here is one:

Every seminarian was required to have a spiritual director. You could pick one on your own or go to the priest who had been assigned as the overall student body spiritual director. Toward the spring of my first year, 1959, feeling I needed more personal attention than I was getting from the man who had been appointed everyone's director, I went to a priest and asked if he would be willing to direct me in my spiritual life. He inquired what my aims for direction were, asked me some other things, including what problems I felt I had with the commandment against impurity, then said he would be willing to start seeing me every week or so. Either of us could drop the sessions if we felt they weren't working out. About six weeks after I began going to this priest, something odd and ambiguous began taking place.

I would go in, sit in a chair beside his desk, talk for a short while, await his nod, unzipper my trousers, take out my penis, rub it while I allowed impure thoughts to flow through my brain, and, at the point where I felt myself fully large and close to emission, say, "Father, I'm ready now." He would then reach over and hand me a black wooden crucifix. The crucifix, narrow and heavy with a gold skull at the base of the Saviour's feet, had been presented to my director some years before at his ordination, as was the custom of this religious community. The cross was a part of a Trinitarian's habit, and when preaching at a retreat or day of recollection a priest in the Order customarily inserted it inside his cincture belt. At my full erection before him in his room, my director would reach over and hand me the Mission Cross (this was its formal name), nod, and I would then begin reciting the various reasons why I wished to conquer this temptation: because God had blessed me with a vocation, because He had given me good health, a fine family, a sound mind. I always held the cross beside my penis, one hand on the crucifix, the other on my erect organ. Having thus systematically provoked myself to the ledge of mortal sin, and letting myself teeter there, I was now just as systematically talking the temptation down. Literally. The power of the crucified Saviour in my left hand was overpowering the evil of impurity and the world in my right.

I participated in this ritual, more or less willingly, from the time I was nearly fifteen until I was past twenty and getting ready to enter my year of novitiate. When he first brought up the idea I had found it repellent, scary. After a time I could take my exposures as a matter of course, of curriculum almost, something I simply did, weekly or biweekly, like writing home or cleaning a locker—almost. If I never completely got used to it, I think I can say I never really despised it, either, at least not until the end. In the middle years the act achieved a sort of weird normality for me, a calendar to my schedule. I think I began to view it just as he promised I would: as a legitimate tool in helping me control my impure thoughts and desires, which seemed to be raging out of control. I badly wanted to acquire the habit of purity, the dominion over self, as it was sometimes called. I knew that grace built on nature and that I must do my part.

In time, when my director suggested it might be more helpful in terms of the therapy (though he never used that word, as I recall) if I slid my trousers and underwear to my ankles, rather than just unzippering, I went along. Occasionally, on the way to erection, I went along with something else: reciting my most recent sexual fantasies. This was hard to do at first, but under his guidance and prodding and, most of all, patience, I got into it. Sometimes these fantasies concerned fellow students, and he would ask me their names and question me in detail about the fantasies, wondering, for example, if I wanted to study their genitals in the showers. He would reassure me that such impulses in an all-male environment were to be expected, indeed they might be inevitable, but that they must be scrupulously watched and worked on and prayed over all the same.

Sometimes my director would bring up—always delicately —the question of autoerotic impulses, wondering, for instance, if I had ever fantasized putting my penis in my mouth. Such an image terrified me; I told him I was certain I could never do anything like that. (I also wondered how you'd do it; you'd have to be a contortionist, I figured.) Once, in the middle of such a conversation, the phone rang and he went to the next room to answer it. There was a book on his shelf titled *Counseling the Catholic*, a popular pastoral tome. I took it down, looked up homosexuality in the index, raced through several pages trying to find out if I was queer or worse. I think I was a little like second-year medical students who become convinced they've caught everything in their pathology books. Why was my director asking me these things?

Before it was over, I found myself going to him even at night. I'd rise from my bed, slip into my cassock, walk softly down the darkened tomblike stairs to tell him I had just come awake from a dream involving myself and three women with fantastic breasts (residue from Michener's novel) and that I was now sorely tempted to "self-abuse." I would knock on his door softly and in a moment he would appear—barefooted, puffy-eyed, paternal. I could see the bottom of his pajamas sticking from under his habit. He had instructed me to come anytime I felt myself weakening—I was the alcoholic, he was the listening line. He would nod, stand aside for me to enter. He would snap on the small light by his desk and we would proceed to go through our brinkmanship. I would get his blessing and return to bed.

This is important: as many times as I performed this scene over nearly six years—and I may have performed in it as many as 150 times—I never once saw or felt him studying me with what seemed like the least erotic urge or lustful desire. I think I would have known. Could he have hidden his true intentions that long? It didn't make any sense that he could be a pervert, although in truth I had only the shakiest notion of what a pervert was. In those first few months I was on guard for what seemed like the least slip. Although I had placed him in charge of my spiritual life, and although he carried considerable weight on the faculty (which doubtless had something to do with why I chose him), I was still prepared to bolt out the door, and maybe the school, if the least overt movement, or even grin, should have escaped from him. But he was never anything but proper, and perverse as this sounds, my hundreds of near orgasms seemed then, and indeed seem now, only in a devout context. Miraculous to say, the worst never happened: I somehow could always rein in at the critical moment of my throbbing light show.

He would appear almost uninterested, restless, as I went about rubbing myself, getting large. And this was the confusing part: what would have been unarguably a sin twenty feet outside his room could take place here under conditions of immediate amnesty. Sometimes he watched me getting erected; more often he turned to his desk and took up papers or his breviary. It was as if this were the warm-up; he waited for the game. Always he sat in the chair behind his desk, and always I sat in the green easy chair adjacent to the desk. Only at the moment when I felt myself close to an emission, and would say so, did he begin to grow alert, solicitous. Hunched forward, arms on his knees, face behind wisps of smoke, he would be poised within two or three feet of my blue-veined adolescent self, nodding intently as I tried to row the boat back to shore. Each time he would urge me to plumb with him for deeper spiritual meanings as to why we were doing all this, metaphysical reasons why I wished to conquer evil, reject Satan, that father of sin and prince of darkness. It was a surreal sexual pilgrimage we were on, a search for the weirdest grail, and I think I can see now that he might have been bringing himself to the very precipice he was bringing me. It was as if we were accompanying each other by the hand on a dark, relentless passage to an Augustinian self-scrutiny. It was a kind of scientific rationalism, it almost seems now; pragmatic, American. It seemed to me as though I had delivered up myself body and spirit to an unearthly caretaker. Numerous times I can recall feeling a profound sense of communion, a conviction that I had stumbled on the right man in the right place at the right moment in my life. Although I have since thought about all of this hard and long, although I have discussed the scene in detail with a psychiatrist—who agrees that things do not always have to be what they seem, and who adds that a sort of canny behavioral modification therapy seemed at work, but who also says it is one of the oddest things he has ever heard—I can still reach no final conclusions about what was going on.

By the middle of my sixth year, soon to graduate to the Order's novitiate, I simply knew I didn't want to do it anymore. My exposures had begun all over again to seem repellent. Besides, I was becoming sure they were clinically and theologically improbable: rolling to the edge of delicious, exempted pleasure, pulling up short. But how to tell him? It would be like announcing an apostasy: after all, we had been in this thing together more than half a decade, had grown in it together. To complicate things, my director had a short fuse on his temper. I wasn't sure how he'd react. At fifteen and still relatively new to the seminary, my conflict had been over a man representing the person of Christ—in a habit and Mission Cross I coveted for my own someday—telling me something was right which seemed inherently insane. At twenty, with some stature in the school, I could no longer suspend disbelief. I just wanted out. I remember trying for several weeks to argue both sides of it with myself, deciding alternately it was sound pastoral therapy and the worst theological perversion. The more I debated it, the more I became confused; typically, I was trying to overuse my intellectual defenses against my emotional conflicts. At length I decided on a kind of truce with myself: maybe the scene was okay, but I wasn't going to perform in it anymore.

When I found the nerve to tell him, his response was an immediate "That's fine, Paul." I remember exactly how he said it—with a small *of course* in his voice, as if he perfectly agreed and in fact was wondering why it had taken me so long to say so. It was as if I had just guessed how many peas were in the Mason jar when the number was pasted on the bottom all along. And he never brought it up again. The ritual was canceled, erased. I saw him for spiritual direction for another several months until school was out, and nothing remotely like this ever happened again. In a dream one night I began to wonder if I had imagined it all.

Six years out of the seminary, between writing jobs on newspapers, married and separated and wanting to fall in love again, I flew to a town in the South for a visit with an old seminary friend. He, too, once had the same man for spiritual direction and perhaps this was the subconscious reason I went to visit him. Sometimes at the seminary the two of us would pass each other in the halls, he leaving spiritual direction, I going to it. I think we both knew. But we never talked of it.

One afternoon during my visit we played a hard game of one-on-one full-court basketball, then sprawled on the grass beside the court, shirts and tongues out. I was trying to spin the ball on my fingertip.

"Say, when you used to go see old Father _____, did anything different ever happen?"

There was only a millisecond of delay, then an insane laughter and the two of us rolling back and forth on the grass, pounding on each another. Later that day, still giddy with delight, we devised an elaborate and sacrilegious outline for a play in which a devout seminarian, in a Pavlovian response, gets an erection every time he enters a church and sees Christ hanging on a cross. (To cure the malady the doctor decides he must go outside the bounds of medicine. He prescribes a cast-iron jock.) It was wicked. *Sancta malitia.* Holy malice. We were having ours.

I know of no other such scene that took place between a spiritual director and a seminarian while I was in the seminary. But it went on here, with this particular priest and some of the boys he saw. One of my old seminary friends, someone several years ahead of me, a law enforcement official now, a gentle and skilled man and deep believer in God, told me he once willfully spilled his seed in front of this priest. We were sitting in a restaurant when he told me. I was forking down meat loaf and mashed potatoes. "How did you feel?" I said, sputtering it a little, grateful for the extreme sense of sanity I was suddenly feeling. "Well," he said, "at first I said, 'But, Father, I can't do that. It would be a mortal sin.' And he said, 'I will take full responsibility.' So I shrugged and went ahead. To tell the truth it didn't feel much different from the rest of it." And just then I knew what he meant: sometimes heresy seems just truth out of proportion. Maybe this explains why I could perform my version of the scene so long. On the other hand, maybe I was enjoying it without really knowing that. Maybe it provided a greater release than I knew. Most of the time now, when I think back on it and try to sort it out, it seems like bawdy comedy. When it doesn't seem bawdy it feels tender, somehow.

Some boys who went to see this priest declined to participate, and apparently that was fine. That argues much on the behalf of our director, I think. But most of us who went to him bought the ranch and uncannily kept a secret. That is one of the most remarkable things about it, I think: Why didn't more people find out? Why didn't a whistle get blown? I think there was a profound level of trust operating—as well as fear. Also, this was part of something called the Internal Form; the checks and balances of the system didn't apply here. I have since tried out the story on a few of my old schoolmates who I had a hunch were always blissfully unaware such a passion play was being enacted under their noses (although behind a closed door). At least one person has told me to my teeth I am either lying or crazy. Perhaps what was running through the minds of those of us who went weekly or biweekly to the green chair was an unthinkable thought: Could I be the only one? Some boys, I've since learned, talked of it among themselves. "Going to the green chair" became a kind of correlative, smirked at. But I never talked of it openly. Thinking the unthinkable bought my silence.

I have traveled a fair distance these last several years to make peace with this story—and I haven't made it yet. Twice I have gone to visit this man. On each occasion I found him warm and sincere and painstaking, someone who seemed genuinely interested to know the various paths my life has taken since the seminary. Each time I found myself scared and vulnerable. I went with the express purpose of asking about our old odd recital together, and each time I lost my nerve at the critical second. Once I brought the conversation right up to the lip of asking and, as the words were coming out, skittered away. I'm not exactly sure why, though I hope some of it was out of a reluctance to hurt or embarrass him. There seemed in his eyes not the least flicker of anxiety or self-doubt or embarrassment or hostility, any more than there had once seemed a flicker of lust, and I wondered whether he would look at me uncomprehendingly were I to bring it up. After all, twenty years had flowed between our lives since I regularly performed the scene for him.

One day I sat down and wrote him a long letter. I wrote it in a bar in Santa Fe, New Mexico, after I had plied myself with two glasses of wine. I wrote it straight through, without pausing to look back at sentences. I said I had been fretting over the matter for some time, and that I regretted very much not being able to ask him about it face to face. I told him I would never use his name in anything I wrote about the scene for publication, and that in fact I would try to do some minor disguising, but that I would be grateful if he could try to express his reasoning then and his feelings now. He wrote back two weeks later. I didn't open the letter for several days, just let it stare at me from the shelf above my typewriter. "Who's the letter from?" my wife asked casually. "Oh, someone in connection with the book," I said. When I did open it, bracing for his temper, I was caught off guard by the letter's tone: not only did it not seem angry or defensive, it sounded contrite, though not pleading. My old director said he had been motivated all along by the idea of impurity as the "worst sin" and the chief obstacle to a boy's vocation; by a desire to help ease the guilt feelings of young boys who in most cases had never received adequate sex orientation at home. He said the act had come about in an era following the Kinsey Report, when some new approaches to guidance were being tried in pastoral circles. "My desire to assist and preserve the vocation contributed to the confusion under which I was working and searching," he wrote. He said self-gratification had never occurred to him. He said that later, away from the environment, he realized the dangerous and unhealthy means he was employing.

He died last year. I might say that I "forgive" him for his part in this node of seminary history, except I feel there is nothing to forgive, at least if a man is to be judged more by his intentions than his actions. Actions have consequences, yes, but finally I side with intentions. Why, I lately have been wondering, should we wish men in the celibate life to be more than they humanly are? If temptation didn't exempt Christ Himself . . .

I guess I have been wondering something else: Why didn't Holy Trinity become one big floating fairyboat? I suppose the resiliency of kids is part of the answer: you can subject them to almost anything and they'll survive. That Holy Trinity was a far cry from a boat of "fairies" is not difficult to recall. That the friendships formed there were true and lasting and deep is not hard to remember. One felt all sorts of odd things, yes, and despite them there was a manliness, a ruggedness, to the place I haven't seen again in precisely the same way. I have heard this quality spoken of as "missionary impact." This ruggedness was more inside than out. It wasn't *machismo* one was tapping into; it was a sinewy spiritual toughness, perhaps of the kind that Dietrich Bonhoeffer, that fierce Christian, referred to when he said, "When Christ calls a man He bids him come and die." Bonhoeffer ended by dying for his spiritual freedom.

But although this character of spiritual strength was more inside than out, the real secret of Holy Trinity may have lain in its exterior primitivism—the very thing the Order was trying to rid itself of when it moved, in the sixties, to civilization and new facilities in the North. I can recall in my first few years at our squeaky clean and glass-enclosed two-and-a-half-million-dollar seminary in Virginia how students seemed to be scattering for the outdoors every chance they got: the steel-and-brick terrarium couldn't hold them. Down in Alabama, nature had rolled at us like a boulder. That hicky leaky school was never a place for soft people, although much softness was there. When we were there we thought of ourselves as wise and tough when actually we were just sophomoric and scared. We didn't know who we were. We were just on a road to somewhere. But the place was a huge ripe adventure, and there was the sense that all of us were in it together. Ideally, at least, we had gone down there with the goal of one day helping people. We threw ourselves toward this goal and this adventure. The Holy Ghost was down there, too, at Holy Trinity, Alabama, but His presence and exactly what He did are harder to say.

PART THREE

PARABLES

———

I think that the world in which we shall live these next thirty years will be a pretty restless and tormented place; I do not think there will be much of a compromise possible between being of it, and being not of it.

—*Robert Oppenheimer,*
in a letter
to his brother,
August 10, 1931

None of us, so far as I know, died in a war. Few of us got rich, though one of us is preposterously wealthy. Most kept the faith, although several are agnostics and one or two say they are nonbelievers. Most of us seem reputable and sane, although one of us was committed to an institution for allegedly shooting his mother in the stomach and intending to kill his father. (He was never brought to trial.) Most of us got married, often as not within one or two years of getting out; there was, I think, a need to try to find order. Often as not we married one-time nuns—evidence, I suppose, that in many cases we were two scared people of similar shared values starting late from ground zero. Most of us have kids and mortgages and sedentary jobs, although more than might be supposed live single, detached, metropolitan lives, on the edge, I think, of a sad asceticism. Divorces have now begun to creep; several have come out of the closet. Many of us still think of ourselves as priests, even if we never quite got there. Our personal relationships, with wives and lovers, seem fraught in many instances with high degrees of tension, and perhaps this is why: as Levites-in-progress we had grandiloquent visions of ourselves. We were preparing to be all things to all men. The minutiae of everyday domestic life—when your nose is running and the car isn't—don't square easily with that. For some of us, I think, there is still the disease of going to another place, as if by this trait or phenomenon or neurosis we might locate something, or exorcise something, or maybe just get even with all that stationary history and rigid schooling. For some of us, I suspect, the true vocation was to search. Seminary was just one of the stops. God writes straight with crooked lines, they told us once.

Brothers:
Charlie and Pat

In the Shreve High football stadium
I think of Polacks nursing long beers in Tiltonsville,
And grey faces of Negroes in the blast furnaces at
    Benwood,
And the ruptured night watchman of Wheeling Steel,
Dreaming of heroes . . .

Therefore,
Their sons grew suicidally beautiful
At the beginning of October
And gallop terribly against each other's bodies.

                  —James Wright,
                  from *Collected Poems*

"Oh, man . . . Oh, my . . . Suppose I didn't have that
    medal. . . . You wouldn't be here, right? You
    wouldn't know me from a hole in the wall. I mean,
    I would be invisible to you. Like a hundred
    thousand other dudes who got themselves sent
    over there to be shot at by a lot of little Chinamen
    hiding up in the trees. Yes, sir! I am an authentic
    hero, a showpiece. One look at me, enlistments go
    up 200 percent. . . . I am a feather in the cap of the
    Army, a flower in the lapel of the military—I

mean, I am *quoting* to you, man! That is what they
say at banquets, given in *my* honor. Yes, sir!"

—Tom Cole,
from *Medal of Honor Rag*

JUNE 1981. San Francisco, California.

The table, small and narrow, sits in the precise middle of
the room. There is a batik over it, and two skinny orange
candles rest in cheap holders on top of the cloth. The room
is dimly lit and cold. Windows rattle in the wells. A knife cuts
through wedges of cheese, coming out onto a china plate with
a thin, small SNATT. Wet afternoon fog nuzzles against
glowering panes, trying to get in, making a mockery of summer. The walls in here are bare except for one print of a
storm-tossed ship.

Charlie Liteky, fifty-one, ex-priest, American hero, comes
stiffly over to the table carrying a plate. He has been working
at the sink with a huge butcher knife, cutting three kinds of
cheese into small, precise slivers, fanning the slivers out on
the plate in neat symmetrical strips. He sets the plate between
us, draws a chair opposite the table, pours wine into a juice
glass and an Oriental ceramic cup. The juice glass he slides
toward me; the Oriental cup he saves for himself. All of this
is done in silence, with fluid grace, making me fantasize some
bizarre deadly ritual I am about to be initiated into.

"I think it's the lightness of it," he says. "And the simplicity.
Particularly Japanese culture. There's an intricacy and a penchant for detail; yet in the end it all comes out so simply."

The first time I found Charlie Liteky, after a year of hap-
hazard trying, he was living in the Drake Hotel in San Francisco's Tenderloin district. He had been there for some
months, I later learned. I wasn't to get out to California to
see him for another three weeks, and by then Charlie had
suddenly relocated. But one sunny San Francisco afternoon
I took a walk down Eddy Street to see his former address.
Platinum-headed ladies in ratty furs lurked at the corners,
waiting to hook. In the lobby of Charlie's transient hotel,
vacant old men sat on the other side of smudged glass looking
back at me like wax oozing figures from Madame Tussaud's.
But Charlie Liteky (you pronounce it lit-key) didn't feel sorry
for himself there, in the bare-bulbed cell he rented for two

hundred a month. For one thing, Charlie has never been much into material comfort. For another, there was a kind of ministry there. In a way the Drake Hotel and the Tenderloin were Charlie's church. Now that he doesn't have to be a priest anymore, he is free to be the deepest Christian imaginable. When he goes to liturgies these days, it is to celebrate his freedom. Liturgy is liberation.

For a time, nearly three years, he had lived by himself on an atoll in Florida. His front yard was the Gulf of Mexico. He built a platform on his roof, and at night he'd go up there to sleep. He got in rhythm with the tides; he got conscious again of his prayer life, of scripture. He had an old truck, and he hauled people's trash, and he got by okay on the government pension that Congressional Medal of Honor winners get for the rest of their lives. One day he moved on. He said later he felt he had some responsibility for the rest of man.

I heard he was in Santa Cruz, California, with his brother Pat. I heard he was in Oakland, living in a community with some Vietnamese Dominican nuns he had brought over during the war. He was in San Francisco. He had gone back to Florida. I kept trying numbers and getting disconnect messages. And then late one night I dialed a number and he picked up the phone on the first ring. He was living in the Tenderloin. By day he worked for the Veterans Administration; by night he was trying to write a novel. From what he said about the day job I knew the stallion wouldn't be long in the harness.

He is tall and gangly, and he is winding his way into the chair opposite me like Rubber Man. He is not unhandsome, though age and enough stressful experience for several lifetimes have caught him. There is shrapnel in his foot. And his back is bad. And sometimes his vision mysteriously blurs for hours on end. And, too, the arthritis that slowly consumed his father over eleven years seems to be creeping in the same way on the son. Also some upper-register hearing is gone, lost to all that shelling in Vietnam. Tonight, in a Vietnamese restaurant, while Charlie and his girlfriend and I eat fisherman's soup and five-spice chicken amid a clatter of dishes and a welter of language, he will ask me three times to repeat a sentence. He will seem old.

Charlie Liteky won the Congressional Medal of Honor as a

chaplain. Fewer than five men in the history of the republic have accomplished that. To read what he did, to hear it described, is to picture a son growing suicidally beautiful, galloping terribly against other men's bodies. The medal Charlie won has an eagle and a wreath on it, and it dangles from a rich blue ribbon. On November 19, 1968, at 1130 hours, the President of the United States, Lyndon B. Johnson, draped it around the neck of one ramrod Captain Angelo Liteky, Catholic Trinitarian priest, Company A, 4th Battalion, 12th Infantry, 199th Light Infantry Brigade. The ceremony was in the East Room of the White House. There were banquets and wire stories and testimonials. ("Son," LBJ said, putting it around Charlie's neck, "I'd rather have one of these babies than be President.") Ed Sullivan's people kept calling up for Charlie to come on the show, but Charlie said he wasn't really interested. Charlie Liteky was a national hero, though later, when he had fallen from grace, and into love, literally overnight, his mama could say, "Yeah, he's the hero of this year, the bum of next."

He has hard, knuckly hands and muscular shoulders and a pair of light sockets for eyes. The lines and creases and leathery seams flow outward from the deep eyes and big bony nose. A semi-wild Lincolnesque beard grows up the side of his V-shaped chin, like patchy ivy. When he smiles, though, the smile crinkles into little affectionate grays down his face over to his ears and across the trapezoidal jaw. He is angular as hell, with arms that don't quite know where to hang. He looks at turns like Mephistopheles, like some wizened and lecherous old Howard Hughes you might see stumbling out of the Nevada desert at 5 A.M., like Natty Bumppo the Deerslayer. When he moves, for all his growing stiffness, it is as if something leonine were moving. He has the grace of a banged-up pro.

The morning of the White House ceremony, a black man from Charlie's company had gone on national television to say what his chaplain had done that day a year earlier in Bien Hoa. "When Captain Liteky went out there the first time, we knew we'd never see him again," the black man said. "And by the end of that day we just knew he could walk on water." The black man told how a weaponless Catholic priest, who had volunteered for the chaplaincy corps, in his first time under fire, crawled to within fifteen meters of an enemy machine gun nest, flipped over onto his back, wrestled a bleeding and moaning man up onto his chest, and started digging backward, with his elbows and heels, for the landing zone. Charlie dug like that for maybe thirty yards, a horizontal scoop shovel, then stood up and dragged the soldier another forty yards to the medevac choppers. Afterward he went back into the woods for another trapped man. All afternoon he was bringing up stretchers, ammunition, water. No one could stop him. He moved upright and helmetless through fields of brightness, anointing the dying. He rose right up, like a man deranged, in full face of rockets and small arms fire, to direct in helicopters. He took off his flak jacket, and then his fatigue shirt, and threw them over the faces of blown-up comrades. The attack lasted from early afternoon until early evening, and in all Angelo Liteky, Catholic priest, saved twenty men. That night the only shirt the chaplain had to wear was his olive T-shirt. Damn cold, too.

"Secretary Resor, General Westmoreland, Distinguished Members of Congress, Distinguished Guests and Members of the Family," Lyndon Johnson began that November day in 1968 at the White House. "Our hearts and our hopes are turned to peace as we assemble here in the East Room this morning. All our efforts are being bent in its pursuit. But in this company we hear again, in our minds, the sounds of distant battle. Five heroic sons of America come to us today from the tortured fields of Vietnam. These five soldiers in their separate moments of supreme testing summoned a degree of courage that stirs wonder and respect and overpowing pride in us all."

Four other American heroes stood at nervous attention with Charlie Liteky on Decoration Day, and one of them was a black man, Spec Five Dwight H. Johnson. There is now a play based on the life of the late Dwight H. Johnson. It's called *Medal of Honor Rag*. The play had a limited run on Broadway. Dwight Johnson had a limited run on life: inside of four years of getting the Medal of Honor in the White House, he was dead in the war zones of Motor City USA, with his obit on the front page of the *New York Times*. Dwight Johnson had held up a corner grocery in Detroit and gotten himself killed, or maybe let himself be killed, in the process.

The American hero had an IQ of 128, and at the funeral his grieving mama could only tell reporters how he used to run home from school just to avoid the neighborhood bullies. Like Charlie Liteky, Dwight Johnson had become a hero in his first occasion under fire. Johnson had seen no action for eleven months and twenty-two days. Then came an ambush on the way to Dakto in the Central Highlands. Spec Five Johnson, who used to run from Detroit bullies, saw a comrade's body alive and burning. Something in his head went snap. He beat into the enemy with a .45, then a machine gun, then the butt of the machine gun. They say he killed twenty men, maybe twenty-five. Some people will now tell you that Dwight Johnson's story is just a replay of the "Ballad of Ira Hayes." Ira Hayes was the Marine and Pima Indian in World War II who helped take Iwo Jima. Two hundred and fifty men battled up that scrap of Pacific sand; twenty-seven came back down. One of them was Ira Hayes, Pima Indian, who would come home afterward and drown in a puddle. He was a drunk. "Call him drunken Ira Hayes/He won't answer anymore," the song goes. As Ira, so Dwight.

I have brought with me in my bag this trip a copy of *Medal of Honor Rag*. Charlie has never heard of the play, seems uninterested in reading it. "The real heroes in that war are all dead," he says quietly, jerking me from reverie. The Oriental ceramic cup is on the table, empty. His fingers are pyramided against each other, as if in prayer, or the way we used to make church steeples as kids. "The company commanders who write up these medal nominations, they know how to pump it up. I'm not saying some of these things didn't happen. I'm just saying it makes them look good, too, you know."

Take the star out of the window; the real heroes are dead.

Maybe what Charlie is trying to tell me is that his military superiors didn't bother to write up the fact that a Catholic priest once got dressed in civies, like anybody else in that dirty little war, and made his way into Saigon, through the plastic-covered wooden shacks and cubicles of discarded cardboard, to a place where he could have sex with a whore. Only this was Charlie's *first* sex. He was thirty-eight and a virgin. He used to watch guys from his company crawling through rolls of barbed wire at night to sneak into the villages to find hookers. He had to find out what sex was like.

"So here's a guy who doesn't believe in sex outside of marriage, a priest, okay? And he has his first sex with a Saigon prostitute. The priest, quote, hero, unquote, who didn't have enough pride to keep himself from paying for his first sexual experience. And you know what? I'm grateful it happened. It brought me closer to the rest of humanity."

In Willa Cather's novel *Death Comes for the Archbishop*, Padre Martinez, who has an illegitimate son, says: "Celibate priests lose their perceptions. No priest can experience repentance and forgiveness of sin unless he himself falls into sin. Since concupiscence is the most common form of temptation, it is better for him to know something about it."

Holy Orders rag. Burnt incense. Break the soul with mortal sin so it can float to forgiveness. Charlie Liteky creaks forward to pour more wine into his cup. We are talking about why and how he left the priesthood eight or nine years ago. The date has always been a little vague. He was in and out for a while, on leave, in limbo, staying with his dying mama in Florida, pumping gas, working at a halfway house for drugged-up vets in Cleveland, making candles. There had been a time in his priesthood when Charlie proclaimed he was having visions, when he felt he was going to suffer the stigmata. Some feared for his sanity.

"I think one of the biggest problems all along was that we were never taught that our happiness was related to anything here and now. I'm not blaming anyone; it's just the way it was. I used to be totally separated from my emotions. I lived in my head. I was into this thing about working yourself out for God. Burnt incense. I think there's an image about burnt incense somewhere in Father Judge's writing. Well, I had to get rid of all that. I had to bury a lot of skeletons about God before I could love Him again. I had to say to God, Okay, Buddy, if that's the kind of God You are, maybe I don't want to believe in You. Where are You, God? I was crying, shaking my fist. I can love a person, you see, because a person can love me back. I can't love an abstraction. I'm a lot more spiritual person now because I'm a lot more loving person. I almost died there for a while before I left the priesthood. My basic human needs were gnawing at me. It was depression in the absence of life. Finally there was the basic Christian conviction that He came to give us life. But I had no life. What is it Aquinas writes about self-mobility? If a thing is not moving . . . ? So that is what I did—choose life, move away from death."

His eyes are tightly closed; he is sitting sideways in his chair. I am longing for the thin small SNATT of the knife.

"I wanted to go someplace where strangers could tell me who I was. Because I didn't know who I was. I was in San Diego for a while. It was like stepping off onto another planet. I was just John Doe. I got an apartment off Balboa Park. The zoo was nearby. I began with long walks. Sometimes I'd talk to people, usually not. The only knowledge I had of myself was what other people were starting to give me back. And that's just as I wanted it. One of my biggest problems in the priesthood all along was that my identity had pretty much gotten swallowed up. When I got out I said: I know I have a body. I'll start there. The intellectual and spiritual parts of me can come later. But first my body. Not desires or wants. But needs. And that's how I started on the road back. From nowhere."

This has come out in soft, almost musical, streams. Now there is a quick laugh, a high, giggly laugh. It startles me. "This one time in the seminary. I woke up from a wet dream and said out loud, probably waking half the house, 'Well, God, You can't take that away from me.' "

I never knew him in the seminary. I knew his younger brother Pat, who was several years ahead of me. By the time I met Charlie he was already a priest, and drowning in the priesthood, too, although I had no idea of that. I met him when I was twenty, in 1964, the same summer I reported to the novitiate. I had gone down to the northern neck of Virginia, where Charlie was stationed at a rural parish, to help out in his summertime Bible program. Charlie had been a priest for four years then, and it was going downhill faster for him every year. What I chiefly remember about him that summer is the way he could mesmerize those rural Virginia kids, probably without half knowing. Father Angelo (this was his religious name) wore black knit sport shirts and black stovepipe pants and seemed to float instead of walk. Every morning Charlie drove an old yellow school bus through that steamy Tidewater countryside, collecting his kids. I'd ride along with him. On the noon hour he would effortlessly toss them footballs or tell them stories outside under a tree. He had a story about three hunting dogs, Maggie, Zeke, and Ella, which I later appropriated. Those kids practically followed this long, laconic drink of water around the yard. Charlie was John Wayne without the *machismo*. He was in his mid-thirties and wore funny wire-rim glasses, and in an ascetic way, I suppose, he was a kind of John Wayne of the priesthood. He looked studious and wasn't. I remember that he prayed a lot.

In the middle of that summer I left the mission and headed for Holy Trinity to start my year of novitiate. A little while later I heard that Charlie had signed up for Vietnam. One of the last things Charlie's brother Pat remembers saying to Charlie, when he heard he was going to the war, is: "Hey, Bud, long as you're over, why don't you pick up the Medal of Honor?" I was out by the time Charlie got decorated by the President. I saw the story in the *New York Times*. "Jesus," I said. "Charlie Liteky."

He has never dreamed about it. It wasn't something that represented trauma for him. It just represented death. It was horrible, but it wasn't shocking, somehow. And he honestly was not afraid. All these people were crying out for help. He was there. He was healthy. He just did what almost anyone in that situation would have done. Besides, it all happened so fast, with hardly time to think, which is one reason he sometimes wonders if it was heroism at all. He's seen men—men, shit, they were boys—stand straight up on their captain's command and walk into fields of fire with an M-16. There's some heroism for you. Anyway, the first guy he came to was a medic. It looked like his leg was blown off. About halfway up where his knee should have been, there was all this gristle and bone. He had been talking to the soldier only the night before. The kid was a musician, and he said he wanted to go home and start up a rock band. The next guy he came to had a big hole in his back. He was lying face down. He knelt and tried to pick the guy up. His name was Perry, a red-haired skinny little kid from the country. Perry was trying to breathe, but the air was just going right out of him. So he anointed him and gave him conditional absolution and moved on. That's when he saw the M-16 lying on the ground. He started to go over and pick it up and he thought: Hell, no, Ange. If a priest is going to get his in here today, they won't find a rifle on him.

Several hours later. We have moved to the front of his flat.
(He has noticed me shivering and put the heat on and suggested we go into the other room, where it will be warmer.)
Charlie's new pad has three rooms—if you count the bathroom, which he does, and which you have to walk through to
get from the front to the rear. There are cat smells in the hall
and a mad kid is next door, but Charlie figures this is the
Ritz, or at least the finest place he's had in a while. He's got
loads of plans for it. Last week Betty helped him paint the
bedroom. Betty is Charlie's current girlfriend, a former nun.
There have been lots of dead ends on female boulevard for
Charlie Liteky. There was a woman in San Diego, several
more in Florida. In Florida, on Pine Island, he saw from afar
a perfect "10." "God, was she beautiful," he says, sucking in
his breath. She was sunning herself on a raft about one
hundred yards from shore. Charlie was on the roof of his
cabin. He got up, climbed down the side of the house, slipped
into the water, breast-stroked over to the raft, and said,
"Hello, I hope I'm not intruding." They became friends, not
lovers.

But Betty might be the right woman at last. Last week
Charlie went down to a Japanese trinket store and bought
her a four-dollar ring. Gave it to her and said, "Betty, this
represents my desire to enter into an engagement with you.
When you feel like putting it on, I'm here. I'll get you a real
one later." Betty got Charlie to sign up at Arthur Murray for
dance lessons. The image of Charlie trying to learn the
mambo amuses me. "Just the other night a thought hit me,"
Charlie says now. "If Betty is really the one, and I marry her,
I can never go back." He means go back to the priesthood.
Despite the fact that he is laicized, that fantasy has long hung
around.

He spraddles on his bed and plows a hand through his
hair. He takes a drink from the Oriental ceramic cup. I am
seated a few feet away from him, by some crates rigged as
end tables. The bed Charlie is on isn't a Westerner's bed. It's
a *futon*, which is layers of compressed fabric resting directly
on the floor. Since Vietnam, *futons* are about all Charlie
wishes to sleep on. Tonight his *futon* will be bed for both of
us.

The room is neat and spare. There is a rack of gray shelving holding a few books, some postcards, a miniature chalice, pictures of his parents and brothers and nephews. The photos rest on a terrycloth towel, smoothed out. All of Charlie's family are dead now, save for his brother Pat. The most arresting picture in the gallery is of Charlie himself. It was snapped somewhere in Vietnam, under canvas tenting. Charlie is in fatigues, scratching a sockless ankle, looking deep and gaunt and poetic. He looks almost emaciated. Charlie doesn't look like a priest in the picture; he looks like a dogface. When he said Mass in Nam, the chaplain never wore vestments, just a stole around his neck. He said Mass on Jeep tops, on crates, anything that was available.

The closet on my right is open, and I see two or three pairs of pants on hangers, a couple of sport shirts, some boxes on the floor which may have files and papers in them. There are a few plants, a couple of floor pillows. Like a man of Galilee, Charlie Liteky travels light.

The day before the decorated priest went back to Vietnam for a second tour, he met a woman named Julie. Julie was the sister of one of Charlie's longtime friends from Florida. Charlie and Julie talked for hours and ended up spending the night together, although Charlie says he refused to have "genital intercourse." The next morning he left for Vietnam. When he got "in-country," to the staging area where thousands of GIs were always coming and going, he hunted up a Franciscan chaplain. He said he wished to go to confession, he had committed a sin with a woman. The Franciscan threw back his head and roared. "You poor sucker," he said. "You're going to be over here a whole damn year and all you'll be thinking about is her." Then the priest said he was leaving Vietnam to return to the States: he was getting married. Not too long afterward Charlie made a tape recording and sent it to his brother Pat and his mother. He told them all about the wonderful woman he had met and fallen in love with on his last night in the States. Pat's mother was sitting at the kitchen table when the tape came. She put her head in her hands. Pat gave the tape to Father Stephen, the head of the Order, and pretty soon Charlie got a letter in the mail. A story with far-reaching consequences had been brought to his attention, Father Stephen said. Our way is the way of the cross, he reminded Charlie. Months later, when Charlie returned from his second tour, he and Julie tried to resume their relationship. It didn't work.

On his second tour the hero-priest discovered there was an unofficial policy in his brigade that if you could verify three enemy kills you would get an in-country R&R. Charlie went to his battalion commander and demanded to know if it was true. The commander hedged. Charlie went to the general of the brigade. He said he couldn't participate in such an environment, that it was tantamount to making bounty hunters out of soldiers. He said that if the policy wasn't changed immediately, he would resign, and that if his resignation was not accepted, he would write a letter to every newspaper in the United States, spilling the beans. The general roared up from his desk. "I'll be goddamned if I'll sit here and let you threaten me like that, Liteky," he said. "I don't give a good goddamn what you won."

Charlie wrote to the Chief of Chaplains in Washington, D.C. Before long there was a special helicopter waiting to take him to Saigon to have dinner with General Creighton Abrams. Abrams had earlier decorated Charlie with the Distinguished Service Cross between a row of armored vehicles. Now he was commander of all U.S. forces in Southeast Asia. Abrams' quarters looked about like any other senior officer's —from the outside. You went through a passageway from the street and emerged into Xanadu. The general had any kind of music Charlie wished to hear. Charlie asked for show music. Over dinner the general said he was appalled to learn of such brigade policies. He seemed genuinely disturbed. "We are all pressured in this war," he said quietly.

Charlie Liteky became close to some Vietnamese Dominican nuns on his second tour. The sisters ran an orphanage on the edge of the village, and Charlie and other GIs would go over to play with the children. Sometimes Charlie brought his altar linens and asked the sisters to launder them. One day Charlie asked the Mother Superior if there was anything he could do for her, and she quickly said, "Yes, you can get four scholarships for my sisters to study in the States."

Charlie said he would see what he could do. He raised money from GIs, wrote to friends back in the States, and eventually got together enough funds to send four Dominicans to America. Today only one of the four remains in religious life. Her name is Elizabeth Lan, and she is a tiny, birdlike lady who lives across the bay from Charlie, in Oakland, and will never forget what a priest did for her when her country was in ruins.

Sister Elizabeth is a refugee resettlement director, and one afternoon two or three years ago I stopped in at her office. Behind her on a wall was a poster: "To Love Someone Is to Give Them Room Enough to Grow." "That he quit the priesthood has nothing whatever to do with what I feel for him," the nun said. We sat talking for about an hour. When I left I had the oddest feeling that she and Charlie could get married.

There are more than 260 living winners of the Medal of Honor. A few recipients go back to World War I. Charlie Liteky is the only living recipient to have received the award as a chaplain. When I called up Colonel Charles Davis (retired), then president of the Medal of Honor Society, who happens to live in the San Francisco area, he said: "I had this Liteky lad over to the house. I quelled some of his fears. He had some wild notion we were going to profit from the Medal of Honor. That's a farfetched idea. He thought we wanted to reap self-glory or something." The Society holds annual conventions. Charlie has gone to a few but has never really liked them. Too much of a mutual admiration society, he thinks. Never been a joiner anyway. A year or so ago Charlie flew over to Hawaii to address the Society's annual meeting. America needs a different kind of hero, not a military one, he told his fellow heroes. Nowadays the priest-hero is a dove. He attends anti-nuke rallies. He works on committees trying to organize demonstrations. The other people on the committees don't know he won the Medal of Honor. "I'm just the guy in the denim jacket. Because that's all I am, really." For a good while, even Betty didn't know he was a hero.

In the three or four times I have gone to visit Charlie these last few years he has never offered to show me his medal. But he has it somewhere; I asked him. "I just haven't had the guts to throw that thing in the river yet. I don't know why."

Holy Orders rag. Burnt incense. He is telling me about the drowning of his brother Jimmy. Jimmy Liteky drowned on September 26, 1959, nine months before Charlie was ordained to the priesthood. Jimmy was the Liteky brother who didn't go to Holy Trinity. He had a new car and a new job and a new fiancée and a freshly minted degree from Florida State. And he was such a fine swimmer, a natural, just like his big brother Charlie. It made no sense he could die this way. Maybe he hit a rock, or a log; nobody knows. He dived in that Saturday and didn't come up.

At the novitiate a movie was in progress when the call came. Father Declan, Master of Novices, poked through the dark and motioned for Pat Liteky to come out in the hall. They went to the Master's office. "Brother Dimitri, I have some serious news for you," Father Declan said. "Your brother is lost." Father Declan didn't say drowned; he just said lost.

At the major seminary in Virginia, Charlie didn't find out until the next morning. He had been in chapel alone the evening before thinking about his family and how lucky he was that no real tragedies had ever occurred. When the head of the house came to tell him, Charlie thought immediately that his father had died. But it was Jimmy.

He left immediately for home. Grappling hooks were already skimming a dark, murky river in north Florida for the eyes or legs or water-blue fingers of a lost boy. Below the chemical riffles, divers labored. They had found nothing. For two days the divers searched. Charlie wanted badly to go down with them, but his mother wouldn't allow it. Then toward dusk of the third day of searching, Charlie and two others went out in a rowboat. Everyone else had come in, had said it was no use. Charlie was determined to give it one more try, for his mama's sake, who was sinking deeper into grief: *Why can't they find my son?*

Charlie and his fellow searchers put their boat toward the point of the island that Jimmy had dived from three days before. They let themselves drift in the current. The boat was drifting past the little green island, and Charlie was standing up in the bow, peering down into the dark waters, saying to himself, Come on, Jimmy, goddammit, come on, when—suddenly—Jimmy appeared, just surfaced, right in front of him, clean and beautiful and smiling, with a gash over his forehead and his arms outstretched. It was as if Jimmy were trying to climb into the boat. The body seemed to want to rise right up out of the water into Charlie's arms. Charlie grabbed for Jimmy, and then the smell was nearly overwhelming.

At the funeral Gertrude Liteky, the boys' mother, had her first heart attack. And the boys' father, Charles Liteky, Sr., the old, hardened, and bedridden Navy Chief, the King Lear of this family, said only this: "God took two of my sons. Now he's got the third."

Charlie has told me this story without interruption. None of it, not even his father's words, arouses passion in him. It is as if the story is too stark for passion. Now he talks of his father.

"He was in the Navy thirty-three years, and then he got medicaled out. He had one name: the Chief. He was Chief of the Deck on the aircraft carrier *Hornet* in World War II. One day the cable that catches the planes when they come in snapped. It whiplashed around the deck and caught the Chief in the spine. He went to the ship's hospital with multiple injuries. They couldn't keep him there very long. When kamikazes sank the *Hornet,* the Chief went into the water with everybody else, although not before he had climbed into the cockpit of a burning Zero and cut the label out of a Jap's glove. He wanted a souvenir.

"This is the sort of person my father was: there was never any pause in him between caution and that terrible moment when you know you have to react. If you and I and he were sitting in a bar somewhere and some guy came up and started being abusive to you, my father would go straight for the guy. He wouldn't give him a chance to quit. He wouldn't ask for an apology. He would just go straight at him. I came home from a parish one time in my civilian clothes, and he said, 'What are you doing dressed like that?' I said, 'I quit the priesthood, Dad.' And he said, 'Why?' I said, 'I got into a problem with the superior of the house, and I hit him in the mouth.' And you know what he said? 'Okay.' He could understand that. Of course none of it was true. It was just a joke, but he could understand.

"None of us could live up to him. He spent the last eleven years of his life flat on his back in a special bedroom. His arthritis, and complications from the spine injury, had crippled him. And right there in that hospital bed next to my father was a .38. It wasn't just being in bed. He couldn't drink because he had an ulcerated stomach. He was in terrible pain all those years, I think. He had had a prosthesis on his hip, and it had broken. But he gained some wisdom in those years. I got him to make some recordings for the blind. He worked eleven and twelve hours a day at it. He taped the entire Bible and then started in on other books. That's the way he was. My father had a wonderfully rich and resonant voice."

Charles Liteky, Sr., the Chief, died on St. Patrick's Day, 1966. He was propped naked at the sink, shaving, when his heart stopped and he fell over dead. It was a year and a half before one surviving son would win the Medal of Honor, a decade before the other would proclaim his homosexuality.

Somehow, when Charlie Liteky feels successful or gets secure, he bolts—people, attachments, jobs. "I have this need to terminate things," I remember him saying once. He didn't say more. The world would doubtless call the need prodigal, or worse. God knows, Charlie seems to have a perverse genius for squandering things, especially his success. Maybe it's because he feels he doesn't deserve an earthly reward, or maybe it's because he feels he was never loved enough as a boy. I can't figure it out and I doubt if he can. His mother was a suffering Monica, people have told me, a selfless, good woman of great religious belief. She loved her husband and sons above all else in life, but she nearly always took the side of her husband against her boys. Charlie has never come right out and said it, but I think he feels his mother held back from him at critical moments. "I was forty-three before I realized that my whole substitution for love when I grew up was a high achievement in sports," he told me once. But there he was talking about his father.

When he was eleven or twelve, Charlie ran away from home, stealing thirty bucks from his mother's pocketbook, riding a bus in stages (so they couldn't track him) from Fort Lauderdale to Norfolk, sleeping all night in the North under dry-docked boats or on streetcars. He ran away because of a terrible fight he had had with his father. He locked himself in the bathroom and his father busted down the door. His father got him down in the bathtub; Charlie can still see that big, angry face over him. After that he got his Palm Beach suit from the closet, stole the thirty dollars, took off. He stayed away two weeks, but he didn't miss Mass. At length his father located him. "He got me on the phone and said, 'If I sent the money would you come back? Your mother is very sick.' He didn't say, 'I want you to come back.' Or, 'I love you, boy.' He just said, 'If I sent the money would you come back?' He picked me up at the depot in the middle of the night. The depot in Fort Lauderdale was far out in the country then, and all during the long, dark drive home we barely said a word. But after that night something shifted. He was kinder toward me. We got into sports together."

You can glance at Charlie Liteky for five seconds and see an old jock. In high school—at Robert E. Lee in Jacksonville, a Florida athletics powerhouse—Charlie became a standout in any sport he tried. There was a basketball hoop in his backyard, and he turned it down so that the ring faced him. He tied a triangle target, made out of rope, in the center of the ring. He would stand all afternoon in one spot, firing footballs at the bull's-eye. Eventually he could hit the middle of the target, even when he put the hoop to swinging. Already, a boy was punishing his body to chasten his mind. The body will quit on you, his father had taught him; the mind will see you through. Coaches began to groom Charlie for the quarterback's slot at the University of Florida. He was sent to a Florida junior college for further grooming. But by then the nudge, or tug, or whatever it was, came. Charlie said he was leaving for Holy Trinity. There are people who will tell you now that had Charlie Liteky kept up football, he would have made all-conference, maybe All-American. Charlie thinks that's absurd.

At Holy Trinity Brother Angelo could throw a football seventy yards. No lie. Someone would hike it to Charlie, and everybody on his team would go out for the pass. Brother Angelo would dance in the backfield, eluding his captors, then heave the bomb at the first seminarian to reach the end zone. It was only pickup football, but legends like that die hard. The other morning I called one of Charlie's old classmates and he said, "Ange was the sort of guy who never knew he had it. We'd be sitting there in the rec room and he'd say, 'Hey, fellas, this Saturday, what do you say we . . .' And the next thing you knew six guys were standing around him."

I have heard people call Charlie Liteky the "superstar."

They haven't any idea where he is these days, what he's up to. But he's the superstar. Charlie loathes that word. "Enough of it is just a medal talking," he says. "You know, these primal scream people scream, but I don't think they know where to go from there. I had to be willing to forgive, not only in the past but in the present."

I remember standing on a street corner in San Francisco one night. Suddenly Charlie said, "This is my old neighborhood, Paul. I got knocked out in a bar right down the street. It was five to two by my watch and the bartender says drink up. I guess I had had a few. 'Whoa, buddy, it's not time yet,' I say, and the next thing I know I'm out on the sidewalk and somebody is trying to kick me in the groin."

Charlie Liteky, superstar.

Charlie Liteky has worked for the Veterans Administration in San Francisco and Cleveland. When he needs a job he knows he can get one at the VA. (Harry Truman thought so highly of the Medal of Honor that he issued an Executive Order guaranteeing work at the VA for any of the award's recipients.)

Charlie told me, the last time he worked for the Veterans Administration, that he intended to pay off some debts and get his teeth fixed and then move on. "Then I'll do whatever it is I'm supposed to do." The next time I saw him he *had* moved on. When he left, his co-workers gave him a small party. Charlie thanked them and then got up and said quietly, with his supervisors standing there, that no one in the building looked happy to him. Jobs like this dehumanize people, grind a man down, he said. Charlie Liteky has long borne strange gifts to authority.

A priest from my old religious congregation once shared with me a letter Charlie had written him. The priest's name is Jim O'Bryan, and he is Charlie's closest friend in religious life, mainly, I suspect, because he allows Charlie the space he must have. Father O'Bryan's great gift and genius is that he is nonjudgmental. At the time of the letter, Charlie had left the priesthood. Jim O'Bryan lay critical in a California hospital with an aneurysm. No one expected him to make it. (He did, though, and Charlie's prayers are probably not the least of the reason). Charlie's letter to his friend began: "Dear Jim, "I'm up extra early today after seeing my brother off to an early flight to Santa Cruz. The early morning silence is so conducive to prayer and reflective reading. I am not one to hold on to anything or anyone anymore, but that doesn't mean I'm immune to the pain of loss. If you go home before I do, God, how I will miss you. Just the mention of it brings tears of loving friendship to my eyes, which is so beautiful for someone who has been so emotionally sterile for so long."

Jim O'Bryan showed me that letter and then told me a story. Once, when he and Charlie were young priests and assigned to the same house in New Jersey, he spilled his guts to Charlie. He was in a bad depression and needed someone to talk to. Charlie secretly tape-recorded the conversation, which took place in Charlie's bedroom. The next week, when O'Bryan came in to talk again, Charlie got out the recorder. He said he had something he wanted O'Bryan to hear. He put on the tape—and started laughing. O'Bryan was furious. He felt humiliated. "I think he was trying to tell me, 'I don't need you, O'Bryan, or anybody else.' But I felt he was wrong. I worked on him hard. I felt he needed me as a friend. I used to tell him, 'Liteky, I don't know what it's about, but I see all this rage in you.' " Jim O'Bryan thinks his friend Charlie is on a strange search for sanctity, not the kind that will get put into stained glass in a cathedral. More the sanctity of being. There is a key to the mystery of Charlie Liteky, Jim O'Bryan says. If it could be found and turned, a fundamental mystery might be solved. But the key has never been found. And so a hero wanders, an ex-priest roams.

"I just have never clung to this life," I remember Charlie saying one night. "I'm not anxious to die, but I look forward to that moment when I can get away from this violence, the cruelty, the uncertainty of the world. I think I'll be happy to go home when the time comes."

A *futon* makes a surprisingly comfortable and roomy bed. In the wet blackness of a San Francisco summer night, a man lying beside me reaches for the Princess phone, punches out seven numbers, and a recording comes on in clean quiet to tell him it is four-eighteen and that the weather in the Bay Area should be clearing today. The dial glistens in the dark like muted lights rising from a pool. Charlie Liteky replaces the phone, turns noiselessly on his side.

I saw Charlie again a year later, in the spring of 1982. The night before, there had been a showing of *Medal of Honor Rag* on TV. Charlie had watched it and followed along with the playscript I had given him. He was writing every day and had finished seven chapters of a novel about a priest in Vietnam. He and Betty were still unresolved about marriage. He had successively brightened his place, though it didn't have any real permanence about it. The wild kid still lived next door, and Charlie was giving the family whatever rice and potatoes he had left over at the end of every month. We talked all afternoon and into the evening. He made a dish called Beggar's Chicken, in an earthen pot he had soaked in water. He chopped some greens into minute slivers, and he stirred some fried rice, and then the two of us stood opposite each other at a counter and ate. As it began to get dark Charlie sat in a window. After a while he got up and lit a candle. He said that were it not for his relationship with Betty, and some friends he had made at a local Catholic parish, and a certain inertia, he doubtless would move on. He didn't know where, though.

The homosexual father, a poet, has two sons, Josh and Jeremy. A few years ago, when Josh was four and just beginning to sort out a sensual world, he said to his father one visiting weekend:

"Dad, do men marry other men?" (The father was living then on a houseboat below Sacramento, separated but not divorced. His big, wild lover was in for the weekend.)

"No, not exactly," the father said. "Not yet."

"Well, do they love each other?" Josh said. (The boy had seen his father and his lover embracing.)

"Yes, like your brother, sort of," the father said.

Two years later, on another visiting weekend, this time at his sons' place, drying dishes, their mom out shopping, Josh, maybe six now, said:

"Dad, are you gay?"

"Yes," the father said. "And what do you think it means?"

"I think it means having sex with a lot of other men." Then Josh flooded in a grin. "I don't think I'm going to be gay when I get big."

"Oh, that's fine," the father said. "And why have you decided that?"

"Because I want to have children."

The story of the Liteky brothers shifts now, to Sacramento, and to Charlie's little brother. The little brother is past forty, a maturing poet and a maturing homosexual. Before I can relate this story, though, I must own up to something: I think I set out to find Pat Liteky several years ago with a small, mean part of me hoping he would be a writable tragedy, not broken, just breaking. Pat Liteky is one of a handful from my years in the seminary who is fully out of the sexual closet. His public gayness takes some heat off all of us, I think. It certainly takes some heat off me. For someone who has long secretly fretted about the seeming ambiguities in his own sexual history, Pat Liteky was Paul Hendrickson's perfect beard. It took a while to see that.

Ten o'clock on a summer morning and I am still in pajamas. I slept out here last night, in the chaotic living room, while Pat slept on the water bed in the other room. He stands across from me now in a blue robe. An omelet is burning on the stove. His left hand is thumbed at the pocket of his robe. He could be an ad for *Gentlemen's Quarterly*. Charlie Liteky's brother is a large man, maybe six feet two, muscled and trim and handsome. He has a swimmer's body, nicely tanned. But somehow the body doesn't seem athletic, at least not in the way Charlie's physical appearance tells you immediately: this is an old jock.

Pat, nine years Charlie's junior, came to Holy Trinity behind his big brother's exploits. Pat went another way. He worked to get on the honor roll. (Charlie had to slog through his studies.) Pat sang in the choir. Pat wrote poems for Father Brendan's English classes. Pat won the Voice of Democracy contest in Russell County. But he wasn't girlish back then; just soft. And spiritual. Pat, in contradistinction to Charlie, knew he wanted to be a priest from boyhood. At nine he was putting on a bathrobe and saying pretend Masses in his room. I called up one of Pat's classmates a week or so ago and he said: "Pat Liteky had a spirituality that anchored the class."

He looks about as "faggoty" as Robert Redford. What he

202 | PAUL HENDRICKSON

looks like, actually, is an account executive for an ad agency, a man not going kicking and screaming toward the body softness of middle age. He has long, smooth, heavily veined hands; thinning hair crinkling into ash-grays at his temples; a loose shrug-shouldered walk. This walk is deceptive. It might suggest a man yukking at life, but I have seen Pat Liteky with a look in his eye that people can get when they need to cry. A better index to his life might be his apartment: it is asprawl in creative tension.

He dresses neatly, almost preppy. Pat is the Liteky brother who is gay—and wears camel sport coats and the right tie and tan oxfords. Charlie is the Liteky brother who starred in football and got the Medal—and he has been known to walk the streets of San Francisco carrying a suede purse. Now you see them, now you don't. The more you look, the more they merge. If the Liteky brothers seem opposites, in far richer ways, I think, they are twins. They watch each other; they ape each other.

I have been here since yesterday. Pat had come into the bar at the Holiday Inn, where I waited for him to get off work, and stuck out a hand. Nothing seemed very different. What was I expecting—a ring in his ear, someone wrapped in silks? Almost immediately an old order seemed to impose itself. One of the chief things I remember about Pat Liteky from our several years together is that he always had time for me. He was kind, and he didn't have to be, in that he was older and lived on the other side of the campus. He used to stop on the walks and speak to me. He knew my parents' names, my father's work. I had mentioned this to him yesterday shortly after we sat down, and he said, "Oh. Well, I guess you never quite know the impression you're registering."

Last night, as we went around town to dinner and in and out of several gay bars, he tried to get every door for me. His courtliness embarrassed me. Did I feel his sexual life now should have canceled the old kindness? It was as if I couldn't square one with the other. When we got back to his place, he had towels laid out, my bed turned down. *Is he up to something?* I wondered.

We had left the Holiday Inn yesterday afternoon and had gone to a Safeway to buy some steaks and vegetables. Both of

us were full of false starts, talking on top of each other, talking about Holy Trinity, about his brief venture into a Trappist monastery in 1959, talking about Charlie and the Medal,
about his ex-wife, about his sons—both of us taking things
off shelves and putting them back, two sitcom fruitballs muff-
ing their lines, Oscar and Felix. Suddenly he had said with
the old shrug-shouldered ease, "I'm gay, you know." We were
in the aisle by the cabbages.

"Oh, fine," I had blurted.

In the years since Pat Liteky and I used to pray by each
other in a narrow wooden building in Alabama, he has, in no
attempt at chronology:

a) gone bankrupt in the firewood business. (He called himself the "Wood Fairy." This was in Santa Cruz, California, six
or seven years ago, and he would spend all day in the woods,
felling huge coastal oaks and madrones, draining six-packs
for lunch, his body turning sinewy and tight, sometimes
working naked save for ragg-wool socks and timber boots.)

b) taught Virgil to Catholic high school boys in Florida.
(This was in the late sixties and he was between seminaries.
One of his students was a kid from a poor family. The boy
always came to school tired, and one day Pat invited him over
to his place. He thought he might be able to help in some
way. "I think I'm homosexual," the boy said. "Now if you
pray very hard on this matter, it will go away," Pat said. He
wasn't kidding. He had been doing the same thing for years.
Six years later, in California, the two met up again. Pat was
out of the closet then. The boy was a soldier back from Vietnam. Pat and his old student had a relationship for a while.
Eventually they went their ways.)

c) struck off for Alaska with a bicycle. (In Fairbanks, Pat
saw black pimps in Caddy convertibles with four girls in the
back. The girls took on the pipeliners for one hundred bucks
a throw, twelve hundred a night. Depressed, out of sync, Pat
wired Charlie for money and came home.)

d) worked for the Governor of California. (Pat and Jerry
Brown first met when Pat was running for county office.
They stood around at a cocktail party one afternoon and
talked of their seminary pasts. Brown had once studied for
the Jesuits.)

e) become a poet, an actor, a restaurant manager, a husband, a father, a rickshaw operator on Fisherman's Wharf in San Francisco.

f) served as chairman of a board of California county supervisors. (He campaigned on a bicycle, on a kind of hippie save-the-environment platform. Only he was the hippie with the theological bent. Teilhard de Chardin was on his campaign flyers. They couldn't figure him out. He won, though not in a walk.)

g) tried to commit suicide.

h) studied theology and epistemology at the University of San Francisco with the vague idea he could and should keep doing something for God.

And somewhere in all this stone-to-stone existence came out, first to himself, then to the world. He's there to stay, he reckons. Doesn't see himself crossing back. "My gayness is only important now insofar as it's one one-hundredth of my humanity."

Pat Liteky has been writing poetry of late about his children and his homosexuality. The ribald ironies of being a homosexual parent may be his poetic apostolate, he says. One of his early poems on the subject is entitled "And So It Starts":

> Driving my old truck down the winding road
> I got my kids in the front seat next to me
> Real close and my oldest who was six today
> And none of us having seen each other
> For some time and he asks
> Daddy, what's a faggot?
> And not taking my eyes from the winding road
> I say a faggot is a stick used to light a fire
> And I casually ask him where he heard the word
> And he says nothing for a moment
> Until he changes the subject and asks
> Something else which I forget just now.

Kids live mythically and they live deep, to borrow Marshall McLuhan's phrase. Pat Liteky's children may not know all the terminology, or technicality, but they know their father is intimate with other men. Pat is sure of it. They will say things like, "Dad, is Allen your *special* friend?" A while ago Pat was with his boys in a park. They came on some of Josh's playmates. "Come on over, Josh, we're playing Kick the Queer," a boy called. Josh got immediately protective. Let's get out of here, Dad, he said. Pat felt tears and held them.

Faggots are for burning, Pat Liteky wrote in a piece of prose a while ago: "We faggots are not the only oppressed passengers in steerage, or even the most abhorred; that is relative to the extent our vilifiers feel threatened."

The omelet in the other room is turning black. Bright and funny Pat Liteky may be; organized he is not. He idles out to the kitchen to tend it, and I glance through sunlight at the confusion around me: his sons' swimming fins and masks on a table; a half-completed plastic model of the U.S.S. *Enterprise;* unhung prints, unshelved books; baskets of dirty laundry; a bed slightly askew of its frame. "I'm just a visitor to this planet, as you know," he says. "Everywhere I go things just seem to stay in process. I've often asked myself why this is so, why I can never seem to finish something."

He *has* finished a trilogy of poems. The first and second volumes were published several years ago and enjoyed a modest West Coast sale. In the introduction to the current unpublished volume, which contains explicit and erotic homosexual poetry, he writes: "Many miles and poems have entered scattered logs since a youth of chosen shelters from real and imagined storms. . . . Journals and diaries from other seminaries, countries, colleges, and barracks now fill cardboard boxes in ever-changing closets from old hotel rooms and boarding houses to homes of friends." If the older Liteky brother travels light, the younger, I think, is a dromedary lugging it all from oasis to oasis.

My eyes have stopped their roam at a bookshelf. A small clay penis is resting atop the case. The penis looks to have a pair of wings attached to it. It is sitting beside a cross and chain. The head of the winged penis is curling over the lip of the shelf. Nearby is another object, small and oval and very hard to the touch, almost bony. The object is flesh-colored and is oddly pleasant to rest in your palm. It looks like nothing I've ever seen before. "It's a representation of two men copulating," Pat says from the other room. "An artist friend of mine did it. He tells his straight friends it's a surreal dolphin's head."

On a wall: photographs of the Liteky clan—Jimmy, Charlie, the old Navy Chief, Gertrude, who looks as lovely and soft as a twenties film star. The picture of Jimmy Liteky was snapped four or five years before his drowning. Jimmy is wearing a Camp Cloudmont T-shirt and looks hauntingly like the Pat Liteky I knew in the seminary. The picture of Charlie is the same one that had caught my attention at Charlie's flat. Pat, coming in, sees me looking at the photo and goes over to stand by it. "Yeah, I guess I'm about the only one left who still calls him Bud," he says.

Five or six years ago, Pat Liteky's life seemed headed for the drain. He got to the point of wanting to take his own life. He doesn't think it was cowardice so much as his inability to understand why everything he had touched seemed to turn to shit, to use his word for it. He had been married—only to find himself unavoidably coming out of a closet. He had tried seminary and monastery, and to no apparent avail. He had gained, and then lost, good-paying jobs. Usually he had lost them because of his impulsiveness. "I just wanted to call the game early," he says now. "I wanted to go up there and say, "Look, God, why is all this happening? I don't really think I'm that bad a person."

So he got some pills. He wrote some letters to his children. On the eve of the day he planned to do it, he hopped on a motorcycle and rode to a hospital to visit his younger son, Jeremy. Jeremy was two and was about to be operated on for a cleft palate. The boy lay doped and bewildered. The father, who hadn't been a very good father in this period, who was living on and off with other men and falling behind in alimony and child support payments, had not seen his sons for over a month. He arrived at the hospital unkempt, lugging a helmet, in a leather coat.

Jeremy saw his father and reached out through his narcotic haze. The boy grabbed his dad and would not let go. Pat tried to wrest himself loose, but a two-year-old's grip was too desperate. "It was just a moment in time," Pat says. "But I think it was the finger of God. I think I saw in that moment a message to start thinking about someone besides myself for once. Jeremy doesn't know it, but he saved my life."

These days the homosexual father has a straight job, at the California Arts Council. He is a project director and he wears a tie. He hops around the state, attending meetings, helping

local communities get art grants. He makes about twenty-five
thousand dollars a year. It almost sounds like . . . stability. "I
think it has to do with passing forty. I'm not going to do
anything crazy anymore." A grin slips through. Although I
should add that my favorite ice cream is still Rocky Road."

Pat and I were supposed to hook up three days ago, in Los
Angeles. But before I could pin him down on a time, which
is what you must do with the Liteky brothers, he had caught
a 6 A.M. flight back to Sacramento. It was a Sunday, and he
had promised his children he would take them to the circus
that day. No matter what he is up to during the week, or with
whom, the father makes sure he is back home with his sons
on weekends. Nowadays Pat and his ex-wife—whose name is
Patricia—get along fine. It was not ever thus. For a while she
wanted Pat out of her sons' lives, and Pat himself wondered
if she wasn't right. But he is through with self-loathing, with
helter-skelter, with self-destruction. He no longer feels bad
about who he is. He's no longer interested in trying to change
himself back to what he never really was. He was washed in
the blood of religion, but he's washed away the guilt, or most
of it. Someday his kids will know what he went through, he
says. "I'm not worried about them now. They're asking the
right questions."

> Your mom and I live apart and love each other
> In different ways than before
> You asked the other day, Josh
> Dad, do men marry each other?
> I was hesitant
> After all, you are only four
> Going on manhood yourself.

The boys continue to live with their mother but see their
father often, and talk with him on the phone during the
week. Patricia's place is a mile or so across Sacramento from
Pat's. Sometimes there is a mixup in phone calls, and then
Patricia Liteky must say to deep-voiced callers, "Excuse me, I
think you have the wrong Pat Liteky." The first time I tried
to reach my old seminary friend, she said that to me.

Like nearly everything else in Pat Liteky's Byzantine biog-
raphy, meeting Patricia seems part serendipity, part dumb
stumble. His former wife is a strong woman. "I know what

it's like to have problems," she says. Pat was in his hippie phase when they met. He was campaigning for office in Santa Cruz, and Pat worked in a dental office, and one day the candidate had an appointment. He already had had some gay experiences but was still trying to convince himself he was a heterosexual. About a week after his first visit, Patricia called to remind him of his next appointment. Pat ended up inviting her to come and watch his softball team, the Utes, which stood for Undesirable Transient Elements. They began going out. Patricia had been married previously; her husband had died in an airplane crash. "Poor dear," Pat says now, shaking his head. "Her first husband gets killed in an airplane and her second turns out to be a fag."

The two Pats began going out. Five months later (on Watergate break-in day, 1972) they made love. Patricia got pregnant. Abortion was unthinkable and so he proposed. She accepted and then got cold feet. Pretty soon, though, the two Pats were posing, heads together, for the local newspaper's photographer. Pat had been out of the seminary less than a year. Four times in the next five years, the two filed for divorce. They would reconcile, break up. Josh, their first son, had come along out of one night's love, and their second son, Jeremy, came along four years later out of the same impossible, hysterical odds: having briefly reconciled the doomsday marriage, the two Pats went for a weekend to Lake Tahoe. They were not intimate in Tahoe, but on the way back stopped in San Francisco, where they had intercourse at a hotel: exactly once. Patricia became pregnant again. Says Patricia: "We like to joke about the two times we made love. And that's Joshua and Jeremy."

> He wonders aloud about life in space
> Among the stars and wanders about
> In space looking for life after birth

The Psychology of Coming Out. For years the thought of sex with another man repelled him. In Florida, in the sixties, when he had left the seminary for the third time, though not the last time, he joined a Y to work out. He was working out, minding his own business, and pretty soon he gets picked up. He would find himself going back to the guy's house and getting royally drunk and only then, anesthetized, exhausted, could he go through with it. "I've been able to enjoy sex with women, though never so totally as with a man. I remember dating some girls at Catholic University in Washington. I was between seminaries again. My seminary career was like a revolving door. Anyway, I would never kiss these girls until about the tenth date, if then. There was this one nurse who took a shine to me, that sort of thing. Actually, I lost my virginity with a woman, not a man."

It's impossible for him to conclude that the seminary "made" him gay, any more than one afternoon in Vietnam made Charlie heroic. In both instances, something, a certain quality, must have already been in place. "I think I was gay from . . . whenever. Even before Holy Trinity, I can remember occasions when I felt attracted to strong male images. Maybe I got arrested in a mental set, though I don't especially hold to that. Maybe it's because I didn't know my father the first five years of my life. The Chief was off fighting the wars. I've thought about that; I've written it down in a poem, in fact."

Like everyone else, he used to lie in his bed in the dorm and fantasize about marriage: what would it be like to have kids? What could it feel like to have sex with a woman? We were all going through that one. "Except with me there was this little corner of worry: This is sickness. You are different from everybody else."

He never heard the word "gay" in the seminary, he says. "Or fag. I heard fairy. I used to watch guys towel off in the shower. Once some of my classmates chased me around the dorm. They were trying to depants me. Five or six of them pinned me on a top bunk. They were all around me, and I was trying to beat them off with a heavy bronze crucifix. I was probably more concerned about committing a sacrilege than getting depantsed. Maybe I was having these Dominic Savio images about not being defiled. You know what I remember about Dominic Savio, the boy saint? He refused to go skinny-dipping with his pals. But anyway, that depantsing humiliated me, angered me—all of that. I kept trying to put it in a spiritual context. I told my confessor I had committed a terrible sacrilege, hitting my classmates like that."

On the road some nights, you get lonely. You go to the baths. At the gay baths, as in most of the world Pat Liteky now inhabits, there is that premium on tidiness. Everything is clean, almost antiseptic. You sit around in soft lighting. There is music. Someone may come up to you and rest his hand on your shoulder. You're not interested, so you say, "I'm resting." It's an old code expression in the baths. Sometimes men go into other rooms and "fist-fuck." Pat Liteky has never done that, he says, nor is he about to try. That is the aberrational outer edge of the gay world, he thinks. And yet a poet is a seeker, a libertarian, and so he acknowledges these things. Lately, he has avoided the baths.

The hedonism of the gay world gets him down. "This implied constant message: if you gain one inch I'm divorcing you as a lover. It's hard sometimes to find people with . . . values. I've got to say it, I get haunted now and then by the vision of these burnt-out old queens, their bodies like wilted lettuce, sitting around at the baths in their skimpy towels and desperate smiles. Christ, is that what it will be like for me in another fifteen years? If there is another man out there intended for me by God . . . maybe in an airport lobby or a hotel bar . . ."

He doesn't finish, but lets it trail off, smooth, tanned hand closing to a loose fist.

> Josh, you saw me caress another man and asked
> Who is going to take care of me?
>
> You gave as much innocent love
> As you received and more
> You understood without knowing the
>   terminology
> I cannot explain, rewrite, or adequately interpret
> History, only make it
> You came from a love between a man and a
>   woman
> You are off to a good start
> With love in your pockets.

Only three or four years ago did he come to full, embracing terms with his gayness. That's when he made the statement: Goddammit, Pat, you're gay, and if you're going to be saved, it will be because of that, not in spite of it. Providing, of course, the other things are there, too.

Even now, all the way out, it is hard for him to say exactly how he went from a disgust for the darker fantasies of it to a recognition of gayness as a legitimate existence to a rooftop shouting acceptance of his own homosexuality. In the end, that is to say the beginning, it was almost an Anselmian proof of the existence of God: I can conceive of a perfect being, therefore He must exist. I can conceive of a pleasurable harmony between two men, therefore it must be good. If a heterosexual marriage can lead to God, why not a homosexual union? He has these urges. And the urges won't go away. And God doesn't create anything evil. That was some of the process. He prayed, too, he says. "I prayed hard."

But what finally turned it around, brought Pat Liteky out, was that he fell in love. "Like never before or since," as he wrote in a piece of his prose. Falling in love threw open the terrible oaken door to the forbidden closet, unlocked the portal of his secret passage. He remembers a line in a book written by a Jesuit, John McNeill, *The Church and the Homosexual*, a line to the effect that you will know you are a homosexual man when you fall in love with another man. That's what happened to him. As never before or since. His lover had covertly followed him for months. One day he sent Pat a letter. He said he felt he was in love with him. Pat met him at the bus station in San Francisco, and they drove toward Santa Cruz. On the way down the coast, they pulled over and lay in windswept reeds on a deserted beach.

Now he knows that the great natural enjoyment of erotic love is a gift to be shared. He also knows that commitment in a hedonistic world has the life span of a mayfly. In the last year or so, Pat has had a relationship with a man he met at Dignity. Dignity is a nationwide association of homosexuals who seek to worship with dignity in the Catholic Church. Some bishops accept them, some don't. In Christian Europe, between the thirteenth and eighteenth centuries, the burnings, hangings, beheadings, judicial drownings, and castrations of homosexuals were a regular occurrence in countries like France, Spain, Italy, and Germany. The roots of Catholic condemnation go far back. Official current Catholic teaching on homosexuality—as expressed in a 1975 declaration from the Sacred Congregation for the Doctrine of the Faith—

holds that although the homosexual orientation is morally neutral, the genital expression of it in any context is sinful. Catch-22.

Headline, San Jose (California) *Mercury*, September 13, 1978:

Ex-Supervisor 'Comes out of Closet' to Fight Prop. 6.

Proposition Six on the California ballot concerned the hiring of homosexual teachers or other employees for schools. Pat Liteky, ever the man of unpredictability and conscience, appeared before the board of supervisors, which he had once headed (he had resigned abruptly over a dispute concerning leaks and disclosures), and publicly declared his homosexuality. A woman was there before the board that day. "You should not pay any attention to these people," she said. "Think of our children, who have a right to grow up naturally."

Sometimes *I* can't help thinking of his children who have a right to grow up naturally. And what, I wonder, is "naturally"? A boy's seminary circa 1958? Just when I am about to judge him, I think of that.

Pat Liteky left the Trinitarian Order and entered a Trappist monastery in the early winter of 1959. He was nineteen. Two months previously, his brother Jimmy had drowned. After Jimmy's death Pat was more resolved than ever to enter a monastery. Seminary, even a novitiate, was not enough for him. He wanted deeper seeds of contemplation. He wanted Thomas Merton's Seven Storey Mountain. He entered the Trappists at Conyers, Georgia. It was cold in December 1959 in Georgia, cold enough "so that the holy water in the tiny plain ceramic font beside the hard straw mattress in the cubicle allotted to me froze solid every night." At two o'clock every morning an old train bell clanged the monks to Matins. They sang centuries-old Gregorian chants for hours on end, it seemed. Brother Celsus (this was his new religious name) would pray in those hours with the heat from his rubbed-together palms warming him. In daylight he pitched silage for cows, washed down pigs in sterile pens, baked monks' bread, read, and prayed. "Oh, those days were glorious." There was never any talking, nor did there seem to be any need for it. "Of course if a fire broke out, we could yell for attention." He remembers a monk cajoling cows, clucking joyfully with the chickens.

Brother Celsus was assigned to the chicken yards. One day, gathering eggs, he found himself next to a hen getting ready to lay one. He could see her quivering orifice opening into a "brilliant red corona" and a white moist oval being nudged out. So a monk did what seemed natural and quickly put his hand in the drop zone. He later described the feeling in a piece of eloquent writing: "The warmth of the egg as it slid gently into my palm, plop, connected me with an earthy and earthly existence I was fleeing unawares." The economy of salvation, the sanity of perfection—and he had his urges. He can still recall the sensuous night sounds of monks grunting and belching and farting as they settled into their straw.

At length the Liteky itch to bolt came back. The abbot tried to dissuade him. "It is a common temptation to want to return to the less rigorous orders," the abbot said. "It will go away." It didn't, and Brother Celsus left. "I wanted to take the silence with me back into the world." He reapplied to our seminary, and they let him back in. It was a practically unheard-of exception to the seminary rule, and they made it, I suspect, precisely because of Pat Liteky's unarguably deep spiritual life. He came back to the Trinitarians in 1960, got back his old name, Brother Dimitri, made over his year of novitiate, stayed through three years of philosophy and a year of theology, then bolted. "You see, I have this history of leaving," Pat says, perfectly seriously, issuing the understatement of the year. "It's always the conscience thing."

From an essay he wrote a while back: "It feels good to be freed from the exclusiveness of the rules of a disorganized ecclesiastical organization which prides itself on being the world's largest. Such rules have built up over centuries of rigid tradition, often crassly political decisions, and unashamed economic considerations. . . . One crimson dawn I woke up in my own unspoiled garden to the fact that union with God was not just for Olympian monks of whatever persuasion. . . ."

Pat Liteky says he used to get this dream. There is an altar and some ordination vestments and young, happy, scrubbed men taking their places before a bishop. There is a place for him, a small opening, but Pat isn't going to get in. And he is the only one who knows. "I used to get the dream about once a week, but it tapered off a while ago," he says.

There is a toothpick hanging at his lip. We have finished eating, and he is knocked back in his chair. He is a handsome, distinguished man. If foppishness were the guide, you wouldn't have a clue that this man is gay. He could be a mortgage banker.

He lights. "Hey, that reminds me: I think I had a dream about you and me last night. Yeah, you and I were in this funky old school bus, a seminary bus. We were searching. We were visiting all these places. You were driving. We were going along picking up our friends."

That evening we make a dreary round of Sacramento homosexual bars. He is driving, I am note-taking. Pat had asked if I cared to go to the baths, but I was too chicken for that. In one bar, a mostly leather place, a mean-looking man, with a Marlon Brando motorcycle cap, studs flashing up and down his sleeves, the seat of his jeans cut out to expose hairy cheeks, gives me the fish-eye. Or am I imagining this? Pat has on a coat and tie. He has changed from what he had on in the afternoon—rugby shirt, white ducks, web belt. He drums his fingers on the bar now and seems a little bored. I am trying to be both bored and cool. He says he has heard of this place in New York where you keep descending to different levels, depending on the depth of your fantasies. On one level there might be a man, naked, in chains; on another, wet-leather boys. We drink up and go on. In the next place we stay for one quick drink. Above jangling music he tells me how he wanted to enter the Trappists nearly the whole time he was at our seminary. "I can remember writing a letter to my mother: 'I want desperately to go to the monastery, but I'm not getting any sympathy from anyone, and if I walk around here with my eyes downcast and my arms folded, people will laugh at me.'"

We are home and in bed before eleven. We are exhausted. I pull out the bed and he scrubs his teeth. "Shit, haven't had much rewarding ever happen to me in a bar anyway," he says. "Bet I haven't been to three bars in the last six months." He says it with a kind of existential weariness, staring at himself in the glass. Pat Liteky and I, I think, are looking for the same things in the wrong places. Home is where we left it.

The next day I left Sacramento and drove back to San Francisco to see Charlie Liteky. I stayed overnight at Charlie's. The next morning the phone rang early. Charlie had left for the VA and so I picked it up. It was Pat. We talked for a while. He said my visit had motivated him to get going again on a play he has been trying to write. It's about former seminarians at a reunion, one of whom announces his homosexuality. Then he said he had been thinking over some of our conversations, and that he couldn't help worrying a little about how he was going to be portrayed, and about what some of our old friends would think. "Dammit, Paul, I still care terribly about those guys; I still want their respect," he said. "I guess it's what the bonding is about." He said he had already picked up a mildly condescending attitude from some people in and out of the Order, "this combination of disdain and pity." He said he was talking mainly of the ones who didn't leave and are priests now. "Because gay, you see, is not an equivocal term. It might mean leather bar. It might mean S&M. It might mean child molester. They're not sure what it means, but they have to put me away. Otherwise it's guilt by association. They have to say to themselves, some of them anyway, 'Oh, Liteky, gay, huh? Poor sucker. Well, forget him.' "

I caught up with Pat a year later, early in 1982, shortly after I had revisited Charlie. Pat had left Sacramento by then and had taken a job in Colorado as a fund raiser for an arts company. He was lonely, he missed his kids, he was experiencing cash flow problems. He showed me a birthday card his sons had sent him. On the front of the card, head to head, were two gay men. On the inside of the card was scrawled this: "Dear Dad, Happy Birthday. A small package is coming. Do you like your job? I hope I can see you soon."

It was Good Friday, 1982. In the seminary we would have

been silent nearly all day. Now it had not even occurred to me to go to church. Easter was forty-eight hours away. The feast was a pagan one, for all I was aware. I wondered if Pat had paused any that week to dwell on old times. Before we went out to dinner that Good Friday evening, Pat called his sons in California. He was speaking to them from his bedroom, and I eavesdropped on the conversation. He said to Jeremy: "Did you say your prayers today? The next time you talk to God, tell Him you want to see your daddy, okay?" When we came back to his apartment that night, Pat put on a tape of the sound track from the movie *Chariots of Fire*. We sat listening to it in the dark, the music swelling and falling like oceans. "Boys of summer, eh?" Pat said from across the room. I could barely make him out.

The next day, Holy Saturday, we rose early. We decided to take a swim and a steam in the club in the basement of his apartment complex. I didn't have my swimsuit with me and felt funny slipping into Pat's spare wildly colored bikini suit. I kept wondering if someone would see us in the hall and figure I was Pat's lover. In the steam room he told me about a closet homosexual he knows with a penchant for little boys. "That's disgusting," I said. "Yes, but by whose values?" his quizzical grin seemed to say. We talked for a while of our mothers, and why a merciful God apparently saw fit for Gertrude Liteky to suffer so greatly in her last years: husband dying on his back, a son drowning, another son leaving the priesthood, a third son seeming to jump from stone to stone, seminary to seminary. "The answers aren't here," Pat said softly. "Everything leads to death. Sand is pouring."

Before I got on an airplane I asked a question I had asked more than a year before: If you could change your sexual preferences, would you? The year before he had said, "Ah, that is the old talk show question. Well, the only thing I'd change is that I didn't come out sooner." I asked the question again now. "Will I always be gay? I suppose, I suppose." He didn't say it with as much enthusiasm as I would have guessed.

At the airport he got out of the car to shake my hand, help me with my bag. "Next time I'll have the pictures hung," he said. "But I don't know in what city."

In the introduction to his current volume of poems, Pat

Liteky wrote this: "And this poet believes in God because he has put his hand, with testy fingers, into the places of the wounds of the daughters and sons of Man, but probably not enough."

Roger and Bertin:
Appalachian February

———

In 1970, the summer before they were ordained, when the three of us were twenty-six, Bertin went to eastern Kentucky to work on a mission. Roger, already running from the outside, went down to Alabama and worked for the Russell County highway department. It was not the textbook way for a deacon to spend the summer preceding his ordination to priesthood. He made $1.22 an hour. The blacks rode in the rear. "There was a guy on the road crew who'd been there for years. He could use a grader like a hand trowel. He was making two cents more an hour than I was," Roger says. Some people in the Order figured Roger was slumming that summer, bleeding with a heart that was somewhere between liberal and radical. That same summer, 1970, I was living in State College, Pennsylvania, working at a public television station, and already busting up with my new wife. We had gotten married less than a year before on the Main Line, outside Philadelphia, and the reception was at a country club where Arnold Palmer modeled golf clothes. I figured I was doing the right thing. I had been out of the seminary four years then.

FEBRUARY 1981, Eastern Kentucky.

They are older, bulkier now, though much else about them seems remarkably the same. We are what we were but not quite. Roger still chews his nails and paces a room and curses infernally. Bertin pushes up his glasses with his index finger the way he did on the day I first met him. That was on a train platform on Michigan Avenue in Chicago in 1958. We were fourteen then and "firsties" and headed for a place called Holy Trinity, Alabama.

Time telescopes, weirdly compacts. Bertin Glennon, Catholic priest, stands behind a table in a purple gown. Bars of leaden Lenten winter light angle in. It is a little after eight o'clock on a February morning, St. Ann's parish, Town Branch Road, Manchester, Kentucky, coal country. I got here last night, driving in from Lexington in a Cumberland dark. I am barely awake this morning.

"This is my body," Bertin says in the same high schoolboy voice I remember as clearly as if the first time it spoke to me were only yesterday. He raises a round wafer of bread, pinching it in his fingertips. Heads bow. Somewhere beyond a window a dog barks. Rain pounds lightly on the roof, shellacs a walk. "This is the cup of my blood," Bertin says, raising a chalice of wine. The chalice is cut with green stones and rimmed with gold. I am barely looking at the cup, though. I am fixed on a rollaway barbecue grill out on the sodden lawn. From where I stand I can see the grill perfectly: it is a dull color and is gathering rust. What is a barbecue grill doing on a lawn in February, my brain idly wonders, perhaps so it doesn't have to wonder on something called Transubstantiation, whereby simple bread and wine, in an old classmate's fingers, somehow become the body and blood of Christ. "It's never like you thought it was going to be, the priesthood," Bertin says after Mass. "But it's not really different, either. It's nothing I didn't expect. Maybe it's not what we schemed and plotted and fantasized in the seminary." That evening, talking by phone to my wife in Bertin's kitchen, I try to summon the emotion I had felt at Mass. "It was hitting me in such a profound way," I say. I don't think she understands. Bertin Glennon is the only one of our original class who made it, who survived. What did he know that day on the train platform I didn't? I say this jokingly before I leave. He shrugs. "Maybe it was the luck of the draw, Paul."

A day and a half later. I am sitting in the dampened glow of a fire across from Roger Recktenwald, another classmate, close friend, "fallen priest." We are talking seminary times, and not all of it is outrage. Roger—shoes off, shirttail and belly out, receding hair gone wild—is propped on the davenport in his living room outside Prestonsburg, Kentucky. Roger has had an eighteen-hour day, twelve of them at his work. His children, Adam and Rebekah, now play at his feet. We have all dined on homemade chili. "Say grace, 'Bekah," he had told his daughter. "God is great, God is good," the child began, giving it up for the chili. We then ate mostly in silence, crumpling crackers, slurping drinks.

Roger lives about eighty crow miles east of Bertin, deeper into mountains. It took me nearly three hours of driving, around blind curves and past dark lamplit places named Hazard and Hindman. Roger is a community organizer, although he doesn't call it that. He maintains rural water systems up hollows and along tributaries named Mud Creek, water systems he is determined not to let be destroyed by pollution from the coal industry. He works out of two offices down in the town, and one of them is a HUD disaster trailer he fast-talked for two hundred dollars. He lives and works in a county where the per capita income is a nudge over six thousand dollars, where people who need dental work don't always get it, people who are described by Washington, D.C., social scientists as the "culturally disadvantaged." That is a term Roger despises. When coal is up in Floyd County, Roger wrote in a paper a while ago, life is up. "I don't think I'm one bit different in what I'm trying to do now than when I was a priest," he says.

Roger built this house, jacked up the two-room slab shack that stood on the lot, widened it, raised the roof, put in ceiling beams, a kitchen, bedrooms. He framed the windows, hung a leaded-glass door, made things mitered, mortared, and tight, none of it plastic and nearly all of it wood, building it on loans and a borrowed down payment, mortgaging himself and his future to the coalfields of Floyd County. In the seminary once, Roger took a cheap motor and a tin can and some crinkly red wrapping paper and made a fake glowing fire for Christmas. We were all a little homesick. He hammered together a mantel from scrounged plywood. "Cut my hand four times trying to get the goddamn thing to flicker," he says. "Practically had myself mesmerized by the drone of a motorized fire. Thought I was going to start warming my hands on it any minute." For a minute he glistens. So do I.

Adam is wrestling for his dad's attention. The son seems a wondrous, eerie re-creation of the father, down to temper and manic energy and pint-sized digital watch. Suddenly Adam cocks a leg and kicks hell out of the easy chair beside the sofa. He is barefooted and howls with pain. He starts to cry, choking back tears and laughter. Roger reaches out and encircles the boy, drawing him to his breast. The father, too, looks bridged beween hilarity and pain, trapped in a middle distance of ironies. "Son," he says, "you're a crock."

A while ago Roger's priesthood seemed trapped. The institutional Church had begun to fray for him like a rope, although in a sense Roger held the knife. A bishop in West Virginia, where Roger was stationed, took away his priestly faculties for alleged willful and flagrant disobedience. Among other things, Roger had participated at the marriage of a priest and appeared on a television show in a suit and tie. Without faculties, a priest can say Mass in front of his congregation, but not preach. He cannot baptize or hear confessions or anoint the sick. "I was a closet priest," Roger says. By then, though, something else had taken him: he was in love. He had met Eileen several years before, when she was still a schoolgirl, and the two had been doubting it and fighting it ever since. "I knew when I went to tell them I was getting married my priesthood was finished," he says, jerking a thumb past his shoulder, an ump calling a clean out. "But it didn't have to be, not really. At first I thought I'd stay and fight. But it was too big, the problems, they were all inclusive . . . pervasive. It was a school bus without a driver; the anger, it was running me." He makes a sweep with his hands, he makes a primordial grunt of frustration: he can't make me understand in a couple of tortured sentences what I doubt he fully understands himself. Eileen, in a plaid flannel shirt, legs tucked up under her on the floor, studies the TV across the room. She says nothing. But she is a direct and forceful woman, I will discover on subsequent visits here. Later this evening, when Roger is on the phone, she will say quietly: "We loved each other. But he was a priest and that was that. I watched him struggle with it."

●

Roger is reading from a bedtime book. He sits on the sofa beneath a funnel of frowsy light, a contented child in pajamas stuck under each arm. Roger's wire rims rest on his knee. He is a big man, with blunt features and a bad hack and nails bitten down. His face might belong to a roughneck on a Texas oil rig. The wearied father begins the story resignedly but rises to it as he goes. "Br'er Rabbit had a way of doing things he had no business doing in the first place," he says. As he reads I muse, try to recollect.

Roger Recktenwald—angry, confused, disillusioned; politically baptized by the sixties; theologically enraged over a 1968 papal encyclical on birth control called *Humanae Vitae;* in love with a woman and "trying not to manage the feeling" but letting it take him where it would—left his priesthood in 1973, not quite two years after he was ordained to it. It took Roger thirteen years to become a priest, from August 1958 until May 1971, and I think he outgrew the goal, or at least the traditional concept of the role, somewhere along the way. But he got ordained anyway: a ball was bowling on a path. And two years later he resigned, although maybe "resigned" is just semantics. Because when the ordaining bishop placed his palms on Roger's head one gorgeous spring morning and said, *"Tu es sacerdos in aeternum,"* he was saying, "You are a priest forever." According to the order of Melchisedech. Until the last cracking ring of doom. You couldn't have grown up Catholic and an altar boy at St. Cecilia's parish in the West End of Louisville, as Roger did, without feeling the finality of those words.

Even at the point when Christ's earthly anointed were going over the boat as though it were a leaky scow, abandoning the priesthood could still seem a little like murdering your father. Doctors left medicine. Husbands quit wives. But priests didn't leave the priesthood. They did, of course, in gangs, and even now accurate figures are hard to come by. The conservative figures, from Rome, report that 13,440 priests worldwide formally left the priesthood between 1964 and 1970, which were the principal years of chaos following the Second Vatican Council. That number says nothing of the thousands of other men who walked off without formal notice or application for dispensation. Corpus, a Chicago-based organization of resigned American priests, estimated a few years ago that there were more than 12,000 Catholic priests living in their own special limbo in this country alone. One of them is Roger Recktenwald, rural water systems man in Prestonsburg, Kentucky. Roger is aware of the paradox, of course. It's his tightrope. Five or six years ago, after I first got back in touch with him, he was holding a drink in my house in Washington, having just come from a National Demonstration Water Project meeting with some White House personnel. He was wearing a three-piece powder-blue suit and I said, not thinking, "So when exactly was it you left the priesthood, Rog?" and he shot back, "Goddammit, Paul, I still am a priest."

That was then. This is now, a sludge-gray winter weekend. I have spent the better part of five days shuttling between Rog and Bertin. This afternoon, plowing down from Mud Creek with Roger in his station wagon, candy wrappers flying off the dash, the baby carrier in the back careening off the door as we took corners like Mario Andretti, Rog said, unable to plug a grin, "Historically, some of these mountain people I work with are really anti-Catholic. They think we're papists, foreigners. I always want to say, when the talk comes up, 'Yes, I know. Kneel down and I'll give you my blessing.'" Some of the people Roger works with know about his fugitive past. He doesn't parade the fact he was once a priest, and neither does he hide from it. It comes up, and it's a little mysterious to people who know him now, because they know him simply as he is now, just Rog, a working stiff, same as they are, somebody you go to Western Sizzlin' with, or K-Mart, or Mud Creek. A woman named Jan who works in Roger's converted HUD trailer says, "He's got to walk when he talks. And the phone better have the longest extension cord the phone company's got." This priest thing doesn't make much sense to her.

What he also said this afternoon was that "I was born to a clock. There are certain things I want to accomplish and by damn I aim to do them. Eileen tells me I take the bumper car approach to life, and I guess I already see some of that in Adam. Remember bumper cars at the amusement park? Suddenly they've cut the juice on you, sparks are flying, and you're slamming the pedal but you're not going anywhere, just sitting there, and . . . it's frustrating as hell."

I remember Roger's frustration, and also his anger, in the seminary. I was a little scared of him, despite our being best friends. He would smolder, then conflagrate, implode and explode at the same time. Once, after one of Father Vincent's loathed "quickies," Roger and the rest of us ganged outside by the rec rooms. We were cursing the Old Roman and his impossible Latin syntactical tests. Roger picked up a cinder block, backed himself away from the building about fifty feet, charged the wall with the block over his head, screaming, cursing, awful-faced. About six feet from the wall he let the thing fly. It was primal therapy and probably we all should have tried it. We didn't much know what to do with anger in the seminary; that was one of the problems. "I had this terrible temper as a kid," says Roger, "and I got the shit kicked out of me every time." The West End wasn't the most pacific neighborhood in Louisville. Muhammad Ali, who was Cassius Clay back then, grew up in that same neighborhood.

Roger has an older sister in religious life. Sister Audrey Recktenwald is a member of the women's branch of the same religious congregation Roger and I belonged to. Audrey is a quiet, proud, independent woman, every bit as tough, I'd wager, as her little brother, although she doesn't drive bumper cars. She is a nurse practitioner and runs a community center in Alabama not far from Holy Trinity. She used to live at Holy Trinity, and one night a few years ago I sat with her and talked about her younger brother. I wanted to know where Roger gets his incredible drive and temper and manic energy. "It never occurred to me till just now," she said, "but if my mother and father had a package to wrap and get in the mail, my mother would do it like this." Her hands blurred as she tied an invisible package the way a rodeo rider might rope a calf and hogtie it in nothing flat. "If my father had the job it would take him all day. But you knew when it was done it was perfect."

The father was process, the mother was product. When I told Roger about Audrey's package analogy, he laughed. "Yeah, I'm like my mother, but I have my father's compulsion to be a perfectionist, only I can never take the time." I met Roger's dad once. I remember a quiet, alert man who seemed worlds brighter than I would have guessed it took to drive a truck for Sinclair. "He had a business degree from the University of Louisville and a minor in chemistry. He worked in a lab and then he lost the job and then it was the Depression and he took anything he could get." One of the jobs Ed Recktenwald took before delivering gas was sorting tools at a Ford plant. The day Audrey was born he took off. He got fired. His father had a tinkering, inventive mind, his son says. "In his semi-retirement he made himself a motorized wheelbarrow so he could futz around in the yard." Roger's dad didn't live to see his son become a priest, or leave the priesthood, either: he died of stomach cancer when Roger was in his last years of study. It had begun with ulcers some years earlier, and I always had the feeling Roger knew what the outcome would be.

The Recktenwald family, German, had a way with machines as far back as anyone can remember. There used to be a Recktenwald Brothers Hardware (cousins) in Louisville, and family historians lay its demise to the rise of chain stores and prepackaging. Roger's great grandfather, Michael Recktenwald, came to the New World in 1847, reports a family history, "to learn the Art, Trade, and Mystery of a Tin and Sheet Iron Smith." The great grandson learned the art, trade, and mystery of priesthood, though he didn't forsake machinery, his love for tooling things.

A rope unraveling: in the major seminary, after I was gone, Roger's superiors were always on him to wear clerical dress. They had made it optional, more or less, as a sort of concession to rapidly changing times. The niggling about clerical clothes made Roger defiant, go deliberately the other way. "I figured we only had the collar for symbolic value anyway." In the fall of 1969 Roger and some others from the Order participated in the Vietnam Moratorium on the Mall in Washington. This time he wore his collar and cleric's suit. "Hell, we were trying to educate ourselves as much as anything. We were still coming out of the woods of Alabama. I stood around down there and passed out Oreo cookies like they were hosts." He giggles, half sheepish, half delighted.

There were more prankish activities. Once, before a talk in the seminary auditorium, Roger stole the papal flag and stuffed it in a closet. It was a juvenile thing to do, a juvenile's cry that he is in trouble. Another time, before a talk on Vietnam, this one presented by the hawk side, he burned an old rag, scorched some brass eyelets, put the charred remains in an envelope on the podium. It was supposed to be a cremated American flag, and he did it to taunt a missionary brother named Shamus Fox, who once had been Regular Army and was still a hard-liner on Vietnam. Brother Shamus and Roger were best friends. He did it anyway.

Another time he carried on a charade about a master key. Brother Shamus was in charge of maintenance at the seminary; he held the master key. "Pulled a nasty one there. I had long thought keys in religious life were an obvious phallic symbol anyway. Anybody who thought he was somebody had to have a key to something, even if it was just to his own room. I borrowed the master key from Shamus and went and got about five duplicates made for myself and then proceeded to go through this charade for damn near six months of borrowing Shamus' key every time I wanted to get into the shop, even though I had one in my pocket all the time. When I needed to open a door and nobody was around, or it wasn't convenient to ask, I'd basically sleuth out the situation and use my own key. If one of the priests was around I'd go through my charade with Shamus. When Shamus found out, he threw one damn shitfit. I think he could probably laugh about it now, but he wasn't laughing then."

Two facts and a personal theory about Roger Recktenwald: in his early seminary career Roger was an immensely likable though undeniable clod from Kentucky who found schoolwork extremely difficult and who didn't possess a lot of athletic coordination. We used to mock his accent, his walk, his clothes. Once, in the rec room, as he flipped through a magazine, I said loud enough for everybody to hear: "Say, Rog, tell me, is the correct pronunciation of Kentucky's capital Looeyville or Lewisville?" "Well, Paul," he drawled, "we always did say Louavul." He said it before he could think about it. I told him the capital was Frankfort. We didn't let him forget that one for years, even after we had elected him our class vice president and he had taken over as a natural leader.

The second fact: Roger's modus operandi, from the start, was to do it first, get permission afterward. Roger Recktenwald was the original seminary red-tape slasher when it came time to scrounge materials for something he was working on. Roger was forever donating his free time to build something for somebody, while the rest of us were loafing in the rec rooms. He might be making a lectern for Father Barnabas's use in the choir, he might be making a set for Father Brendan's latest play. Father Brendan used to give out the annual Generous Rog Award. When Jim Recktenwald, Roger's little brother, came along to the seminary, *he* won the Generous Rog Award. Jim Recktenwald, like me, didn't get ordained to the priesthood, although he was in for a number of years. Jim and Roger ended up marrying two sisters. Jim is divorced now.

My theory: Everything Roger became, he was back then, only we couldn't see it because it was channeled differently. When the seminary moved to new facilities in the North, when things didn't have to be jerry-rigged and held together with baling wire anymore, he had to look elsewhere, go outside the walls, for his deep-seated needs for struggle, for taking on the establishment. I think urbanity and clean new buildings swamped him. But he wasn't inconsistent in the side he fought on.

When I was in the novitiate with Roger, I decided I was going to craft something for my mother with my own hands. I decided on a pair of chalice bookends. I spent countless time and blocks of wood on the lathe down at the shop, and then one Saturday afternoon Roger came over and nudged me aside. He finished the bookends, trimmed them in gold, dropped them off on my bed before supper prayers. I never told my mother the present was really my classmate's work.

The rope unraveling: a new superior came to the seminary. Tough cookie. He summoned Roger. "You have broken two of my predecessors. You will not break me." *He* left the priesthood before Roger did. At the end of his third year of theology, a year before his ordination, holding minor orders, Roger was supposed to go on the missions for three months. He said he wanted to go to Alabama to work at a regular job, see how it felt. He went down to Alabama, slept at Holy Trinity, hitchhiked into town every morning till he found work at the highway department. Few knew he was a clergyman. The crew grouped at the garage every morning, went out to the site on a truck. Because he was white Roger was supposed to ride up front in the cab. Just get in and keep his mouth shut. One day he climbed in the back with the blacks and promptly caused an altercation. After a while the crew found itself working near Holy Trinity. "We put this great big ass rain tile in a creek. It felt great, stinking with sweat like that." A few times they worked side by side with the county prison gangs. They had to tell the Man with No Eyes, who stood up above with a shotgun, when they were taking a leak. Taking a leak here, Boss. "I thought I was living a goddamn movie." Cool Hand Roger.

At the end of the summer, a couple hundred bucks in his pocket, Roger got a notion he'd like to go back up North on a motorbike. Don't want a pickle, just want to ride my motor sickle. He bought an old German scooter for ninety bucks, retooled the gears, bought three new Michelin tires, bought flag mounts, bought goggles and a helmet, and struck off to see America. He got about halfway to Phenix City "and the fricking thing catches fire. Blue flame shooting out the rear and some old lady on the side of the road hollering at me to pull over."

In that final year of study before ordination, Roger did a thesis on the theology of priesthood. He was nearly feverish in his research. He wanted to understand the disciplining of priests by hierarchy and superiors. He could find no rational basis for a mandatory celibacy—other than Church rule since 1139. Ecclesiastical celibacy became Church law with the passage of the seventh canon of the Second Lateran Council. But it wasn't dogma; just policy. The Pope could remove it with a stroke of a pen. "I don't know . . . maybe I was trying to prove what I already felt," says Roger. He had known Eileen for several years then. She was a high school senior when they first met and had then gone on to the University of Maryland. The two had kept in touch in Roger's last years by letter and phone call and occasional sneaked visit. Typically, he had met Eileen through an act of generosity. Eileen's mother knew some of the priests in the Order, and one day Roger went over to her house to help fix something that had gone wrong in the plumbing. Eileen was there that day. Roger was taken pretty fast.

He was, that final year, a kind of Rasputin, a tortured saint, a holy Lucifer, full of ice and fire, his devil the measure of his angel. There was a vague idea percolating in his head, although he couldn't articulate it. It had to do with the concept of the worker-priest, a tradition in France and other places among clerics who go out to work amid the poor in factories. But in any case the old seminary notion of Sacramental Priest, the parson who waits in his rectory for baptisms and marriages and funerals ("Hatch, Match, Dispatch"), had gone dry in Roger's head before he even got to try it. Which may explain, as I come to think about it, the truth in a cryptic remark he once made to me in my house: "I can't miss what I never had, Paul."

He got ordained. "These young priests, oh, so beautiful, so happy, so holy, but what of their future?" Father Judge, the founder of Holy Trinity, had written half a century earlier. "What souls does the Evil One covet more than theirs?" Roger was sent for a summertime fill-in assignment at Kiln, Mississippi. In every way he was the somewhat different parish priest. "If I had a collection on Sunday I'd give half to the pastor and the other half to help some poor old lady get moved who'd lost everything. I was constantly ripping the collection basket and slipping people rent money." Sure, he knew the old classroom moral arguments, means justifying ends. He didn't care about classroom moral arguments. He gave a sermon that summer, on the Eucharist and liturgy, just speaking from his heart because the notes were full of rhetoric and he always got balled up with them anyway. Liturgy isn't some black-magic hocus-pocus, he said; it's communing, it's opening yourself and being vulnerable. Afterward, as Roger was disrobing in the three-by-five sacristy, a man came in and started quietly crying. "He just kept saying, 'Thanks. Thanks.' He'd been trying to find a more personal God."

Two kids in the parish were getting married. "We figured, what the shit, both of them don't have two pennies to rub together." So he and a co-conspirator nun took the collection plate that Sunday and rolled out for New Orleans: a clerical Bonnie and Clyde with the pastor's car. "Right on the outskirts of town there's this great big discount house. We went through the appliance section of that place and bought it out. I mean, we bought toasters, we bought this thing, that thing, the other damn thing. And then we gift-wrapped all of it and sent one from Pope Paul, one from the bishop, one from the pastor. We were signing names on those damn things till three o'clock in the morning."

That fall Roger got assigned to a permanent job in Wheeling, West Virginia. He worked for Catholic Charities, got involved in community organizing in East Wheeling. He witnessed the marriage of a Franciscan priest. Though Roger presided at the ceremony, he didn't sign the license. (The wedding was across the border, in Ohio, where Roger wasn't bonded as a marriage minister.) But he threw rice and distributed communion and celebrated the Mass and kissed the bride. The day following, Father Stephen, the head of the order, called from Washington; he had heard about the ceremony. He said he wanted Roger in Washington immediately. Before Roger could leave, the bishop of Wheeling was on the wire. He wanted to see Roger in his office on Monday morning. Roger called Father Stephen back. "I had gotten both of them pissed off and had to deal with them one at a time." He went to see the bishop first. The bishop yanked his faculties. Roger was now a "closet priest."

In September 1972, little more than a year from his ordination, going down fast, he went to see Father Stephen again. He said he intended to enroll at the University of Kentucky, get a master's in social work. Father Stephen said, no, we want you to take an assignment on the missions. Roger said, no, I'm going to Lexington. He went to Lexington, where, with his typical genius for cutting tape and shaving points and tucking it to the bureaucrats, he wangled in-state tuition. But it was the Order's money, not his, and he can appreciate that now. He worked on his degree, arranged for a practicum in Floyd County, deep in Appalachia coalfields, got involved with a planning agency called the Big Sandy Area Development District. Big Sandy, covering a five-county area, was trying to take Washington and Frankfort monies and put dignity into people's lives by getting the people involved in their own decision-making processes. Big Sandy, named after a river, was sandy—and gritty with coal dust from the ravages of coal companies that make people rich and rob them of something deeper.

At first Roger got involved with recreation programs. Then rural water. That May he went back to Washington to see

Father Stephen again. "I didn't go empty-handed. I had pretty well briefed myself. I knew what I felt about Eileen and Kentucky and my priesthood. And I wanted all three. I said, 'Stephen, I want to get married. And I want to stay in this Order.' He didn't bat an eye. He said, 'That's impossible, you know that.' I said, cutting him right off, 'No, it's not impossible; it could happen if you and I and the bishop and the Pope and whoever damn else really wanted it to happen. I'm not talking about getting married and working in a big city somewhere where there are layers of tradition. I'm talking about working in eastern Kentucky, where I'm needed.' Well, it went on, and needless to say, he didn't buy my line. But to me, at least, my thinking was a natural progression."

Father Stephen brought in Father David, the Order's ace canon lawyer. In the minor seminary, fourteen years before, Father David had taught Roger and Bertin and me sophomore Latin, drilling us through any number of Latin proverbs: *Vestis virum non facit*. (Clothes don't make the man.) *Dum vivi bibi libenter*. (While I lived I drank freely.) "I'll help you write your papers," Father David said. No, you won't, Roger said. And that's the way it stood for a while: he was getting married and to hell with laicization. It was a term he always despised—"laicized." He hated it for its reductionism, its implied condescension. "Reduced to what, for Chrissakes? Who said priests are automatically higher?"

But after Roger and Eileen were married a while, he capitulated to paper, to use his phrase, to help ease his mom's pain. "My leaving was just a wrenching for her. She has never really accepted it, what I did or the way I did it, and she will tell you that flat out till the last breath she takes. She was classically gracious where I was classically bullheaded. The dispensation thing was just such a constant tension. She couldn't reconcile herself to it. She had reconciled herself to a lot, but she couldn't reconcile to that."

Eileen was upset, too; the question of Roger's dispensation had become a small obsession for the family. So he let out his breath and sent in the official papers to be canonically removed from the priesthood—but with a last salvo: "I wrote a letter I knew the Order or Rome would never accept as a reason for leaving, an absolutely frank and true letter, then gave them four blank pieces of paper with my signature on the bottom. If they didn't like what I had written they could write whatever reasons they damn pleased." Father Stephen, now no longer head of the Order, denies he ever saw those four blank pieces of paper. "We don't invent reasons to get people out of the priesthood," he told me a little hotly. "We were trying to help this young man." Roger, for his part, will now say that his refusal to submit papers was "half belligerence, half indifference." But he will also say his superiors were consistent with him and tough on him. "And I was grateful for the consistency. As I look back on this whole painful period, I guess you'd have to say their efforts were really pastoral, trying to help some guys like me who had gotten into trouble. I was scared shitless at the time. My defiance was studied but not acidic. I was intellectually convinced but emotionally guessing and stumbling."

Roger Recktenwald got married by a justice of the peace in a courthouse in Rockville, Maryland, on May 26, 1973. On the following Saturday, at eleven o'clock in the morning, under not bright skies, Roger and Eileen had their own ceremony, the one that counted in their hearts, in the backyard of her apartment across from a Naval Surface Weapons Center in Silver Spring, Maryland. A priest friend from the seminary was supposed to witness; he backed out, though he came to the ceremony. Another priest from the seminary, Father Eric, who had been one of Roger's teachers and close friends, brought his trumpet. Maybe sixty people were there, a number of them Eileen's friends. Maybe half a dozen ex-priests and their spouses were there, a reunion of outlaws bringing covered dishes, which were set up on folding tables in the garage. "We weren't trying to have ourselves some hip, bund affair," Roger says. "It was a celebration." Ed Recktenwald, Roger's oldest brother, flew over from Louisville with his wife, although Roger's mom stayed away. So did Eileen's. Sister Audrey Recktenwald stayed away also, although in other less painful circumstances she might have come. At noon that day, Father Roger Recktenwald, "renegade priest," standing maybe two miles from the spot where he had been consecrated almost exactly two years earlier, consecrated a few loaves and passed around a cup of table wine. The next day he and Eileen packed a car with books, some clothes, their gifts, and drove off to Kentucky to begin jobs and a new life.

The day I left the novitiate, in 1965, one of the quotes I took down from my wall was from John Henry Newman, the nineteenth-century English cardinal, humanist, and theologian. The quote was this: "In a higher world it is otherwise, but here below to live is to change, and to grow perfect is to have changed often." At the time I taped it there the quote meant a lot to me.

I remember asking Roger if he thought he had changed much. We were standing outside his office beneath sun glinting off new snow. It was raw and cold, although a day not without promise. Roger had on a tie and sleeveless cabled sweater that didn't quite cover his growing paunch. He stood rattling the change in his pocket, scuffing at an air-conditioning unit with his squeegee-soled shoes. (He's always walked duck-footed, and it makes a comical sight.) We had been talking furiously for several days. I was getting ready to leave. Roger blew into his hands. "Damn, it's cold," he said. "You should see this place in the summer, though. It's a jungle, it's so green. Eileen puts out so many flowers." Then he answered my question about change, but not until he had cleared his throat a couple of times. (He's always been a phlegm factory, and the habit has passed to his son, Adam. Clearing his throat buys Roger time.) "I think I've given more thought to my actions these last several years. I've witnessed this phenomenon a number of times: I'll place an action and then try to figure out what the hell it was I did." He laughed. "I guess I don't brandish the sword as much now. I've stopped trying to convince the bureaucrats."

A while ago Roger and Eileen started going to church again at their local parish in Prestonsburg. But the sermons turned them off. Sometimes Roger and Eileen take the kids to a service and find they miss it. Roger still frets about his "salvation," still gets down on his knees some nights, as I do, to say he isn't worthy. When they are in Louisville visiting his mother, they go to church with her. Roger and his mom are one again.

I asked him if he thought the climate might ever change so

that he would be tempted to take up some form of active ministry again. He yawned. Didn't guess so, he said. We let it drop. "I don't think I would have survived the sixties had not the basic questioning happened. On the other hand, if the sixties and Vatican Two and all our seminary hassles hadn't come along, I might still be a priest. And probably I'd be celibate. But you've got to play the cards they dealt you. Or you dealt yourself."

I thought he was finished. He cleared his throat. "My overall feeling about the experience is one of sadness, I think. I don't mean sadness because I rejected them, or they rejected me. I don't mean that I ever went down there in the first place. I mean a sadness that it all worked out as it did. Because what you're talking about is a group of people—Father Judge, Mother Boniface, you, me—who went down to Alabama with a dream. You can call it humanistic or pietistic or whatever you wish. But it was still a dream. And somewhere along the line the dream got out of focus."

A minute later Roger reached over and cuffed me. It is impossible to know all he meant by this light slap, but I'd like to think it had to do with an essential camaraderie, with bad times and great times, with a sense of the transcendent, with a certain quirky ribald history of the distance between two points, there to here. We shook hands and I left. I could see him in the rear-view mirror of my rental car, diminishing only in my vision.

Father Bertin Glennon, the kid I met on Track 9 in a railway depot in Chicago in 1958, stands in his own country rectory in Manchester, Kentucky. It is past midnight, and through the window behind his bulky form I can see a lace cloth of clouds gliding beneath a winter moon. I feel lonely, tired, vaguely depressed. Home is somewhere else.

We have been talking, gabbing, nonstop since I arrived five hours ago, catching up on our families, mutual friends, our jobs. The pastor is in a collarless clerical shirt, work boots, jeans, a puffy goose down vest. The vest only makes him seem rounder, more guileless. If Roger is *Angst* and fire, Bertin on the surface is contented chaos. Going to see Bertin is like stepping into a J. F. Powers short story about clerics: Bingo and irony at the foot of the cross. But looks deceive.

A briar pipe is clenched between Bertin's teeth: a commander at the helm of a perilous ship. A silver pocket watch, umbilicaled by a chain to his belt loop, makes a small bulge in his right front pocket. The sisters at the parish gave him the watch. He had another one, but it ticked so furiously at Mass it drove one of the nuns nuts.

At Bertin's feet, in harm's way, snores an aged elegant Irish setter named Boo. Bertin has had Boo for ten years, since ordination. For the first several years of Boo's life the dog rode around on the back seat of Bertin's car. It was the dog's only reality. Bertin was on vocation work in the Midwest then. Sometimes Bertin wonders if he would have made it on the road if it weren't for Boo. One Thanksgiving a few years ago Boo swiped the rectory's turkey. It had just come from the oven. Boo got a swat.

We are inspecting the pastor's prize hunting gun. There are lots of guns around the place, and the rectory is piled high with stacks of *Outdoor Life* and *Field & Stream*. Fishing paraphernalia clutters corners. One of his parishoners gave Bertin his first gun; that started him off. "Course, nobody in eastern Kentucky ever gives you anything right out. They say, 'Here, take this shotgun, I don't have any use for it, and if I need it I'll know where to come get it.' " Bertin loves to go hunting with the men of the parish—grouse, deer, fox— not that he's ever been in much danger of bagging anything: he's a pretty lousy shot when it comes to breathing things. Doubts if he could squeeze the trigger on a doe hanging between crosshairs. Mostly, getting involved with guns is a way of getting involved with Kentucky. Hunting gets Bertin out of his pastor's duds. "Fox hunting," he says, breaking up. "You know what fox hunting is down here? You sit around a fire all night, drink whiskey, tell lies. Heck, I guess I'm just one of these *macho* guys who feels he has to carry a gun through the woods." On Sunday after church Bertin hosts turkey shoots out back of the rectory. The winner gets a frozen bird. Likely as not Bertin wins.

We wander upstairs, atop the rectory, to his personal hideaway, where the pastor makes tapes for his half-hour radio show and sometimes prepares his Sunday sermons. "I write them out," he says, referring to the sermons. "I get all this deep theological insight and then just get up there and bull-crap." His radio show comes on every Sunday at noon. The idea is to play a little religious folk music, sermonize in between. The owners of the station like Bertin because he doesn't wail and rant, hurl lightning bolts, or thump his Bible. "I get them coming home from church," he says, the "them" being Baptists and Pentecostals and Methodists, almost anybody in town but Catholics, since there are but about fifty practicing Catholics in all of Clay County. One of the fifty is Montgomery C. Hounchell, turnkey at the county jail. Montgomery used to be bedrock fundamentalist till Bertin got hold of him during half times at local basketball games; though, really, people say it was the other way around: Montgomery was the seeker. He had the questions, Bertin had the answers, and today the jailer, who converted, writes a religious column for the weekly *Manchester Enterprise*. Montgomery calls Bertin "the padre" and attends church with his wife, Pam, and their two babies. Pam is a Pentecostal, but that doesn't stop her from playing aching gospel tunes on the piano for the Catholic services when the regular pianist is off sick. Pam sways and lilts through numbers called "Learning to Lean on Jesus." Doesn't read a note. Sometimes Montgomery goes to her church, where he's seen preachers get so bug-eyed and excited they leap, like bullfrogs sprouting wings, plumb over the podium right into the middle of the congregation. At funerals in eastern Kentucky you sometimes see a Princess phone sitting atop the casket with a little message under it: He Called.

On a stereo speaker cabinet, I see a photograph of Bertin and Roger and two others who joined our class in later years. The picture was snapped on ordination day, in the spring of 1971, and the four freshly minted priests in the photograph are beaming. I attended the ordination. I drove down from State College, Pennsylvania, the night before, took a room in a Holiday Inn near the seminary. I hadn't told anybody I was coming. The next day, at the reception for the new priests, I lied every time someone came up and asked me about my wife. We had separated a few months before and I was too ashamed to say it.

Bertin goes over and lifts the picture off the stereo cabinet. Father Judge, Holy Trinity's founder, once wrote: "Men who for the mere nod could possess kingdoms discarded the tawdry raiment of the world to clothe themselves in the livery of Jesus Christ." I stand behind Bertin as he studies the picture; I try to peer over his shoulder. Roger's clerical collar is different from those of the other priests in the photo. Roger's collar doesn't have the little break in it that indicates a Catholic priest. Roger's collar is the full round collar of Protestant clergymen. "Maybe it's just Rog's role to be different, to fight himself and everybody else until he dies," Bertin says, talking to the picture. "Some people are called to greatness, I think, and if they don't achieve it, invariably they begin to see themselves as tragic figures. The rest of us just stumble and bumble along." He puts the picture back, hits the light, locks the door behind him as we go out. He locks up at night nowadays. The first couple years he was here he didn't know where the keys to the rectory were. Not too long ago some kids on dope broke in and stole all the liquor in the house. "There's a large truancy in the high school. A lot of drugs here. Kids have nothing to do. One of the local sports is shooting out the overhead traffic light down by the Chevron where you came in. Course you don't have to be in high school to participate in that." (Big yuk.)

We go into his office, where he conducts parish business. A snapped-on lamp cuts the darkness, though not the quiet. There are black brooding ridges out there, but I won't see them until tomorrow morning. He plugs in a space heater at his feet, and it wangs on, orange coils glowing like tubes of neon, taking the chill off. I look around: plaques, books, papers, pipe tamps; the parish baptismal ledger (on the floor behind him); wonderfully aromatic tins of Borkum Riff and Kentucky Club and Granger tobaccos; a zippered breviary with its colored flutter of placemark ribbons; stacks of last Sunday's parish bulletin (typos and crossed-over words, the text running downhill on the page); a framed certificate naming him a Kentucky Mounted Rifleman; technicolor signs that say: BLESS THIS MESS and I'M THE BOSS AROUND HERE; a calendar askew of its nail but turned to the right month (February) with an inscription from Luke, chapter 15: "What man among you would not leave the ninety-nine sheep in the wilderness and go after the missing one until he found it?" Bertin's college room in the seminary was exactly like this. I know: I was his roommate.

He sees me looking around. "Hell, Paul, if I was organized I'd be dangerous, you know that." He doffs the blue captain's hat on his noggin to reveal a pate going bald. Two or three long strands of dark hair comb all the way over, the way Sinatra used to do before he took to a rug. Bertin selects a new pipe from the pipe stand, holding a fraction over the decision. He gouges for tobacco. He ignites a flame, knocks back, folds his hands over his stomach, whistles air through the pipe, surveys me: Sherlock on a case. We have seen each other twice in fifteen years. "It ain't awkward, is it, Paul?" he says. I wag my head in a no. Bertin always had the gift of putting you at ease, making you feel palsy.

"Do you get lonely?"

"Sure. Everybody gets lonely anywhere. But there's a nun who's company to me, Sister Alice. And there's usually a couple of lay volunteer college kids who come to the mission and sign up for six months or a year. I know I can come home at night and there are people in the house who care what kind of day I had."

"Do people in town think you sleep with the nun?" (Tomorrow, in fact, at the Gospel Variety Shoppe, someone will confide to me he figures the Catholic priest "up there on Town Branch Road is married to Sister Alice.")

"Oh, hell, probably. There are three females here at the moment with me—Sister Alice and two lay volunteers. I think the town understands about me and Sister Alice. A rumor races through Manchester like a weed fire. In a week nobody can remember it."

Bertin Glennon is a priest in an Appalachian coal county where about 60 percent of the families are on some form of public assistance, where 40 percent live below the poverty level, where nearly half the roads are unpaved, where some people live in hollows in shacks they rent for maybe ten, fifteen bucks a month. When it gets bitter cold in those hollows the people stoke up their pot-belly stoves so fiercely that the chimney can't take it and the shack goes up like a tinder box. "Burnouts," they call it. Happens all the time. (Tomorrow a burnout victim will show up at Bertin's door. The man will have one change of clothes. Bertin will get him a bed and mattress.)

"The social concern is so apparent. You're a material

helper first, a spiritual helper second. You can't turn around
in Clay County without meeting someone who's hungry or
wants you to pay his light bill. I bet I get five requests a month
to pay a light bill. The culture of poverty is strange. It's not
strange to see somebody with a Monte Carlo parked in front
of one of these pineboard shacks. People here can make a lot
of quick money, in the mines and other places, and they blow
it. You take alcohol. It's such a forbidden fruit, once you get
some, you drink the whole thing, you drink everything in
sight. That's the way some poor folk adapt. They have a real
sense that everything's fleeting. And welfare is the enemy,
except we'd die without it. The big thing is disability. You get
a lawyer. A doctor. You cough three times. How can they
disprove it? In some cases you're dealing with four generations of welfare. People would rather sit home and collect
and rock."

None of it comes out disparagingly or condescendingly,
any more than did the comment upstairs about Roger.

There are 474 square miles in Clay County, Kentucky,
23,000 people. Bertin has ten families on the parish rolls. He
has an outpost church down in Hyden—a double-wide trailer
with an altar in it and a turgid green river glittering out the
window. Can it be worth it, sticking here, in this Appalachian
February? I think of Bertin's calendar and Luke 15: "What
man among you would not leave the ninety-nine sheep in the
wilderness . . . ?" Bertin yuks, and the yuk answers my question. "Last night, at the Sunday vigil, had maybe eight people
for Mass. Usual crowd. Depends on the season." He bolts
forward, burrows on the desk, comes up with a small paper-
clipped wad of checks, starts thumbing through them like a
bank teller. "If I collect fifty bucks a Sunday it's a major deal.
I have to deposit these babies first thing in the morning so
Holy Mother Church doesn't go broke. Let's see, twenty-five,
thirty, thirty-five, fifty, sixty, *seventy.* Hey, sports fans, seventy
bucks, how do you like it?" He is waving the wad triumphantly. Once a month or so a Chinese lady doctor in town
might kick in a hundred bucks. The mayor of Manchester
(Daugh White, pronounced Doug; has the Chevy dealership
with his brother) is a Baptist. He and Bertin are cronies. The
mayor calls Bertin "Manchester's priest," never mind that
Manchester's priest hasn't been invited by the other ministers

in town to join the ministerial society—after seven years. This is still the frontier of the faith. Catholics, for all the padre's civic involvement, are still looked on a little xenophobically. At Christmastime Daugh White might slip a five-hundred-dollar check into Bertin's collection basket. Then Manchester's priest is rich as cream. A while ago White gave Bertin a moped. It belonged to the town and nobody was using it. The mayor knows where to come find it when he needs it.

The temptation sitting here opposite my old classmate is to say Bertin just glided through while Roger raged about tomorrow. When they were in the major seminary, after I was gone, Bertin would sit of an evening in his room in an easy chair beneath the weak wattage of a long-stemmed lamp with a fringed shade, feet up, pipe clenched between his teeth, while out beyond the open door, Roger was whipping the troops to mutiny, or trying to. Used to drive Roger bonkers, people say, seeing Bertin sitting there like that, while all Jericho was coming down.

But practically nothing is that monolithic, and it is easy to forget that Bertin Glennon, even when I knew him, was concealing demons, as all of us were. Father Constantine once put Bertin on the diet table in the refectory, and suddenly the roly-poly kid from Mundelein, Illinois, whose dad worked for the Soo Line, began to take on an alarming blue tint. Bertin dropped weight so viciously he nearly stopped looking like Bertin Glennon or anyone remotely related to him. The more he lost the more viciously he dieted. His fingers began to resemble waxy pegs. He wouldn't talk about it to us. The prefect almost couldn't get him to stop. I think it must have been some sort of anorexia, maybe tied to studies, and later, when we were in the novitiate, it would come back: I used to sit across from Bertin in my final year and I remember whole weeks when he'd take the plate I proffered but refused to take anything off it. He got by on bread and lots of iced tea. He didn't explain and I didn't ask.

I find out this evening that, in his fifth year, when we had graduated from the high school section and gone on to the college department and thought of ourselves suddenly as "old boys," Bertin secretly packed his bags one night, hid them in the bottom of his locker, then went to see Father Constantine about getting a ticket home. He was going to sneak out the next day while we were at lunch, catch the one o'clock train, avoid his own wake. "I was determined not to go through the death scene. I went to see Father Constantine, and he said, 'Glennon, you have to have a reason.' I couldn't think of one. I just wanted out. He made me agree to wait a week. Thank him for that."

My bed was three feet from Bertin's that year. I never knew.

"When did you know you wanted to be a priest?" I ask.

"When I was in second grade. The nun I had, Sister Apollonia—what was I? seven?—told us to put our heads down on our desks. It was our First Communion week. She said, 'This is a very special day you're getting ready for. Anything you ask Baby Jesus for, if it's good, He'll give it to you.' And she came up to my desk and whispered, 'You ask to be a priest.' So I did. I was seven years old. I'd just made my life decisions. I went home and said, 'Hey, I'm going to be a priest.' My dad was on the sofa reading the paper. He said, 'Oh, that's nice.' "

All the ironies. All the years. "In eighth grade Monsignor Meegan used to call me up at ten o'clock at night and say, 'We're going over to the hospital to visit the sick. I'll be over for you in ten minutes.' My whole eighth-grade year I never went home from school without first checking in at the rectory. I used to sweep the parking lot after school for the monsignor—that was a big one. He made me do my homework at the rectory, eat dinner with him. I had my own room at the rectory, just like I was an assistant pastor. My house was two blocks away. I could be there in a minute."

"You lived on Archer Street," I say. He grins. We used to know by heart each other's towns and streets and parishes and pastors' names. For some of us they were like baseball stats.

He guesses he went to the seminary out of hero worship for priests as much as anything. "The way a kid might go to a ballpark hoping to get an autograph." One of Bertin's favorite players was an Irishman named Father Adrian Doherty. Father Adrian was one of the vocation recruiters for Holy Trinity. One afternoon in Bertin's sixth-grade year, Father Adrian pulled into the parking lot at Santa Maria del Popolo parish in Mundelein, Illinois. He bounded over to the grade school. He showed a movie. He talked. Bertin was stroked. "I signed the card. I helped him pack up the projector and carry it out to the car. I just stood there, trying to think up a question so I didn't have to go back in. I wanted him to take me with him right then."

A year later, in rural Minnesota, Father Adrian was on his way back to Chicago from interviewing a seminary candidate. It was late at night, a lonely road. The car went out of control, overturned. Father Adrian was crushed beneath the vehicle. In one of the dispatches of his death there was this: "A trail of Roman collars, spilled out of the careening car, pointed the way to the body. The scene of the accident was about thirty miles from a town called Adrian." For years that story was told in the seminary. The inexplicability of it only made the ways of God more absorbing.

Hero worship passed, of course. "That held me for maybe three years. It started wearing thin by my senior year." Other schoolboy notions of what priesthood means passed too. But that is just process. Bertin Glennon signed up at eleven, applied at thirteen, went in at fourteen, got ordained at twenty-seven. And now he is a priest in Manchester, Kentucky, and I am here with him, and both our eyelids have begun to droop. We are twin sleepyheads, breathing on forty. "C'mon," he growls, "I'll show you to your bunk."

The next morning he is moving across the hall, and through my sleep, before it is light. At seven he pounds on my door. He is fresh-shaven, redolent of Old Spice, beaming. "We're a little late this morning. I gotta do a lot of piddly stuff, errands downtown and things. Want to ride with me?"

"What time did you get up?"

" 'Bout five-thirty. Old habits. I like it then. You can think."

I see the grounds for the first time in daylight: a triad of yellow buildings; a convent on one side across a dried-up creek spanned by a footbridge; the church in the middle; Bert's house on the other side. St. Ann's parish sits below a bank of ridges and, today, a glowering sky.

We take breakfast standing up. I eat cereal, Bertin has a piece of sausage jammed in a hot dog bun. All morning, just as he threatened, we piddle downtown with errands, batting around in his snappy compact (he used to have a pickup, which he loved, but it got to be a gas hog), tooting at people,

SEMINARY | 243

pecking on windows, jawboning, dropping off things to be fixed or typed or filled out. In his Greek fisherman's hat and work boots and old jeans, the padre doesn't look so much like a padre. Outside Rice's Shoes we stop to talk with the postman. Outside H&N Drugs, by a doctor's shingle (Moises P. Langub) and just over from a doorway advertising SLEEPING ROOMS FOR RENT, we stop to jaw with someone whose name I don't catch but who greets me as if I'd been in town all my life. I'm a friend of Bertin's, that's enough. We go over to the town hall to see Wanda, the clerk. Wanda sits behind a bare desk in a bare room on a second floor. She has the hard generational face of an Appalachian woman. "Hello, Father," she says. "How long have you been here?" I ask her after Bertin has made an introduction. "Whole life, 'cept for that year's stretch in Ohio once," she says, like a refrain from a hurting country song. Before I can ask her more, Bertin has me back into the snappy compact, scooting me over to see the new swimming pool and rec center, the new jail, the city park he helped build his second year in town, the seventy-nine new low-income housing units going up at Goose Creek. Bertin's lay volunteers run a rummage sale down at Goose Creek several mornings a week. You can get a shirt for a dime, somebody's cast-off underwear for a nickel.

We head for Fox Holler but can't get through a soup of mud. Bert turns the car and we slide like butter on a skillet. Doesn't faze him. "This was all stripped. This was a mountain down to here. Mountains are useless to us. They don't feed anybody. They're filling in this land. They could put one hundred houses in here, a factory."

All morning I scribble and Bertin jaws and bats. I wait outside while he ducks in to see a legal assistance lawyer. (Child abuse case.) He comes out, sees me scribbling in my notebook by a parking meter. "What are ya, writing a ticket?" he says loud enough for the whole block to hear. The more we make rounds, the more countrified his accent gets. "Why, we wuz just comin' over to see ya," he says to a jeweler, back-slapping, a happy cracker. Back in the car I ask him to be immodest for a moment and name me his civic positions. Bertin is chairman of the transit authority (no buses yet, but they're working on it), of the zoning board, of the RCIP (Regional Capital Improvement Program). He is on the ADD

(Area Development District); he's the veep of the Clay County Development Association. There are more memberships and posts and acronyms, but I can't get them down fast enough. Bertin isn't bragging. This is flat-out civic pride, priestly Rotarian pride. Bertin Glennon, Manchester's priest, is a shepherd who has found his place, his stake, in a town where every car seems layered with coal grit. Manchester and Clay County depress hell out of me—and I am flat envious. He has something I don't. "Priests from the Order come to visit me and they shake their heads and say, 'But, Bert, how do you adapt?' Adapt? I love it here. This is me."

We take lunch at the Last Roundup, where wrestling posters are stapled into walls and patrons wear perforated Agway caps. Bertin knows everybody in the joint. I'm the only stranger for miles. "You sometimes wonder: Am I doing something worthwhile, or am I just wasting my time? The temptation when you're a priest is to go out and sit with some old lady whose sister has just died, because . . . it's priestly and it's safe."

The waitress has jammed the pencil back in her hair and gone to fetch our coffees.

"Do you think about the seminary much?"

"Truthfully, no, Paul. Most of it is a blur. They weren't the greatest years of my life, and they weren't the worst. It was something I had to do, I guess, to get here."

"What do you remember about me?"

"Well, I remember that when Roger Skifton left, you didn't get up off the sofa to tell him goodbye. You were taking a nap or something, and Skifton came around to shake hands with everybody. It was his worst moment. And you said, 'Okay, goodbye, Roger.' "

Blurted (heads turning): "Hey, remember our second year, when you and Moose Gerken and me and I forget who else got in all that shit for being gripers, the class complainers?" I nod enthusiastically, although until just now I had forgotten it. The prefect of discipline had pegged Bert and me as the class's chief malcontents. I always figured it was a bum rap. We had to make a "visitation" to see the seminary rector. I remember Bertin and me sitting outside Father Killian's office thumbing wetly through *National Geographics*. Later I learned some priests on the faculty had voted to toss me out.

When he was in theology, after I had left, Bertin fell in love with a nun. I had heard something about it a while ago. "Oh, everybody fell in love with a nun. It was the time, I think. This nun and I carried on this positively torrid correspondence. Then she left the convent—I think her hemlines were a little too short—and one weekend I used my clergy discount pass and flew up to Newark to see her. We were supposed to have this big hairy romantic secret union in the Newark airport restaurant. I was going to make my decision then and there. I was ready to leave and all of the things that go with that. She could have me if she wanted.

"But when we talked, she knew, perhaps better than me, that I was not ready. She felt that she would never be able to have me. I got up there and she said, 'This is goodbye. I have to figure out the rest of my life and, sadly, you're not in it. You have to get ordained.' She was very kind. I said to myself, 'Well, I'll be dipped in shit.' "

So he was ordained. Roger went to Kiln, Mississippi, and began pinching the collection basket, and Bertin prepared himself for a three-year nomadic job: they had tagged him to be the new Midwest vocation director, recruiting kiddies even as he had been recruited. A month or so into the job, twenty-seven, three months a priest, with an Irish setter puppy and his life's goal attained, he found himself one lonely night in downstate Illinois, in a little place called Centralia. The local pastor wasn't home, there weren't any motels. He was exhausted. He pulled the car into an empty lot, cradled Boo in his arms. "I started bawling my head off. It scared me. I wondered what the hell I was doing in the priesthood. The job suddenly didn't make any sense. The next day I went to a gas station and cleaned up in the john. I looked terrible. I went to a phone and dialed the motherhouse in Washington and got Father Stephen on the phone. I said, 'Look here, did you guys really go through prayer and council when you gave me this job?' It must have knocked him flat because he ordered me to drop everything and come immediately to Washington. I said I had a talk to give to some school kids. I gave the talk and drove to Washington and laid around a few days, getting myself back together. Then I went out on the road again."

In the afternoon he takes me up on Hector Hill, past a

246 | PAUL HENDRICKSON

pawnshop (ANYTHING OF VALUE BOUGHT OR SOLD), past Lo-
chards Creek, where tire rims and punctured mattresses and
emaciated chickens go with every front yard, past mare's tails
of smoke curling from crumbling chimneys. "Over there," he
says, his hand leaving the wheel. "See, somebody was living
in that shack. They've used those Sylvania boxes for insula-
tion." He sucks in his breath. "This is the metaphysical es-
sence of poverty." He climbs the car up a rutted path to a fire
tower. We get out and begin our own climbing. He is puffing
before I am, though it is nearly a tie. We make it about halfway up the tower. "Look at it, Paul. Isn't it something? Down
there's Tennessee." I don't see Tennessee; I see scepters of
smoke, inky-blue whale humps marching off in four directions, streaks of sky the color of canvas, beauty a mask for all
the ugliness. "I find it strange for people to come to eastern
Kentucky and say, 'This must be very depressing for you.' I
think this is the starkest, fiercest beauty there is. You've got
to fight it, sure."

Bertin and Roger don't see each other much nowadays. It
may be ironic to me that two people who know each other so
well and have gone such different directions have ended up
doing their jobs within eighty or ninety miles of each other.
It isn't ironic to Bertin; he doesn't really think about it; irony
is for writers. A while ago Roger and Bertin turned up at the
same area development meeting. It was a little stiff. But they
tried. "When Roger and I were in the seminary I always felt
so inferior to him. He was so talented. Everybody considered
him the rising sun. He could do anything with his hands.
Once, when he and I were on a summertime mission assignment down here in Kentucky, he took a plank and told me to
hold it. Damn, if he didn't build a bathroom around me while
I stood there."

"But you're the only one of us who lasted."

"Aw, don't make a big deal outta that, Paul. Sometimes I
think the wheat fell away, the chaff stayed."

"Bet you don't believe that."

He shrugs, sticks out a paw. "Probably don't."

Apocalypse Then,
Paradox Now

Nam. At night they'd go out on "fireflies." They'd run them from about eleven until three, and the air usually felt soft then, though sometimes there was that funny burnt smell in your nostrils, acrid and a little scary, as when the transformer on a kid's electric train shorts out. Anyway, he'd be up there in the Command & Control chopper with his maps and flashlights and .45 and two canteens—one filled with water, the other with cognac, just in case this time was the last time he could go out in a swill of glory. Down below, strobing the darkness, was the light ship, and on either side were the Cobras, though his word for them was "snakes": two-man choppers with rocket pods dangling off their sides, cannons on their hook noses. It was beautiful, the way those damn snakes could roll in, blades beating air, churning it, thunking at the night, mortars and B-40s whumping and spattering up, the lights and green tracers turning on the darkness like daylight.

"Ever hit the wrong target?" I say.

"Huh?" He is startled. "Hey, those are free fire zones down there, buddy. Anything that moves you can fire at it." He makes a little kissing *pfft* sound with his lips, the way you might giddyap a mount. *Pfft.* I think I remember it.

"But wonder if they're friendlies?"

"Hey, baby, there aren't supposed to be any friendlies down there. Those are free fire zones. And if there are, well . . . t.s."

Bombs away, babies. He seems trancelike, frozen, a cutthroat trout held over a limpid pool. His blond arm suspends for another instant, then dive-bombs toward the coffee table and some far green icon ten thousand miles away.

APRIL 1980. Tucson, Arizona.

He has seen men wrap other men's testicles in live telephone wire, then sit back with a smoke and a Victoria Falls beer, waiting for the next call to come in. It works better if you force the guy to sit in a tray of water. A jolt from something like that won't kill you, just snap your head around as if it's on a pivot. After this, the prisoner usually talked. He refused to participate in such interrogations, he says. "I had . . . psychological ways of getting my prisoners to talk. Hey, I could have you eating out of my hand."

Cauterizing desert sun burns in, scraping the day white as the scar on a soldier's cheek. Steel-blue hummingbirds, like tiny helicopters, hum at glass feeders by the front door for the tubes of sugar water Dick Ohrt has put out. It is a modest and attractive house, ranch-styled, with a pool and built-in barbecue pit out back. Behind the pool is a high pastel wall cutting off the neighbors. "You put up some barbed wire and sandbags, it's about the height of our compounds in Nam," he says. He's had the house since the fall of 1979, when he and Ruth and the girls came back from Germany. He was over there thirty-seven months, and it turned out to be his last overseas assignment. For the first eighteen months in Germany, he commanded an MI office (military intelligence). Then he got the letter notifying him he'd been passed over for promotion. For the second time. "Not selected" was their phrase. It ended Captain Richard Ohrt's sixteen-year Army career.

An airy smile I remember from somewhere deep inside me scissors sideways on Dick Ohrt's mouth. Once, I recall, this smile and its owner ragged me mercilessly after I had muffed an easy pop fly in an intramural softball game. In his fingers now is an unlit Kool. The Kool is all the way down in the crook of his first two fingers. He sits tilted backward from the edge of the sofa, balanced by a muscular leg, his pale blue eyes inert, placid. Now he holds the Kool like a tiny baton.

Now he tamps it against his thumbnail. "Course, there have
been times when I thought an enemy was lying to me. Then
I haven't been so nice." On the other side of the sliding glass
door, his three-year-old, Justina, played on her new swing set
from K-Mart. Justina is just up from a nap. Her peals bounce
against the glass, harmless mortars. "Hiya, Piggypoo," her
daddy calls, mugging.

Apocalypse then, paradox now. He had status, I had zits.
He was going on to the novitiate and to the major seminary
to study Kant and the *Summa Theologica*. I was still working
to get down Latin declensions and keep people from calling
me Boneyard. He was in the college department and wore a
cassock and lived in a room on the other side of chapel. I was
a wretched freshman and wore high-water pants and took
showers in a bunker with lots of nozzles coming out of the
wall. Our lives should have passed at barely intersecting an-
gles, except that "luck" put me on the waiter crew he ran like
Bismarck, the softball team he captained, the slave galleys
that shined candlesticks under his Prussian eye on the back
steps of chapel during work periods. I remember him as head
of our waiter crew: he'd give us maybe seven minutes to bang
down our food. He'd time us, grin on, blond arm out. "Let's
don't dork around, you guys," he'd say.

Even back then, walking in silent lines to the refectory,
fretting about homework and my vocation—whether I really
had one and what would happen if I lost it—I think I could
sense something fantastically two-tracked about Dick Ohrt. I
could almost feel brittle tensions tangoing in him, between
his impulses for good—those things that had gotten him into
the school and made him a leader—and those things he must
have wanted to act out from his darkest fantasies. All of us
are two-tracked, of course; it was just that Dick Ohrt's tracks
flashed brighter, like tinfoil crumpled in sunlight. Or they
did for me. I think there was something in him I wanted to
be. Not that I was able to articulate any of this for myself. I
could barely articulate anything. I was fourteen, he was
twenty. He was a quarterback, I was on the scrubs.

Prussian: it was both a nickname and an ancestry. From
the 1956 yearbook: "Dick is very proud of his Prussian ancestry. And believe it or not, he has all the characteristics of
some brilliant German scientist: good marks in school, a

bright smile, and a vast expanse of forehead." From the 1957 yearbook: "Just ask any of the hapless boys who have worked under him and they'll testify Dick can exact more work from an unwilling laborer than a queen bee. . . ."

He had a less-used name, too—Lugerhead. Though I think he secretly loved that name, reveled in it, gloated that God or blind stupid luck had stamped him out Germanic "while the rest of you slobs just muck along," you wouldn't have dared call him that to his face. Not if you were his junior. He'd cut your fingers off at the first knuckle, or make you think he would. And yet, if you hurt too much, if you could show him need, he'd pick you up, stroke you. He did that for me a lot. That was part of his other side: a mushy spot somewhere in the middle for the underdog, the down-beaten, even if he was (willingly) the beater.

Once he called a fat kid in his class a dirty name. The kid came after him, and they fought. Later Ohrt found the kid and apologized. He knew he was wrong; he just couldn't say it in front of the others. Afterward, the two became friends, later roommates. The fat kid became Father Pierre Hissey, the only member of Dick Ohrt's original seminary class to survive. It was a large class, much larger than mine, with a total of fifty-one through the years. At night, breaking the Silence, Hissey and Ohrt would lie in their college bunks on their backs and tell each other stories. The red bulb that they kept for studying after lights-out would cast a strange filmy glow on the room. Sometimes Dick would talk about his dad. "Boy, would he kick ass at this messy room," he'd tell Hissey. He'd say it proudly.

He was in the seminary ten years. He was three years from ordination. Then one June evening at the major seminary, after exams were over and most of the building had emptied for summer assignments, Brother Meredith Ohrt shook several hands, went to Washington, boarded a train, changed the next afternoon in Chicago (where he also changed to a new green sharkskin suit), and rode across field-sheets of summer corn to Davenport, Iowa, the place where he had grown up. He arrived about quarter to four. He took a cab out to 2307 College Avenue, past Sacred Heart Cathedral parish. He hadn't told anybody what time he'd be in; he wanted to see how freedom felt. His dad was home from his job as a plant foreman at John Deere across the river in Moline. His mom was setting out supper. He just walked in the back screened door. "I'm home," he said.

He was twenty-four then, and today he is forty, about to turn forty-one, and I am pressing him to recall that moment. "Where else was I going to go? I had maybe two hundred bucks they gave me when I left, some of which I'd already blown in Chicago on the suit. I didn't know anybody. I didn't even own a driver's license. I figured I'd go home and try to get it screwed on, tightened up, bolted down."

The body is lean, trim, tanned. His face is that same remarkable wide wedge of smoothness, although its blondness has browned out a little. His hair is longer, combed flat to the top of his ears; when I knew him it stuck up like a prickly brush. When he got out of the Army last year his wife said, "Listen, Dick, let it grow a little, will you? You're out now." So far, longer hair hasn't helped him find the right job. A while ago some Arizona joker called up and offered him a security investigation job: $3.95 an hour, 17 cents a mile for the use of his own car. Dick laughed. Then stuck the phone down. He's been unemployed five months.

Pieces of art he and Ruth have collected from Greece, Spain, other places in their military travels, decorate the room. He goes over to a delicate wood carving, explains it, replaces it precisely where it was. The red Princess phone in the corner has a ballpoint magnetized to its side. (There is another ballpoint magnetized to the dash of the Horizon in the carport.) In the bathroom there are two soap dishes, side by side, fresh bars in them. Exactitude.

Ruth is in the military, a captain, as he was, though she wants out now: she is bitter over her husband's nonselection and the Army's general attitude toward women. She and Dick met in 1973, after his second tour in Vietnam. He had just been assigned to Fort Huachuca, Arizona, as an instructor at the U.S. Army Intelligence Center and School, and somehow on his first day there wound up in the wrong quarters. Ruth: "I was across the hall, and he knocked on my door and said something flippant, like, 'The refrigerator's out of beer.' He was getting over a divorce. He kept pestering me with notes and calls. He always wanted to drive up to Tucson for dinner. At eighty miles an hour."

Ruth—tall, dark-haired, soft-spoken, a feminist—was raised a fundamentalist Baptist. The brass nameplate on the door reads "THE TAGGART-OHRTS." She has become something of an informal Catholic, attending Mass with Dick and the family, although she says she could never accept confession. This morning, a Sunday, all the Ohrts went to nine o'clock Mass. Dick gets them out of bed and moving. For a time, while he was getting divorced, he had stopped going to church. He takes communion now, even though, technically, that's a sacrilege if you're a divorced Catholic. "I stopped going during the dissolution," he says, emphasizing "dissolution" as if to savor it. "It was part of the depression."

"I think he's a very religious person, basically," says Ruth.

"What kind of officer was he?"

"Old Army. Hard-nosed."

"Why not?" says Dick.

Why not? That's what he had said on the phone two weeks earlier when I asked if I could come out. I had called from a phone booth in the basement of the Library of Congress in Washington, and I couldn't keep my voice from trembling. "Have at it," he had said. This morning, coming down the walk at my motel to get me, wearing shades, arm already out to rap at my door, I knew him instantly. "How'd you find me?" he said, as we drove back to the house in his car. "Tracked down your parents," I answered. He had nodded a small approval.

Justina scampers in. She has on red knee socks, a frilly dress with polka dot trim. A crumb of cheese hangs at her lower lip. "Still sleepy, Piggy?" her father taunts. "Well, why don't you go back to bed then? Did you slide on your new sliding board yet today?" She doesn't answer, darting off to the bedroom for a comb. "You going to watch Walt Disney tonight?" She doesn't respond to this, either. Dick gets his younger daughter off to nursery school every morning, and since he's not working at the moment, he collects her every midday afternoon, too. "House husband," he says of himself derisively. At night he'll do the dishes. On good nights he falls asleep about ten. Since Vietnam, he usually can't go to sleep in quiet, so he plays the radio or the TV. He might wake up about three or four, read for a while, drift off again. At five forty-five he's up, making eggs for the kids.

Besides Ruth and Dick and Justina, Jocelynne Ohrt, a teen-ager, lives here. Jocelynne is from her father's first marriage. There is a son from that marriage, too, Dickie Junior, but he lives in Boston with his mother. Father and daughter have their normal problems, only sometimes this father likes to play drill instructor, the Great Santini of Tucson. "I get a case of the ass with her, sure. Ruth thinks I'm turning her into Casparina Milquetoast." But it is Dick, not Ruth, who coaches her in French, frets about it. When male friends call up and ask if Jocelynne is there, Dick says: "Yeah, as long as you've got a name."

I have not laid eyes on him in twenty-one years, since June 1959, just before he and his class entered the novitiate. But I never forgot him, not even what he looked like. Years after the seminary, when other things had faded, I could still see a phosphorescent smile biting into cigarettes (as if he held them with his teeth instead of his lips), a popped-up chest, a torpedo-drive down enemy throats on our old basketball court. Ohrt played guard. You'd see this blond blur and black tennis shoes, legs tucked up under him like a contortionist. Father Vincent always pushed him, he says: "Ohrt, you don't move fast enough." Once, in a game against Open Door Community Center, his torpedo-drive backfired and he ended up sprawled on the floor with part of his mouth beside him. "They had this little shit playing for them. I mean, little. He must have been five feet five. I was going in on one of my patented lay-ups, and he stepped in front of me. I lost some teeth that time, but the next time we played him I went in feet first. I got that sucker." Father Shaun, who was coach by then, benched him. Ohrt didn't care. "Get in my way, you chew rubber" is how he explained it to me the following week on waiter duty.

So I never forgot him. I couldn't forget him. He was stamped inside me. And years later, when I began to hear some unsettling secondhand stories, stories about throwing people out of helicopters in Vietnam when they wouldn't talk, stories about castrations, stories about even darker things than that, I felt myself drawn to him again, wherever he was, with my old fascinations. The stories I heard had only the loosest connection with Ohrt. He had gone into the Army within nine weeks of leaving the seminary. He entered military intelligence school in Baltimore and eventually did two year-long tours as a military advisor and intelligence officer in a green, jungly, mountainous place on the lip of the Pacific called Phuoc Tuy Province. He lived in a tin-roof hootch with screening coming halfway down the walls.

In early 1966, after he had completed several TDY (temporary duty) stints in the far Pacific, a freshly commissioned officer, Ohrt came back to the major seminary to visit his old friends. I was gone from the seminary by then, but I heard about the visit. He brought his first wife. Only three members of his class were left, shortly to be ordained, although there were others there he knew. The stories that I heard grew from this visit, although no one who was there will swear to them now, and besides, they say, it was never quite clear whether Ohrt was merely talking, or talking in earnest, whether he was describing other people, or talking about things he witnessed, or heard about, or tried to stop, or what. Of course. That is one of the essential seductive things about Dick Ohrt. You never quite know. There always seemed a vague delight in him for the possibilities of horror, for the heart of darkness, but nothing more than that. He could take you to the edge and get away clean.

Dick Ohrt insists he never participated in any illegal or immoral activities in Vietnam, although he says that others around him did. There is no evidence he isn't telling the truth. I checked as best I could. Additionally, I have long letters about him from his commanding officer in Vietnam and from an Australian intelligence officer who knew Ohrt well. Both men describe Ohrt as an exemplary soldier. Ohrt himself will say, with varying emotion and over several days of talk, some of it with a tape recorder in front of him, seeming at points almost desirous of confessing something: "Wartime can make an individual very cruel. I think all of us . . . in our deep consciousness have a certain amount of cruelty we want to inflict. What was preying on an individual's mind, my own included, was that there were three or four other Americans lying down there in the sun, had been for a day or two, bloating. You ever see a body that's been lying out in ninety percent humidity? Mmmmm. Not too nice. Don't plan on eating lunch or breakfast or supper for a few days. . . . He [an informant] knows if he fucks me over I'll get his stuff blown away. I have no compunction about that." This last he will say moving his hands up to his eyes and rubbing blond fists into the sockets.

I had not gone to Vietnam, or anywhere else for my country, and perhaps this was some of my fascination about Dick Ohrt. I had trumped up a mild asthmatic history in graduate school, gotten a doctor to sign a statement about my nervous stomach, and had then ridden down to the Cumberland Army Depot below Harrisburg with a busload of other would-be draft dodgers. At the physical I had to drop underwear and spread my buttocks along with everyone else while an Army doctor came along and peered up my behind. Later I went in a room and showed my papers to a man sitting behind a desk. He grunted and stamped them. I had to come back to Cumberland once or twice more, but eventually I got off scot-free. If you lived in a college town, it was an easy thing to brag about.

Afternoon of a Midwestern boy. I am gazing at a small black-and-white photograph of Dick Ohrt. The picture is stapled in a small, glossy photo booklet, the kind you got from drugstores in the fifties. On the cover are three words: Sem Week Souvenir. A boy is seated on the ground in the picture. He is with some other boys. Ahead and to the boy's right is a monk. The boy in the picture is fair and skinny, almost frail-looking. His knees are pulled up under him, and he is wearing an old ball cap with a long bill, and though he is seated beside these other boys, he seems somehow not quite of them. It is the summer of 1953. The boy has just turned fourteen. He is an acolyte at the cathedral parish in his home town. He is the student manager of his grade school basketball team. Already the boy has made application at, and has been accepted to, a preparatory seminary at Holy Trinity, Alabama. His parents have brought him here, to a Benedictine abbey in Conception, Missouri, so he can try on for a week the life of a seminarian, make sure it fits before going away to Alabama in the fall. Alabama is a long way from Iowa, and Dickie Ohrt's folks want him to be certain. If he is certain, he can go.

The boy is a house painter and an arrowhead collector and an avid fisherman with his father in the sloughs and lakes along the Mississippi River near his home in Davenport. Already he has developed keen interests in history and archeology, in the ways of Plains Indians. The boy's folks are devout Catholics. (His dad is a convert from Lutheranism.) The boy has two older brothers, Don and Harry, Jr., both grown and gone from home. In years past, the boy has lain in his bed at night listening to his parents, especially his father, arguing bitterly with the older boys. Violence seems always ready to erupt. This scares the boy.

At Conception, Missouri, in June of 1953, the acolyte prays, makes his own bed, plays baseball, gets introduced to Latin. The life of a seminarian—its prayer, its study, its rituals, its camaraderies, its dim, certain feeling that this is something important—works on the boy. At the end of the Sem Week, Dickie Ohrt tells his family he's sure. A month and a half later he leaves for Holy Trinity.

We are talking about why he left. He isn't sure, really, anymore that he knows exactly how he got in. "Grace," he says, the grin up, letting the word cut both ways. Fair enough: I can't figure mine out either. He guesses the decision to leave had steadily grown in him, not always on a conscious level. Even before vows, in '60, there was this . . . twinge. "Two years earlier, when I was walking off the basketball court at the Bibb City Tournament, this stranger comes up and says, 'My daughter and I were watching you closely during the game. She thinks you're wasting yourself in a seminary.' It startled me. It may have been the first time since I entered that it had really occurred to me I could have an existence outside the seminary. A girl I didn't even know thought I was good-looking. I was twenty, and I fantasized about her for weeks."

Toward the end of first theology, in temporary vows, he had gone to see his spiritual director, Father Warner. "I said, 'Father, I've got this problem. I'm not sure I should be in here talking to you because I don't even know what the problem is.' " The priest was unresponsive, he says. He went back. The priest was still unresponsive, Ohrt feels. He is telling me this, and a tooth bites a lower lip. The lip is spread thin and tight across his gums. His right arm is out in a stiff-arm on the table. His fingers are lightly drumming. "I think Ruth would agree . . . that as it reflects itself in my relationship with the family . . . I probably still resent the guy's attitude."

I talked to Ohrt's old spiritual director. He isn't a priest anymore. He is a scholar at a respected Eastern university, married, with kids, a man who insisted on his anonymity. He declined to talk specifics about Ohrt, citing confidentiality of spiritual direction and a basic respect for the people he had tried to help. But when I said something about Ohrt the Prussian, he said, "I think maybe I saw through that."

I figured I'd go home and try to get it screwed on, tightened up, bolted down. He was on his way back from class at St. Ambrose College in Davenport that first summer after he left. He had decided to pick up some philosophy credits. Basically he was biding time, cooling. "Anyway, this one day I got off the bus in downtown Davenport to transfer—I didn't have a driver's license yet—and there's the U.S. Post Office. I figured: What the hell? The first door on the right was the Army recruiter's. I figured, What the hell: the oldest brother was in the Navy, the other one was in the Air Force, I'll try these guys. I walked in with my usual tongue-in-cheek manner, and there's this sergeant sitting there. His name was Lloyd B. Fish. I said, 'What does the Army have to offer me?' He said, 'What do you have to offer the Army?' I said, 'Oh, four years of college, lots of philosophy, lots of theology, whatever.' So we sat down and talked for two, maybe three, hours. He said, 'Really, with your background, you shouldn't waste yourself in infantry or armor. In fact, we've got a big push on now for Army intelligence.' I said, 'Oh, tell me about it.' He said, 'I can't, it's classified.' At that time there was maybe one little paragraph in a recruiting book that said you'd be doing special duties for Uncle Sam. He told me he could set up an interview with the resident intelligence agent of the Rock Island office the next day. He said I'd have to take a written exam and undergo stress testing. I figured I just came out of a stress-testing environment."

A couple of days later the Rock Island resident agent was looking over Dick Ohrt's personal history statement. "He said, 'Mmmm, I see you were in the seminary. What are you, some sort of fag?' I said right back, 'Probably not any more a fag than people who are in the Army, sir.' It stopped him cold. If he had wanted to pursue it I would have said, 'Give me five minutes and I'll go get a skirt and you can judge for yourself.' Then he said, 'I see in your autobiographical statement you've had a lot of Latin. Well, if we accept you, maybe we'll send you to the goddamn Vatican.' I said, 'Well, sir, it might be better than going to the place where you go after Rock Island.' "

He had passed. Sergeant Fish called up in several days and asked if he could be ready in twenty-four hours to get on a bus for Fort Leonard Wood, Missouri. He went away at night, with one suitcase.

"It sounds a little like . . ."

"Re-entering the seminary." He is way ahead of me. "I've thought about that, and about why I might have adapted so well. These people were getting up at—what?—six o'clock? That wasn't hard. Scrubbing down toilets? Hey, I'd already done it."

At intelligence school, at Fort Holabird, Baltimore, fourteen of twenty-seven in Dick Ohrt's class were former divinity students. I am startled when he tells me this. He shrugs, making the little *pfft* sound. "Sure. We make great security clearances. They knew right where we were all those years." But of course it is more than this, and Ohrt knows it. On reflection I can understand how, on several levels of psychological motivation, a job in the CIA, the FBI, the service intelligence units would appeal immensely to a man fresh from the seminary or his priesthood. For one thing, such a job would give him belonging, a new corps of moral fellowship. For another, it would accommodate deep feelings for authority, for structure, for order, for discipline, even if such things may also be ambivalent in him. Two Holy Trinity classmates of Ohrt are in the FBI today; a third was an Air Force intelligence operative; a fourth may have been in the CIA. That's just Ohrt's class alone.

At Fort Holabird, Ohrt quickly took to intelligence training. The atmosphere was more collegiate than military, although the students marched to classes, which were conducted in pre-1942 wood barracks not unlike what he had slept in as a seminarian. He studied investigative procedures, interrogation techniques, sabotage, espionage, the legal rights of people, *portrait parler,* which is the skill of storing a "subject" in your memory as you converse with him—what he has on, specifics of mannerism, cues in his speech. Ohrt would come to excel at this. As well as at psychological interrogation.

He picks up a magazine, skims it quickly, as if it's a dossier. Then he talks without looking at me, through smoke from his cigarette. "Hendrickson, Paul, eh? Mmmm. Jesus, we got a whole bunch of good shit about you in here, friend, goddamn, we do."

You don't always come on like that. "You break the guy down any way that you think will work. I remember this one time we had several North Vietnamese and VC wounded on a chopper pad. It was the first day of Tet, late in the afternoon. We had a couple U.S. Rangers with us, happy horseshit types, Special Forces. They were going to do their interrogation bit, knives against the throat. I had these two prisoners lying over by a fence. One had been shot in the shoulder, and we had bandaged him and were waiting for a chopper. I told my interpreter, 'Let's go talk to this guy.' First I tried to console him. I got down right next to him, squatted by him. My weapon was right there; he could have made a grab for it. I said, 'Hey, you feeling okay?' I gave him some cognac from my canteen. Eventually I found out the guy had been in Paris and spoke some broken English and was really an educated man. He told me he was shot up bad. I found out about his family in North Vietnam, that he was an equivalent of a corporal. I learned some valuable stuff about the Order of Battle. It took about an hour, though, and the other way I might have gotten nothing."

At Holabird, Ohrt was earmarked for counterintelligence work, and before he went to Southeast Asia he got a chance to use some of it. He was assigned to the Twenty-fifth Military Intelligence Detachment, Schofield Barracks, Hawaii. Then he was named to a special operations team, ranging the Pacific, involving surveillance and special investigations. Some of the investigations involved U.S. forces; some involved the enemy. He was only an enlisted man, but he had power. Once he investigated a whole building of gays and tucked it to them. The Prussian who never got below a B in the seminary (Father Columban gave him the equivalent of a B-minus in trig once) was back on track, laying line to a new station.

He sits stroking his ten-year-old dachshund, Licorice, asleep in his lap. Licorice belongs to the family, but she is Dick's dog. Last year Licorice had the runny eye. Her master nursed her back, put the salve in a couple times a day. Licorice flew over to Germany with the family. A Haydn symphony is floating over from the other room. The head of the house likes listening to Haydn in the morning; the man's simplicity. Too often we try to muck up our minds with complexity. "I don't know, maybe you could call it a James Bond complex, although I never had the Porsches with the machine guns behind the headlights. Still, there was something direct and right-to-the-edge about it. You could walk into a colonel's office in civilian clothes, at least then, lay your dope on the desk, and proceed to watch him crap in his pants. I'll admit, I'll still admit, I'm a damn good intelligence officer. I know I did a good job. I have the record that shows I did a good job. Maybe I used unorthodox methods in certain ways. Decidedly I'm too blunt at times. But I figure if people can't stand bluntness I'm not going to cry for them."

His face splits in laughter, the way a pumpkin might smash against a walk. "This one time in the minor seminary. We were in class with Father Barnabas. You remember those old stifling classrooms in Alabama. The windows were open, and Barney is sitting there swatting flies, and before I can stop myself I say right out, 'The flies aren't bothering me. Guess I'm not a big enough pile.' Well, he hauls me outside and gives me hell. But after that we were pals."

The next day. Dick Ohrt seems looser. Maybe he has dropped some old images. Maybe I've dropped them. Maybe we had both come to this ruled by our preconceptions. Last night, exhausted, I had gone back to my room, too tired to fill in notes, but bothered by one thought: Why should a person of such iron character and high achievement be out of work so long? It didn't make sense. Ohrt had said something yesterday about his age being against him for the jobs he really wanted on the outside, but I found that hard to believe.

Before I could think about it anymore this morning, he came for me at the motel. He was there at the door at ten o'clock and announced that we were going for a drive into the Sonoran desert. We drove out on the edge of Tucson, into a red dead zone, got out, and walked around. I found him expert—and amazingly gentle—with the desert flora: the cholla and prickly pear and the great looping saguaro cacti. He seemed to love the desert, be protective of it. "You should see the seeds of these saguaro," he said, bending down, cupping his palms. "Talk about the parable of the mustard seed."

I have begun to pay attention to Ohrt's speech; it is veined with military and religious jargon. He'll say "One November" and "that's affirmative," then stick an *"ad aeternum"* in an odd context. When I asked where a light switch in the bathroom was, he said, "On the gospel side." When I asked him how to spell Phuoc Tuy, he said, "Papa, Hotel, Uniform, Oscar, Charlie. Tango, Uniform, Yankee."

We dined last night by candlelight in the kitchen, with the sliding glass door open, letting in the desert air, while the girls ate on TV trays in the den and kept the tube at low levels. (On top of the television sat a picture of their father, ramrod in dress blues.) Dick had bought the food and cooked it outdoors: peppery ranch beans, huge toasted steaks. He set out cold bottles of Löwenbräu—a pale substitute, he said, for his favorite, Australia's Victoria Falls. Once, on his first tour, they got shelled at five o'clock in the morning. He had been awake since three, waiting. The first round hit maybe one hundred yards behind the hootch. Then a mortar came in and shredded his fridge. Got him mad as hell.

He was a rigorous gentlemen last night: I was a guest in his house. And I think I had begun to feel not only affection but a worry he might forget I was an interviewer, not just someone he knew from the seminary twenty years ago. At one point in the evening I said, "A lot of this is going on tape, you know." He didn't look up, and I knew instantly I had made a mistake. "I haven't forgotten for a second," he said a little haughtily. "I never lose control. There was one time I lost it, I guess. You may find that out in your research." He did not elaborate.

When we sat down to eat, he had come at me with the old spin: "If you don't like the best Texas beef the grocery stores will sell, then the hell with you." I had fumbled for a comeback, as if there had to be one. But we had talked freely during the meal. He told me about his first marriage and how green he was (he was hitched within two years of leaving), about how wrenching and protracted and guilt-ridden and angry the split was. He also told me about his various assignments. He hated the part of Germany he was in last year. "Hessians. Too rigid, too cold." Actually, it was his father who was the Prussian, he says. His mother was Bavarian. They're softer.

For a time, midway in his career, he headed an intelligence field office in St. Louis, where among other things he "covered" the mail of suspected subversives. No question that gentlemen should read other gentlemen's mail if the situation warrants. "Hey, I know guys who could take a letter you sent me, look at the envelope, and tell you what kind of glue was used, who made the paper. I could probably get a letter opened and sealed back up just using the stuff in my kitchen."

For a moment last evening, he had talked of getting passed over for promotion, for the second time, last year and therefore having to leave the Army. He said it was bothering him worse than he probably knew. He said he got riffed because he wouldn't bend. Because he came up against superiors who couldn't handle his style. They wanted to fudge; he refused. He blew the whistle on several of them. "In seminary you were trained to try to accept everybody. Maybe I'm too much of a straight arrow, too letter-of-the-law. Basically I don't kowtow to anybody. Why should I? I have to live with myself and what goals I have for myself. Knowing my own weakness at being a snap-judge of character—well, I don't know if it's such a weakness, because ninety-nine times out of a hundred if the guy's a shithead . . ."

Ruth had looked over; he broke off.

I had asked if he would go back to Nam. "Sure. That's what I told those guys at the D.A. [Department of Army] when I volunteered for a second tour. I said at least over there you knew who was shooting at you. I like the Asian mind. It's very direct, like mine. It's not like the mind of the Occidental. The Occidental will never deal with you straight up but will keep coming at you sideways." He had looked at me pointedly.

All this was last night. Hunched now on a stool, back from our drive in the desert, cigs and tube lighter beside him, late morning streaming in, he talks of his second tour. To his surprise he got reassigned to Phuoc Tuy, by then a military backwater, pacified. When he got back to the province, in early 1972, the mountains no longer looked so green. A lot of the handsome French colonial architecture was gone. He went down to the province on Highway 15; four years earlier 15 was a cow track, but now it was a three-lane highway. On the way into the capital he waved at faces he thought he recognized. He rode over the handsome iron bridge south of town which had been put up by the Eiffel Tower Bridge Works. He got to the compound about suppertime. Damn, if he didn't get assigned to the same room he had last time. He unpacked and went over to the general mess. The same *ma-masans* were there in the kitchen. *Dai'Uy* Ohrt is back, they said, fussing. *Dai'Uy* means captain. They brought him rice tea and double helpings while everybody else in the mess watched: Who is this joker? He was finishing supper when a gate guard stuck his head in the door and said there were some people outside to see Captain Ohrt. He went out and found a dozen of his old operatives and informants standing by a fence. Word had spread within three hours. His operatives took him to a restaurant where there were South China Sea lobsters and cognac in sixteen-ounce glasses and toasts that ran on for hours. Then they gave him the plaque. The plaque is a painting of a wild stallion, and it sits now on a shelf in a closet in the family room. There are four Vietnamese characters in the upper left hand corner of the plaque. They mean: A horse returns a second time to its place of victory. He almost pitched it, Ruth tells me later.

"It really means a dog comes back to its vomit," Dick says.

Five minutes later, though, raking his hand past his eye, ragging it, digging the butt of his palm into his eye socket: "I always seemed such a soft touch for those people. That's what everyone kept telling me. Some of the other advisors, they had problems, but anything I wanted to get done, I could get done. And, shit, after hours I almost had to hire myself a social secretary. I don't know . . . maybe I had empathy."

Again: "Was there more I should have known to help these people?" He grew to loathe, he says, the State Department advisor he reported to in his first days back. That was before the Thirty-third Regiment of the NVA launched its full-scale attack. "He refused my briefings. He'd sit there and take my reports over bacon and eggs. He was a real colonial. He had no regard for these people, no feelings for them. 'You god-damn military types are all war-mongers,' he told me. I nod-ded. 'Aye-aye sir,' I said to myself. 'Three bags full.' " A couple of mornings later, Ohrt and the rest of the compound woke to find themselves in control of little more of the prov-ince than the ground they stood on. The State Department official was shipped out.

Shaking his head in disgust (but is he amused?): "Some of what you'd see. I remember this one Air Cav guy who came through. He called himself Earth Hog. He used to oink."

It was the nonsensical things that tore you up (talking al-most to himself): "During Tet, the VC would go by this one little orphanage, this Catholic orphanage on the outskirts of town, and just toss in grenades from their scooters. During play periods."

I start to say something; he cuts me off. "I'm not saying our side was so pure. I had a Vietnamese counterpart. We were good friends. If he was interrogating somebody he knew was VC or North Vietnamese and the guy wouldn't talk, he'd say, 'Okay, baby, get up and start walking. You just became the mine-clearing person.' " Another time they found out the Deputy Province Chief was really VC. (They planted false info.)

"What happened to him?"

"He didn't show up for work the next day."

"Oh."

Dick Ohrt's commander in Phuoc Tuy on his second tour was Colonel Giac Modica, career Army, a fellow Catholic, alumnus of St. Bonaventure University. When the chaplain choppered in for Mass once or twice a month, he'd sometimes use Ohrt's trailer for a church, and Modica and a few others would attend. Once, the Viet Province Chief, a Buddhist, came. One Sunday night, after the chaplain had gone, Ohrt and Modica were in quarters talking. It had been a rough day, lots of fire.

Modica: "Ohrt, how come you give a damn about these Vietnamese?"

Ohrt, carefully, evenly, trying to get this right: "Well, Giac, probably for the same reasons you do. Only with me there might be one thing more. Maybe I'm extending to these people what I always wanted to be as a priest."

I wrote to Giac Modica in care of an APO Miami address. He was in Central America, still in the service. He wrote back four legal sheets' worth about Ohrt. He said he hadn't heard Ohrt had been passed over, regretted it deeply. If he had access to Ohrt's 201 file, he could pinpoint the reasons, he said. "The system probably failed where Dick was concerned," he wrote. "Dick was in my view a rare young officer. He was able to do all things well. I was proud to serve with him, and even more proud to have him as a friend."

I tried to get access to Ohrt's 201 file. The 201 file contains the complete record of a man's time in service. The people in St. Louis, where the file currently is, told me that only certain information is releasable through the Freedom of Information Act. Why a soldier is "not selected" is not releasable information, I was told. It may not even be in the file.

I also wrote to Colonel Geoff Carter in Australia, a career military officer who had served with Ohrt. "I had no occasion to see Dick physically scared, though he did scary things," he wrote. "He was determined to be right, not for its own sake but because of the penalty attendant in being wrong. He was less inclined to forgive than most, especially when the event under scrutiny resulted from laziness or incompetence."

Dick Ohrt won three Bronze Stars in Vietnam, two Army Commendation Medals, one Meritorious Service Medal, three Vietnam Crosses of Gallantry, the Vietnam Campaign Medal, the National Defense Service Medal, a Meritorious Unit Commendation, four Overseas Service Bars, and other lesser decorations. After he left the country for the second time, and the province fell, the North Vietnamese Army lined some friends of Ohrt's against a wall. One of them was his Vietnamese intelligence counterpart. The man was Buddhist, his wife Catholic. They had eleven children. The officer, his wife, and some of the children were put against the wall. Then their heads were blown off. Ohrt says he has almost nothing left in the way of mementos of the two-plus years he spent in Vietnam, not even a photograph. "I burned everything when Saigon fell," he says, stubbing his cigarette.

●

This is the riddle of the story, and it is in two parts. Here is part one: What happened to Dick Ohrt's class in novitiate? On August 1, 1959, as I was about to start my second year at Holy Trinity, Dick Ohrt and thirteen classmates reported to Silver Lake, Pennsylvania, to begin the year and a day of novitiate prescribed in Church law for candidates for the religious orders. The class had completed its six years of minor seminary, and in another year would begin six more years of philosophy and theology in the major seminary. But now, in their novitiate, books were to be set aside so that the class, like every other Trinitarian novice class before it, could be trained and tested in the ways of the common life. Novitiate was a school of religious perfection, a year devoted to the soul and to the spirit, with the bone of manual labor tossed in. It was the toughest year of the thirteen, a spiritual boot camp. Demons came, and came often to novices while they fasted and prayed and worked in the desert of novitiate.

Ohrt and his class reported to an old stone and wood estate on a lake in northeast Pennsylvania, just below the New York line. (The place had come into the hands of the Trinitarians via benefactions.) Across the lake were summer resort cabins. Silver Lake was contemplative, remote—a kind of made-to-order Gethsemane. Dick Ohrt was twenty. Thirty-six boys had started out at Holy Trinity, Alabama, six years previously; fourteen were now left. A few in the class had joined up along the way, although most of the class consisted of the originals. (It was always status to be an "original.") It was an exceptionally bright and talented class, everybody said, an almost inspired mix of scholars, athletes, actors, and mavericks. It was as if the recruiters of 1952 and 1953 had stumbled on a mother lode. From the beginning the class seemed destined. As freshmen they whipped the seniors in basketball. They challenged other classes in intramural debates and won. It is true there were several factions in the class—the much-feared "cliques"—and this concerned the faculty. In the group's sophomore year, as an attempt at breaking the cliques, the faculty had the class put on a minstrel show in the gym under the direction of Father Benedict. One of the numbers was "Thirty Super Sophomores, That's Us, We Never Gamble, Chew, or Cuss." The show and the number

were hits, and after this the class seemed to jell. Dick Ohrt
and Will Booth became leaders on the basketball court, while
off the court the class could put forth Tony Lachner and
Tom Molloy and Art LaChapelle, Latin whizzes all, three of
the brightest students the seminary had ever enrolled. In the
fall of 1956, the class's senior year, Pat Liteky brought honor
to Holy Trinity by winning the Russell County Voice of Democracy contest. (On a summer vacation the next year, Gerry
Cieslinski wins a contest of a different sort—a Michigan
polka contest. This is not so prized.)

Only four from the class would be destined to be ordained
to the priesthood in 1966. Of those four, three would eventually resign their priesthood, although one of the three who
resigned would become a priest in the Episcopal Church. The
lone survivor of Dick Ohrt's class, the only one who would
make it out of a total of fifty-six boys who came and went
through the years, would acknowledge years later that what
might have kept him in while everyone else dropped out was
a cold, stark fear of going to hell: his first year, a priest took
Leo Hissey aside and told him it would be easier for a camel
to pass through the eye of a needle than for a boy who had
given up his vocation to get to heaven. Father Leo Hissey,
whose religious name is Pierre, is still a priest.

But who could know such things that August 1, 1959, when
the future looked so bright for Dick Ohrt and his class?
Chances were good, even favorable, that all fourteen postu-
lants entering their novitiate would make it through the year.
That year, 1959, a letter went out from the Holy See's Sacred
Congregation of Seminaries and Universities. The letter went
to bishops throughout the world and talked of a seminary's
role as a supreme court sitting in judgment of vocations. The
letter said: "Let discipline, therefore, joyously embraced, be
the touchstone by which superiors test the vocations of their
students. Let them demand an obedience, not merely theo-
retical, but effective, singleminded, and complete in all
things, great and small, contained in the seminary rule. Let
them always remember that obedience primarily involves 'ob-
sequium,' that is, a total submission of mind and heart which
makes our actions pleasing to God. If superiors can achieve
this much, they can be assured that their students will also
acquire the other virtues proper to a priest, especially those,

like chastity, which require manly will power and perfect self-control."

What the letter was essentially talking about was a Greek word found in the epistles of St. Paul: *kenosis*. *Kenosis* is an "emptying of self."

Before they met at Silver Lake, the members of the class decided to hold a get-together in New York City, a sort of black-suited last fling. Nearly everyone showed up. One night the class took in a play. Another night Maury Flood's folks hosted a spaghetti dinner at their home in Larchmont, New York. Still another evening several from the class got up in Your Father's Mustache in madras sport coats (borrowed for the occasion) to sing some impromptu seminary songs, startling patrons. At the end of the week, money spent, fourteen boys verging on their manhood went to Silver Lake, Pennsylvania.

On their first afternoon, so several now recall, Father Declan sent the class out in silence to pick up stones in bushel baskets. Then he told them to dump them on the ground and begin over. This was nothing new. It was part of the testing. Several days later Father Declan sent for Art LaChapelle, perhaps the brightest seminarian in a bright class. He immediately brought up the question of LaChapelle's vocation. A week later LaChapelle was summoned again. He was given a two-day special novena to make to the Blessed Mother. Father Declan "ordered" him, says LaChapelle, to make the private novena and told him that when he was finished with it he would know whether he should remain or leave. The Lord or the Virgin would give him a sign. "He told me he had used this novena before in very difficult circumstances and that it had never failed him. I thought, 'Well, this is a crock, but I'll try it.'" Three mornings later, so LaChapelle now insists, he woke, having completed his private novena the night before, and knew one thing: he was leaving. "I can't explain it, but suddenly I hated the place. Despised it. I had to get out. I had never really questioned before whether I belonged in a seminary, had pretty much never thought about another kind of life. I knew I wanted to be a priest from second grade, and told people so. And I don't break my word. And on the third day of the Master's novena, I know one thing: I'm getting out. How do you explain that?"

Art LaChapelle did leave, almost immediately, though not before the Master took him aside and said, or so LaChapelle claims: "You have opened the floodgates." A year later, still a little stunned, LaChapelle came back to Holy Trinity and stayed around a few days. He was trying to write a novel about the seminary. Today he is a Minnesota lawyer. The novel aborted.

True to the Master's prediction, the floodgates opened. Tom Molloy left. John Pryle left. Mike Keown. Pat Liteky. Tony Lachner. Fourteen candidates entered, six emerged, and though there were different reasons for different departures, it was still a stunning development, at least for 1959.

What went wrong? Why did eight out of fourteen fall? That was the question filtering down to those of us at Holy Trinity. The six years of minor seminary were expressly designed to weed out those candidates not serious about their vocation. The work of a minor seminary has been described in Church literature as "the happy elimination of the unfit." A boy began his studies at thirteen or fourteen, but by the time of his entrance to novitiate, at twenty, with six years of study and prayer and direction behind him, he was considered an adult, and one would think that Las Vegas odds would have to be in his favor, no matter the year's hardships. A few novices had been known to drop out in previous years, but nothing like this had ever happened. (In 1952 eighteen had entered the Trinitarian novitiate, and twelve emerged, an attrition of six.) While a seminarian was making his year of novitiate, his life was under the autocratic rule of the Master of Novices. In the minor seminary a boy's fate was in the hands of a senate of men, but in the novitiate one's fortunes were directed by a single priest to whom the Order's constitution gave power and authority in a nearly absolutist sense. The Master of Novices of the Trinitarians was a red-faced rhetorical middle-aged Irish-American from Kearny, New Jersey, named Declan Boynes. Father Declan had entered in 1927 as a teenager. He had become Master in 1942, not long after his ordination, and by 1960, when Dick Ohrt's class was going through, it was estimated that Father Declan had trained fully half of all Trinitarians for the vows of poverty, chastity, and obedience. Father Declan was practically Mister Missionary Servant. His reputation for prayerfulness and wisdom and high hilarity was practically above question. Imagine then the puzzle at the sudden mass exodus of 1959. I can remember the mood at Holy Trinity when word began filtering back to us. The priests on the minor seminary faculty didn't talk of it openly, though we did. It seemed both scary and euphoric in an odd, vague way. But what did it mean?

It might have meant nothing more than what lightning means in a summer sky: something luminous and electric and darkly exciting, but a freakish phenomenon all the same. Or it might have meant something deeper, more mysterious. It might have meant that an old system of things had begun to crack and that a new way had begun. Was this the fore-shadowing of the decade to come? In the five years following, while Father Declan remained at his post, no other Trinitarian novitiate class would suffer such drastic attrition.

Three voices:

Father Pierre Hissey, sole survivor of the class of 1953: "Look, these guys weren't about to take this crap from Father Declan, no matter who he was. This was an outstanding class, and here's this guy in total charge of their breathing telling them to go pick up cobblestones. Come on."

Tony Lachner, Episcopal priest: "It may have been some kind of semiconscious squaring off in our heads of what I would call Self-Preference versus Divine Election. The old concept of vocation may have been drying up and we didn't know. On the other hand, maybe it was quite conscious on our part, though I don't think we were seers, particularly. We were living a moment of time. Maybe we were never a unit. Maybe we were never that serious. Maybe the novice master got to us. I can remember he once made me water the lawn in the rain. I thought it was kind of funny, actually."

Gerry Cieslinski, accountant, Dow Chemical: "I wasn't going to buckle under that nickel and dime shit, no matter what."

That is part one of the riddle, and here is part two, the part that directly involves Brother Meredith Ohrt: In the middle of a moonless late spring night, with three quarters of his novitiate year successfully elapsed, Brother Meredith rises from his bed and begins tearing off his pajamas. His roommate, Brother Mel Kiernan, wakes, half-conscious, dreamy. "What are you doing?" he says. Ohrt doesn't answer. Brother Pierre Hissey is across the hall. Brother Pierre comes awake at the noise. He sees Ohrt trotting down the hall. He may be naked—Brother Pierre can no longer be sure. The trot becomes a run. The door bangs. Brother Pierre gets up and rouses Brother Ronald Booth and Brother Ronan Cieslinski.

A search begins. At first only a few novices are in on it. Father Declan is said to be away from the building for the evening. Maybe Brother Meredith can be found, and everyone can get back to bed and the Master will be none the wiser. Brother Mel and Brother Ronald and Brother Pierre beam through the darkness with flashlights. Somebody takes a van from the barn and drives down the main road to hunt. Some time later—no one is sure how long the search went on— Brother Merdeith is located down by the lake sitting in a rowboat beneath the boathouse. The boathouse is stuck up on pilings and extends out over the water. Brother Meredith is sitting in the boat, motionless, noncommunicative. He is wearing a swimsuit, and this in itself seems odd because Brother Meredith never swims, not that anyone recalls. When the class goes swimming on free days, Brother Meredith usually sits on the side, tanning and reading. But the biggest mystery is this: there are a rope and a knife above Brother Meredith's head on the dock. (Ohrt denies this.) At length Brother Meredith climbs out of the boat, comes in, gets back into his pajamas, and goes to bed.

The next day there are only embarrassed smiles. But of course word about the night before is out. The Master must be told the full story. Just before he goes in to see Father Declan, Brother Meredith tells his friend Brother Pierre: "This is it. They'll kick me out for sure." But a half-hour later, when he emerges, Brother Meredith seems his old contained, controlled self. And nothing more is said about the incident, not a word. From that day on Brother Meredith and Father Declan seem to enjoy a special relationship. Several years later, after Ohrt has left religious life, he receives an irked letter from Father Declan, who wants to know why he wasn't consulted about the departure. And once, when he is in the Army and stationed for a time in Carolina, Ohrt rides a bus up to the northern neck of Virginia to see Father

Declan, who by now has been reassigned and given a rural parish to tend. Father Declan's reputation as Mister Missionary Servant is already in revision.

"Under the veneer of Ohrt is somebody who really wants to help people, okay? But dammit if somebody doesn't take and follow my directions I'll kick his ass into next week."

"Why does it have to be either or?"

The shoulders dip, the palms turn up, the grin is on. "My fault."

A month later. I have come back to Tuscon. On the phone and in a letter I had said there were some unasked questions, some holes in my notebook; could I come out again? My fault. "Have at it," he had said.

We sit now in the waxless, darkened air of a Marriott Hotel lounge. I am trying to get drunk. There is the thin, weary smell of old drinks, of cigarettes, of Naugahyde. Across the room somebody is banging a piano. Around the piano, faces flicker like alcoholic ghosts above butane lighters. I am nervous because I must ask him about that strange night in the novitiate. Just before I had left last time he had gone to the back of his house and brought out a piece of Navajo pottery. I had said earlier that day I admired Indian pottery. "Here," he had said, sticking it at me, "it's a souvenir of your trip." Earlier that evening, talked out, we had sat numbly in front of the television, watching the Academy Awards, neither of us saying very much, glad for the silence and the set's empty noise, distances of space and time halved between us, at least in my head. I had begun to sustain the illusion that I was fourteen and he was twenty and I had just gotten off his waiter crew. I had tried to say what I felt, and given up. What I had felt was kinship, a bonding, a loss of my objectivity, although it was probably pretense all along.

The conversation is racing tonight. He hasn't found the job he wants. The CIA got in touch saying that maybe if he wanted to think about relocating to Washington . . . (He doesn't.) IBM is building a new plant east of town, and he's got a résumé in. "They're big on internal security."

He talks about his family. Hasn't seen his brother Harry since 1951, his brother Don since 1971. His folks have retired to Arizona now; he tries to be the faithful son. His father's fire is mostly banked, although the coals still ignite once in a while. He sucks in his breath, shakes his head. "I've got to say it, sometimes I think I went into the place just to get away from him. He was management. I think he carried that over into our lives. 'Let's get it done,' he'd say. 'Let's don't dork around.' "

"Why did you want to be a priest?"

"Little bit of Crusader Rabbit, maybe."

"Did you want to save souls?"

"Why not?"

Without pausing, catching me off balance: "Ruth has lately talked about chucking real jobs altogether and maybe going into some sort of lay service volunteer work. Maybe that's what we should do."

"So what happened to your class in novitiate?"

"We were a group of individuals. I don't care what anybody says. We never got things out in the open. When it started to cave, it caved badly."

Above the mindless bang of the piano: "So what were you doing that night in novitiate when they found you down by the lake? I've spoken to most of your classmates. Somebody said you'd cracked. Somebody even thought suicide. Somebody said he remembered a rope and a knife."

The robin-egg blue eyes are perfectly serene, locked with the inquisitor's. The old interrogator handles the blurted question like a groove pitch to Ted Williams. "I had been out fishing a couple of days before that night. There was this woman across the lake, outside one of the cabins. We'd seen her once or twice before, on hikes and stuff, and even had a name for her: Jessebel. Anyway, I'm fishing by myself and she calls out, 'Hey, why don't you come over Wednesday night. We're having a party.' I didn't think any more about it. Then Wednesday night came. Call it the Animal Urge, okay? Okay, so how am I going to get over? Swim or row the boat, of course. I decide to take the boat. Only thing, I got about three-quarters across and chickened out. I lost the urge. I rowed back and was sitting there by the dock trying to catch my breath when they found me."

"Why didn't you tell anybody?"

"I did. I told Father Declan."

"Why none of your classmates?"

"I guess we were like that."

In the journals and diaries of medieval monasteries there are accounts of men so stricken with Eros they rise from their cells and streak into the night with rashes and welts rising on their bodies.

The next morning, before the desert sun has drilled its way to noon, Dick Ohrt and I are on the floor of his living room, listening to recordings of Gregorian chant. The house is silent except for the cool mesmeric music coming from his stereo. Ruth is at work, the kids are at school. I listen to this soothing music and I picture robed men, pale as candle wax, moving liquidly down water-beaded stone passageways in Abyssinia or maybe Coptic Egypt. "I enjoy playing chant on Sunday when we get home from Mass," says Dick Ohrt. "This one's called the *Paschale Mysterium*. The Paschal Mystery."

I didn't see Ohrt after that for several more months. In August of 1980 he turned up at Holy Trinity for our reunion. He was one of the first to arrive, in a fast, flashy car. At the rosary procession on Saturday, from the Blessed Mother's shrine up to the chapel, he led one decade of the beads, intoning them as if this were exactly what he did with his own family every weekend. During Father Vincent's emotional talk, he looked over at me and slowly nodded. The next morning, Sunday, he came up to me on the walk in front of chapel and said, "Listen, Paul, some of these people here this weekend are really pissed at you for some of this stuff you've been writing about the seminary. I told them, 'Hey, the guy's gotta make a living, doesn't he?' "

It caught me completely off guard. After the chapel service he came up behind me and took me by the arm. "Let's go down to the gym; I'll show you where I creamed that little shit from Open Door Community Center." We went down to the gym and walked the old oily floor. Ohrt was gregarious. He said he wanted to buy me a drink in town. I said I had to leave for Washington. "Have at it," he said.

I didn't see him again for nearly a year. We wrote to each other several times in that interval. He had done an eight-month stint of work for the Army. (When he left active duty he secured a captain's commission in the United States Army

Reserve.) He had done this and that but still had found no permanent work.

One day in the summer of 1981 I called him from San Francisco, where I had been visiting Charlie Liteky. Eighteen months had now elapsed since Ohrt had left the Regular Army, fifteen months since I had first gone to see him, and he was still without full-time employment. On the phone he said he was doing some "sleazy domestic stuff" and that he would fill me in when he saw me. Before he hung up he asked if I wanted to stay overnight. "We've got the room. You know you're always welcome." I said I'd have to catch a flight back to Washington but that I appreciated his thoughtfulness. "Whatever," he said. After I hung up I wondered what shape his ego could be in, whether the Prussian was so Prussian now.

We met a few days later at the hotel where we had stopped for a lunch the year before when I was interviewing him. He was there waiting for me when I walked into the bar. Immediately he seemed his old rigorous, gentlemanly, bastard self —god of light, god of dark. If he was hurting he didn't show signs of it. Ruth was pregnant with their second, he said, and Licorice had died on Valentine's Day. "Don't worry," he said, "we cried for two days." He was willing to bet me that the coming child, due later that summer, would be a boy. "I've made the decision."

"Can you make Ruth cry?" I suddenly said.

"Yes, and she can make me cry, too."

I cared for him and I hated him. *Why can't you bend?*

Presently he began hassling the waitress in a friendly sort of way. "Does this sort of approach ever backfire?" I asked. "I mean, wonder if she told you to stick it?"

"Then I'd say, 'What's your problem, lady? You mean you're not in control of yourself?'"

His part-time job amounted to tailing unfaithful husbands and wives for divorce proceedings, he said. He had been doing the work for several months and despised it. It was a private investigation firm, maybe fifteen investigators, and the owner thought he could call up his people at two o'clock in the morning and get them out on a case. "He called me up last night. We had company. I told him to get lost. He's small time. He was paying me five bucks an hour, and I said I wanted seven and a half or I was leaving. He gave it to me, but now he won't pay my mileage."

He had reapplied to the Army, he said, for a personnel officer's job at the St. Louis administrative division in reserve officers' intelligence. His papers had been in nearly five months. "I guess they're deciding whether I'm worthy. I don't expect to get it, actually. Too many enemies at Department of the Army, even though those people in St. Louis like me a lot. It won't bother me one way or the other."

He made the tiny familiar kissing *pfft* sound with his mouth, and his eyes seemed to be watering a little. But then I thought I had remembered them watering a year ago, too.

"Did you think it would take this long to find the work you wanted?"

"Truthfully, no. I figured it would take six or nine months, tops."

"Would you really like that desk job back in St. Louis?"

"Sure. Why not? Of course it's true that the work I really care for is being able to get somebody right by the throat and just keep my hand poised at his Adam's apple, waiting for him to move a fraction of an inch." He reached over during this and locked his smooth brown hand at my throat. The only thing between my neck and Dick Ohrt's hand was air. He laughed. So did I. His hand fell away.

"You're one of the most . . ." I began.

"I know: obnoxious and likable bastards you've ever met."

"That about covers it. I think you're really marshmallow underneath. And you're terrified of letting people find that out. This is the way you cope. You think it's the only way. Did you ever wonder that you might be working against yourself with all this uncompromising shit of yours?" It felt incredibly good, speaking up.

"Could be." He said it weakly.

"Do you still go to church?"

"Every Sunday. It's a time for the family. It's a time for Ruth and me."

"And you still believe in God?"

"Got anybody else in mind?"

Outside, in fierce light, Richard Ohrt got in the family's second car (he had insisted Ruth take the one with air-conditioning) and drove down a sun-blinded Tucson street. I watched him go, a slumming angel, a forty-two-year-old ex-sem, a private dick waiting for the chance to burn again. All the way home to Washington I thought about him. The sun glinted brilliantly off the plane's wings. Maybe Dick Ohrt stayed in the seminary and the Army too long. Maybe the world was too gray by the time he got out. Maybe he is living out of time, a high achiever in the wrong season. Well, he would have made a helluva priest, I thought, making that soft *pfft* sound, not so much in imitation as in wonder. I couldn't help thinking that someday, somewhere, he'd be back. He'd *snap* back.

PART FOUR

LIKE A

SHEPHERD'S TENT

———

The rainbow trout has an instinctive attraction for wandering. Once introduced to a body of water, a rainbow's first inclination is to head downstream, looking for a lake or a larger river. One rainbow, tagged and introduced into a tributary of Lake Michigan in January, 1958, was found eight months later in the Bay of Quinte, Lake Ontario. The fish had traveled about six hundred miles and survived a descent of Niagara Falls.

—Tom Rosenbauer,
Plain Old Rainbows

Transition:
Wood into Brick, 1960-1964

The dream ceased working, or maybe we did. Something called Vatican Two, and a spiritual restiveness,
and a controversial papal encyclical on birth control, and
the wider crashing world of the sixties themselves
seemed to be changing the rules, although in our case I
think the disarray we suffered also had greatly to do
with the move from Alabama to Virginia. I don't mean
this purely on the level of symbol. The missionary congregation I was preparing for had begun to change, had
gotten computers and millionaire donors and increasingly urban, had seemed to move away from, as perhaps
was inevitable, its primitive spirit of poverty. The Order
was changing, as the Church was changing, as the country was changing, as we were changing. And what resulted, I think, was a growth imbalance, like a kid
shooting out of his shoes. The waters got too roiled. The
center didn't hold, just as it wasn't holding in other seminaries, just as it wasn't holding on college campuses for
a different set of reasons, though at bottom, I think,
there was the same revolt against the alleged sins of the
fathers.

Once the flow began, it could not be stanched. A way
of life had suddenly become obsolete, anachronistic, a
yawning dinosaur. Or it seemed that way.

ON SEPTEMBER 1, 1960, the Missionary Servants of the Most
Holy Trinity relocated their apostolic training program from

the woods of Alabama to a high green plateau off Route 655 in Amherst County, Virginia. In the annals of the Catholic Church, this was not the watershed moment, though for the small bullish American missionary congregation in question, it unequivocally was.

New land had been bought in the foothills of the Blue Ridge, near Lynchburg, in the curving folds of Tobacco Row Mountain. A $2.5 million building, on 325 acres, all brick and glass and native greenstone, was opening neatly with the new decade. The place seemed to hoist itself up out of the land as you drove up, snaring your attention with a 100-foot gold-colored aluminum cross on a bell tower that was filled with 5,900 pounds of bells. The bells were controlled electrically and rung three times daily to announce that this was the Lord's place. A magazine article on this gleaming new green-house, the envy of religious communities everywhere, said: "In the spirit that popes commissioned da Vinci and Michel-angelo, distinguished artists from all over the United States were commissioned to create statuary, altars, tabernacles, and glorious stained glass to make a living entity of contemporary beauty in which the young seminarians develop." Thousands of young men hungry for Christ and souls and their "orders" would pass over those glossy terrazzo floors and through those airy glass breezeways in the decades to come. They would acquire their sense of beauty almost by osmosis, and one day they would go out into a world where there wasn't much beauty, laboring amid migrants and sharecroppers and rural blacks and inner-city Hispanics. This was the dream. The dream had many shades, but the primary color was this: getting chrismed with oils so you could save the faith. That was the motto of my old Order: *Ad fidem servandam.* For pre-serving the faith. We were all going to be preservers, savers.

Norman Mailer once portrayed John F. Kennedy's succes-sion to Dwight Eisenhower as a victory of city over small town in America. Well, in a sense, I think the Second Vatican Council and the 1960s were a triumph of urban over rural in the Catholic Church. And it was in this precise time frame— after Pope John XXIII's Council had been summoned in 1959, but before it could formally convene on October 11, 1962—that my order and my seminary seemed to undergo, both actively and passively, a series of critical shifts: from backwoods to edge of the town; from Army barrack to new brick; from hickdom to relative urbanity; from obscurity to mainstream recognition; from poverty to relative affluence. I am not saying the move itself accomplished all this. The move was only the most tangible symbol of a deeper, more subtle transformation which had been going on for a number of years. Even if we had stayed down in the woods, change and the world would have caught up. I doubt seriously if the losses my old Order was to sustain in the latter half of the sixties and into the seventies (whole classes wiped out, several years passing without a single ordination) were any worse on a percentage basis than the losses other Catholic religious groups were sustaining. (In some cases, I *know* the losses of other Orders were worse.) It was just that the smallness and newness and tremendous spirit of my religious group—less than half a century old, fewer than two hundred full-fledged members—made the eventual departures more painful, the chaos more glaring.

I have two seminary alma maters, one in Alabama, one in Virginia, and neither exists anymore, at least as a seminary. At Holy Trinity they've bulldozed most of the old wooden buildings and turned the place into a parish for the sprinkle of Catholics, black and white, who live in the area. But our hulking old gym that used to freeze us every winter and parboil us every spring still stands, wheezing against time. So does the chapel. Only they've put in an orange rug and a cry room and pads on the kneelers.

My Virginia alma mater, christened Father Judge Mission Seminary, is now the Old Dominion Job Corps Center. For a while it was a training center for the mentally retarded, a fact that gives me small inward amusement. When it closed, in 1973, they didn't quite know what to do with the place. There were stories it was going to be sold for a private air terminal, for a training site for the Olympics, for a Baptist seminary. Four or five years ago, on a spring Sunday, I stopped in to see the place. It was then in a transition period from a facility for the retarded to a federal property. My wife and I had to climb over a gate and walk in half a mile to the seminary grounds. There was a security guard sitting at the front desk, where Brother Vianney used to sit. He told me I was trespassing. I said once I went to school here, could I look around? He led me through the empty buildings suddenly wide awake with questions. He was a Baptist divinity student holding a part-time job and was eager to know about the symbols in the stained glass in the chapel, about the statues standing dusty and strangely monolithic, like a religious Stonehenge. In the library, in a bottom drawer, I found a couple of old due cards with signatures I knew. I wanted to feel more for the place, but it was like a cut that had whitened over.

Decades of days, cycles of seasons. If getting in, in the fifties, seems a swirl of confusing forces, getting out, in the sixties, appears impossible to unravel. And still I try, bumble on. I look back on all that eventual late-sixties turmoil now— in me, in the Catholic Church, in my country, in confreres and Christ figures who still populate my days and dreams— and it seems like a series of concentric circles, each circle with its own terribly acute center-seeking force. Had there been no external change, no move to new quarters, no Vatican Two, no seeming loss in the Order's spirit of poverty, I suspect I would have ended up leaving the seminary one day anyway. Such were the shifts and changes and concentric circles going on inside me. But all these shifts and changes and concentric circles were coming together at once, or it seemed that way, and so it is really hard to know now, it is really difficult to separate what is real from what is imagined.

For forty years a firetrap, rattletrap school held together by prayer and will and baling wire and a spiritual recklessness had stood on the founding hallowed ground in Alabama. An old plantation house and two frame cabins had served as the first classrooms and dormitories, added to and nailed over as the years went by. But now, in 1960, there was a new seminary, for a new decade, made of brick and glass and reinforced concrete, up in the Old Dominion, close to the necklace of East Coast megalopolis. The Trinitarians were moving toward the Center, and this was their emblem of it. Seven bishops and hundreds of priests came for the formal dedication ceremonies. Out front of this splendid building stood a twelve-foot cast-bronze statue of Thomas Judge by world-renowned sculptor Ivan Mestrovic. In the courtyards, visible from the glass-enclosed breezeways, were two kinds of sodded grass. The walls in the hallways had been color-coordinated by an interior designer so as to perfectly reflect and refract the afternoon sun. Down below the gym was an Olympic-sized swimming pool, said to be the finest prep school facility of its kind on the Eastern Seaboard. Suddenly, with the opening of the new Father Judge Mission Seminary, there seemed a chance for everyone—student, priest, bene-factor—to be tied to something fabulous. Suddenly the Mis-sionary Servants of the Most Holy Trinity didn't seem so radically poor anymore.

I had no idea when I first went down to Alabama in 1958 that there was even going to be a new seminary. The first time I can remember hearing anything substantive about it was when Father Gerard, who was the vice head of the com-munity, came down from his office in the North to tell us about bids being taken and land being graded. He stood at the lector's stand in the refectory one dreary Sunday after the noon meal and talked about blueprints and facilities that sounded like the World of Tomorrow at Disneyland.

Actually a new seminary had been in the minds of the master builders since at least 1955. That was when 325 acres, twelve miles outside of Lynchburg, Virginia, by Harris Creek, were purchased from an E. W. Woody. "Catholics Plan Sem-inary Here," headlined the Lynchburg Daily Advance one day in 1957. It would take three years, from grading to the bless-ing of bells, but finally the dream was realized. The seminary would remain open for thirteen years, until 1973. I, of course, would be long gone by then. Many boys would come and leave in this time. In the end the enrollment would be down to a pathetic forty-three, hardly enough for an in-house volleyball league. By then, too, odd stories would have begun to circulate: the school was, some feared, turning into a floating fairyboat. Toward the end, some priests were get-ting into the seminary cars and going out to recruit girls to bring them back to the school for weekend interaction with the seminarians. The faculty had become badly fragmented; individual priests found themselves leaving the grounds to find their own measure of sanity.

A press statement went out on April 15, 1972: "Among the several reasons" for the school's closing the following year, the statement said, "are a definite national vocation fall-off, continued escalating expense, the question of suitability of this enclosed type of training in today's society, and the de-layed life decisions in today's youth." The idea of a boys' seminary was bankrupt. Father Judge Seminary was the land of the walking dead.

I had no idea in 1958 that the religious community I had joined at the fringe, like a foreign legionnaire, was just then in the pained, subtle process of facing up to conflicts of change. In a book called *Cloud by Day, Fire by Night*, a Catholic writer named David M. Knight writes: "It seems to be a fact of history that the beginning and the renewal of religious orders are marked by an impulse toward radical material poverty, as in a womb, and the reform of monasteries is spearheaded by a return to poverty and prayer."

I had arrived in Alabama at neither the beginning nor the renewal, but at the moment of seeming fame, or at least success. The hard years of the Depression, after the founder's death, were over. The forties had seen a floodtide of GIs. The fifties had witnessed an increasingly steady growth and approbation from the institutional Church. And now, with the start of the sixties, with a new preparatory seminary crammed with expensive religious artwork, it almost seemed as if the founding ethos of radical material poverty had been forsaken. There were millionaire benefactors, such as Bolton Sullivan of the Skil Corporation in Chicago. (His father had developed the portable saw.) Other wealthy benefactors (a lingerie mogul) were being wooed and won. There were already, or eventually would be, investment counselors; an IBM 370/125 computer; a Donor List with half a million names on it. These benefactors, according to a subsequent donor profile, were mostly middle-class women, conservative, of strong faith, mission-minded, many of them retired and living on social security and pensions. Perhaps they could give only two dollars a month, but there were hundreds, even thousands of two-dollar envelopes coming in. There were now burgeoning and psychologically sophisticated fund-rais-ing techniques, such as the Foster Parent Program, which essentially was a way of fleshing out the giving, putting a face on it. Donors would be given a major seminarian as their own "adopted son." They would be given the chance to help pay for their "son's" education and clothing from that moment until ordination four or five years hence. Maggie Murphy, in her Iowa pew, might give two dollars for her seminarian-son monthly, but a better-heeled foster family in Manhattan might be able to offer fifty. Each seminarian was assigned his list of Foster Parents ("FPs," everybody called them) and was expected to write several times a year in gratitude and with chitchat. This was usually done by form letter, and to keep it from looking so, an automatic typewriter cranked out the copies and the seminarian-son signed them all one afternoon in a cramping swoop. (There were signature wheels that could duplicate a handwriting perfectly, but these were not used in the FP program.) In fairness it should be said that some seminarians became genuinely close to their FPs in the years before ordination, and vice versa. Some would come to look upon them as their real family.

By 1960 the Missionary Servants of the Most Holy Trinity not only had a $2.5 million junior seminary to show off—the admitted envy of much older congregations—they also had commissioned a coat of arms for themselves and were breaking ground for a new building in Rome to house doctoral students and serve as a second novitiate for ordained members. "The first house built in Rome by an American-founded congregation," the Order's religious magazine to benefactors proudly said. For a time it seemed as though every graduate student in the Order was preparing himself for an academic career, not a missionary one. What is a hick little missionary outfit doing getting so many doctorates, some in the community wanted to know.

But the most important step upward, at least in terms of Church approval, was that the founder's name was about to be entered for the long and tedious process of beatification and canonization. Thomas Judge's cause—the Ordinary Process, it is often termed—would formally open on August 16, 1963, between my fifth and sixth years of study. There would be stories in every Catholic paper in America and in much of the secular press, too. Judge was the first American-born priest to be so considered; it was a tremendous surge of prestige and pride for the obscure American Order known alternately as Trinity Missions or the Trinitarians or the Missionary Servants. What was essentially needed to advance the cause of canonization was proof of miracles. A lock of the founder's hair was being applied to the body of a young man dying of cancer in Birmingham. A girl incurably ill of brain damage in Puerto Rico lay with a piece of the founder's clothing pinned to her pajamas. A plea for word of miraculous intercession in the founder's name began. The Order subtly "advertised" for word of miraculous cures in its magazine. Some thought this unseemly.

The Ordinary Process would go on two years, until 1965. Many witnesses to Judge's saintliness would be called before a tribunal in Philadelphia. But essentially no miracles could be found. There would be "cure" stories, but they wouldn't hold up. Already, I think, a retrenching had begun. The cause was not so much dropped as put in limbo. Already, some within the Order were openly raising questions about the cost of trying to canonize Thomas Judge, about the priority of the endeavor. It would take maybe fifty thousand dollars, at bare minimum, to get the cause through the Church's labyrinthian bureaucracies. Some causes took decades, even centuries. Maybe the money put toward the cause was better spent out on the missions, some said, among the poor. The Mission Procure Office in Silver Spring, Maryland, would still have startling success, it was true, and would continue to have it all through this period and the decade to come. Between 1967 and 1972 the Order would raise nearly $14 million to sustain itself; between 1973 and 1979, $18.5 million. One priest in the Order, who would eventually be elected to the top office, would study at the Wharton School in Philadelphia. By then there would be 17,000 Mission of the Month givers, 4,000 Foster Parents. There would be provisions for benefactors' wills, trusts, memorials, life insurance bequests. The Order wasn't exactly rich, and the money was being put to God's use, but things had moved far from the reckless material poverty of the founder praying by oil lantern in his Alabama cell. There were huge, splendid buildings to heat and pay for, payrolls to meet in the Procure Office. Thomas Judge's had been a primitive charism lit with a small fierce flame, and though his spirit was much alive in people like Vincent Fitzpatrick and Brendan Smith, the numbers had vastly changed.

And what I'm wondering is this: Could all this gain and change and success, some of it inevitable and much of it hoped for, have made nonetheless for a severe, hidden, collective angst—not so much on our part at first as on the part of our role models? I am speaking now not of the last years of the sixties, but of those first opening years—when a new seminary was opening in the Blue Ridge, when Vatican Two was opening in Rome, when America herself seemed to be entering vast uncharted places. (Astronaut Alan B. Shepard went into suborbital flight in the spring of my first year in Virginia.) Could our own shepherds at the new Father Judge Mission Seminary have been giving off involuntarily some cues and distress signals—of doubt, of guilt, of internal crisis about their priesthood, their vows, their rapidly changing congregation? And giving them off before they or we really knew? This much would be certain: We would have been the immediate recipients of any such distant early warnings of distress. After all, we were the ones on whom they daily tested out their ideas and emotions in a classroom and on an altar and on ballfields and in rec rooms and in spiritual direction. We were disposed, at least then, to swallowing their gospels whole. In Systems Psychology there is a view that once one part of a particular root system becomes diseased, the other parts will inevitably become affected, too. Consider, for instance, the nuclear family. If one member of that family gets seriously ill, all members in some measure will feel the pain. Their behavior will show it, even if a brother is in Spain and a sister is in New Delhi. In the root system I am thinking of, one hundred men and boys lived under the same gold roof, in a gorgeous new brick and glass building. Perhaps what happened ultimately in the Order can be explained as a kind of surface tension. You can take a glass, fill it to the brim with water, rest a thin piece of cardboard on top, turn it over, and the water will hold—until you break the seal. Then all of it will pour out.

Marty. Two pictures freeze in my mind from my first days there, and both have to do with my brother. I can see Marty standing outside on the steps of the new seminary on the night the student body arrives there for the first time. Marty has been in the seminary four years to my two and is now a first-year collegian. As is the custom for fifth-year students, Marty has returned to school a month early to help get things ready for the arrival of the student body in September. In Alabama the advance team mowed lawns and cleaned the pool, but here, at the new place, the fifth-year men have been assembling new beds, putting metal lockers into place. Marty is standing on the steps in the dark when the buses pull up. He is in work clothes and is holding a push broom. I jump off the bus and run up to my brother and say, Hey, Marty, how do you like this place? I've got something for you from Mom." "Great," he says, and somehow I know he is lying. In all the years following, I will wonder if his small lie could have something to do with the fact that Marty was alone in the new seminary with his classmates for a month. Did the group turn on him, or he on them? After he leaves the seminary, Marty never brings up his old friends.

The second picture: a frosty morning six weeks after school has begun. All of us are still new to this place, still trying to find our way in these glossy cavernous corridors. I was sitting in the rec room last night after supper when Marty stuck his head in the door and asked me to come out in the hall. He looked nervous. Except to exchange mail from our mother and to converse illegally now and then in the halls, Marty and I haven't seen each other much. We're not supposed to see each other. High schoolies are supposed to keep away from collegians, even if the collegian is your brother. Upper-lower friendships are frowned on in any category. They lead to "particular friendships." Particular friendships lead to homosexuality.

In the last year or so I am aware of a subtle shift taking place between my brother and me. For as long as I have been able to recall, I have lived under Marty's shadow. Sixteen months older, two grades ahead, he has always been a little faster on his feet, a few pounds heavier, a split second quicker, and more sure with any kind of ball. This remains true now, although I have begun over these last months to feel the slightest edge of superiority. It is because of books. Marty senses it, too, I think.

Out in the hall Marty hitches at his cassock. The tip of his tongue is edged at the corner of his lip, an odd habit he has had as long as I can remember. The habit shows up when Marty is angry or under strain. He comes straightaway to the point: "Look, um, Paul, I know this will probably surprise you, but I'm leaving in the morning."

I don't get it. He says it again. The sentence has the wallop of an iron safe dropped from a roof. I have witnessed the departure of dozens of boys, but this one is viciously unlike any of the others. This one is my brother. "But why . . ." I stammer, my brain fighting for time so I can decipher its meaning, find a way to talk him out of it. "Why didn't you tell me?" He shakes his head. He can't go into the whys; it is too late for that. It is just something he has been coming to for a long time.

After Benediction, when everyone else goes to study hall, Marty and I walk down the basement hall to the trunk room. (Father Constantine has told me I can help him go.) We fish around and find his trunk and carry it in silence the three floors to his room. He says he can pack okay by himself. I stand around several more minutes, watching, then edge out the door. Sleeping will be impossible this night.

It is now the next morning, and right after Mass, my brother is gone. Brother Basil and I help him lift the trunk into the back of the car. He skips breakfast. I stand on the steps watching him go. Then I walk over to the refectory, where the rest of the school is doing dishes. "What's the matter?" Roger Recktenwald whispers. "My brother just left," I whisper back. We are breaking the silence. I feel bewildered. Marty's leaving is my leaving, somehow. In reality, my own leaving is a full five years off from this moment, but nonetheless I think my life has now begun to move in the direction of a dominant thought: getting out.

In truth, life didn't seem so different when we first got up there. We still rose at the same dark hour. The days were still crammed with prayer and learning. Only now space seemed as discretely measured out as time had always been. And nothing looked or felt jerry-rigged anymore. Thomas Judge's words had been chiseled into plaques in the halls: SILENCE IS THE HANDMAIDEN OF PRAYER AND RECOLLECTION. Special machines had been purchased to buff the floors, special polish to shine the brass on the doors leading to the chapel.

It was only later that something vital appeared missing. But what was it? I'm still not sure, although I think some of it had to do with a glut of synthetic surfaces. Father Judge Mission Seminary was built of incredibly sturdy materials, all right, and had an overall integral design where form followed function: a series of tight boxes, with little window openings, as in a monastery; each box had a connection to another box, from chapel to refectory to classroom to dorm to gym. The sheer brick face of the five major building units, backed by concrete block, gave a spare, monolithic, almost primitive quality to the school. You could say, and several of us profanely did, that they built it like a brick shithouse.

And yet much of the interior furnishings turned out to be what I would call "unborn." For some reason they built the walls like the Great Wall of China and went cheap inside. In the classroom, for example, we sat on pastel-colored Brunswick pre-molded plastic chairs; you could never get all four legs to rest even. The desks we studied at had aluminum legs and Formica tops; they were cheap and tinny. Most of the furniture for the new place had been bought by Father Norbert, Holy Trinity's Procurator. Father Norbert bought $100,000 worth of industrial and school furniture at Gene Malone's furniture store in Columbus, Georgia, and had it shipped north. Father Thomas, who was head of the Order in the initial building phase and into our first days there, had stipulated that as far as possible he wanted every desk and table surface to be Formica. The only exceptions he would allow were the library. (There was wood here and there elsewhere in the building, but you had to look for it.) Father Thomas, who had run the Order for twenty-two years, nearly since Father Judge's death, was an enigma. For a time he had refused to allow his vocation recruiters out on the road to have radios in their cars. For himself he cared nothing for the world and its comforts. But yet when it came time to erect the multimillion-dollar memorial to the founder, he insisted on the best architectural plans, the finest building materials. Father Norbert told Father Thomas one day that his brother Jack, who was a stockbroker in Chicago, might be able to arrange for an architect free of charge, and Father Thomas snapped: "No. That's where we've come from."

A shell of steel and an interior glut of Formica may sound

like a trivial matter when you're trying to piece together a vast disarray of people, but I don't think so. I have talked to too many of my old confreres who have said yes, come to think of it, one of the things they recall after getting out was the strongest urge to be in a place where they could touch wood again. Wood is a warm form. The materials with which the new seminary was constructed were far superior to wood in their strength and durability, though not in warmth. There was next to nothing warm in my mind about terrazzo floors and concrete stairwells and hundreds of square feet of sheer brick, not to speak of pre-molded plastic chairs and wobbly aluminum desks. Artful as the damn building was, nothing about it was endearing, at least for me. I am not saying I was actively aware of this. But I think it was working on me all the same.

Just across the tobacco fields from our property lay Sweet Briar, a tony girls' college. We had almost no contact with the Sweet Briar women, who always looked imperially slim to me. Every once in a while we might see them riding by on horseback in their boots and blousy pants and short-billed caps. Father Benedict became a more or less official chaplain to the Catholic girls at the college, and one day in French class he took off his spectacles, balanced them on his fingertip, swung the stems, and said: "They've got a name for you: the Untouchables." He said it and roared. Once I saw Father Benedict and a Sweet Briarite holding hands out by the bell tower, preening and giggling like a proud daddy and daughter on her graduation day. She had come over for Sunday Mass. Her heels spiked on the terrazzo floor behind my pew. I didn't dare turn around. Later we were complimented on "custody of the eyes."

Once, I remember, we were bused over to Sweet Briar for a reading by Robert Frost. The cranky old poet came on stage in high-topped boots and a thick suit and an even thicker shock of snow-white hair. He was in the middle of a poem called "Once by the Pacific" when he stopped cold, peered out into the semi-darkened auditorium, and said: "Someone is knitting. I've been reading my poetry up and down this country for decades, and I don't think I've ever been so insulted as I am right now—by that lady out there in the fifth row who would rather knit her damn sweater than listen to a poem." He pointed out his innocent victim and every head in the place turned. The thing about the incident that is nearly incredible to me is that twenty minutes later the damned old New England cur had us all back in his palm.

Another time we went to Sweet Briar for a symposium on religion and the arts. Flannery O'Connor was on the panel. That great dry-eyed satirist, fierce in her faith, was just a year or so away from her death by lupus. She was puffy and homely and brilliant. Father Brendan, our English teacher, had already exposed us to her stories and novels, but there was no way I could fully appreciate the art of a woman who, as Thomas Merton wrote later in elegy of her, "could keep looking the South in the face without bleeding or even sobbing."

But the person on the panel I remember best was John Ciardi of the *Saturday Review*. He was an avowed agnostic, maybe even atheist, and had probably been invited on that basis. He said something to the effect that the mysteries of creation were as arbitrary and senseless to him as some polliwogs you might happen on in the stagnant water formed by a jeep track. He had written a war poem with such an image, I believe. Why should there be something instead of nothing? He said that if he could somehow learn he was going to die in the morning he would want for tonight a) a woman, b) a steak, and c) a good bottle of liquor. The nakedness of his admission both shocked and embarrassed me. But I was embarrassed also because he had said it in the presence of my Christ figures.

I spent four important years at Father Judge Mission Seminary, from 1960 to 1964, before I returned to Alabama to make my novitiate in that seventh and final disastrous year. My consciousness widened in Virginia in all sorts of ways. I got rid of my skin condition, I put on pounds and inches, I registered for the Selective Service, I made the honor roll, I went from squeaky first-tenor to second-bass in the choir, I became a debater and extemporaneous speaker, I became a seminary driver. (Students drivers got to go to town for shopping or to ferry a schoolmate to the doctor when no faculty member or missionary brother was available to do the chore. They picked out five or six of us a year to get a Virginia driver's license, and in my fifth year, I was tapped.)

I had begun to find a small, tentative writing voice. Books were a world to lose myself in. Eventually I became editor of the school paper (*The Prepster*) and of the yearbook (*Spes Gregis*—"hope of the flock"). When John Kennedy dies I am moved to write an In Memoriam: "One hundred and eighty-five million Americans slumped in their seats as the assassin's bullet ripped through their heads. President Kennedy wasn't one of us. He was a part of us. That is why the nightmare of his death refuses to leave us. It isn't because he had so much charm or such a fine family or even because he had such devotion to duty. No, the reason we cannot forget him is that when we lost him, we lost something deep down inside of us. We cannot describe it, we cannot picture it, we do not even know what it is—but it is gone and we can feel its absence."

I remember when Kennedy got elected; the outside world barreled in. Father Constantine kept us informed of events. On the morning after the election, he came into the refectory beaming but serious, too. It was as if now we all had an extra burden to shoulder. Kennedy was ours. The night before, putting out the lights, he had told us that it looked extremely good for Kennedy. The next morning, in the refectory, he slapped the little silver bell on his table. "It's all but official the Senator has won," he said. He dispensed with the reading of scripture and the *Lives of the Saints*. Jokes flew from table to table that Pope John XXIII's papal 707 had been spotted overhead on its way to a new home at Andrews Air Force Base.

And three years later, when Kennedy was dead, routine was again briefly broken. Father Constantine had TVs set up in the refectory, and I remember sitting there all Saturday afternoon watching De Gaulle and other heads of state arrive at Dulles Airport. Even more than three years earlier, the world had busted in.

I remember the strange feeling I had the first time I read James Baldwin's *Notes of a Native Son*. I read that fierce book at a point when I had begun to fight hard with my vocation. Perhaps I was seventeen. Baldwin's book seemed to galvanize me, and I couldn't exactly say why. There seemed special hidden messages in it for me, if only I could ferret them out. James Baldwin had become a boy preacher at fourteen, in Harlem, as I had become a kind of a boy preacher at fourteen in another time and place. The wages of sin had been everywhere around him, he wrote, "in every wine-stained and urine-splashed hallway." And so he had fled into the church. His flight to religion was not so much out of salvation as refuge, sanctuary. It lasted, this holy fire, three hysteria-tinged years until he found, or refound, the fire of literature and the power to rage there with his own voice. And yet, as James Baldwin wrote in that beautiful essay, ". . . nothing that has happened to me since equals the power and glory that I sometimes felt . . . when the church and I were one." I had never been anywhere near Harlem then. Nor did I have any conscious idea that I, too, might have fled into my faith not so much out of salvation as out of sanctuary, refuge. I knew only that James Baldwin spoke the truth. He had touched me with the Word. He was wringing wet with it. His holy fire, his hysteria tinges—those were the things I felt.

Father Gavin Mooney joined the seminary faculty in these years. Father Gavin was a fair and brainy man and tried hard at his job, but he was extremely nervous, too, and this tied to a seeming inability to answer in a simple sentence even the simplest question made it natural we should mock nearly everything he said or did. Father Gavin had a sense of humor, but it was off in its timing, and this only fueled the mockeries. "Hot glass looks like cold glass," he'd say gravely in chem lab, after you had cursed and yanked your hand off a beaker. He'd say it with his lips pursed, nodding. Then he'd turn sideways and crack with laughter. He had an analogy for kinetic energy that involved one thousand monkeys. I forget how it went but every year he used the same analogy. New physics classes would wait for the kinetic energy chapter. That meant the monkeys. In a way he was our mad scientist, and what my puny mind couldn't grasp was that he camped on a high shimmering plain of breakdown. Once, serving his Mass at a side altar, I saw him trembling and perspiring so badly I turned away. I laid off for a few days.

Finding ourselves with an Olympic swimming pool motivated another priest, Father Claude, who was an old jock, to teach a course in water safety and senior lifesaving. Father Claude ran the course, and Father Gavin volunteered to be the victim. Every afternoon at three-thirty sharp, there was Father Gavin treading water in the middle of the pool, waiting to be "rescued." Each of us got to take a turn at swimming out to save him. He'd be hanging with his head visible, nostrils just above the water line, beady eyes following your every stroke. He had hardly any hair, so you knew you couldn't pull him in that way. When you got within a foot or two of him he'd begin screaming and thrashing. All the way in he'd try to drown you. At the end he'd thank you.

Before coming to religious life, Father Gavin studied premed at Holy Cross College in Massachusetts. Once, on an oppressive winter afternoon, he got his old Holy Cross classmate Bob Cousy to come by and give a talk on sports and hand out jayvee basketball awards. The Couz, Boston Celtic immortal, struggled for inspiration while Father Gavin beamed behind him, as if to say, "There'll be no mocking me at table tonight, boys."

October 13, 1961. The day held no particular significance then, although I have carried it with me ever since. On the outskirts of a farm town in western Wisconsin, a Corvair Monza with seven hundred miles on its odometer slammed head on into a green Dodge. It was just an instant in eternity, and at the seminary we didn't know of it until a week or so later when a note went up on the board. Four boys were riding in the Corvair that afternoon, but only the one in the back seat on the right-hand side was killed. He was hurled forward into the windshield and suffered a compound fracture of his cerebral cortex.

Father Constantine put the note up just before retiring prayers. I stood looking at it, scuffing my shoe on a smooth terrazzo tile, thinking: "If I leave, will this happen to me, too?" I shivered. I went into chapel, brushed my fingers in the holy water font, prayed hard—not for the repose of Patrick Power, who only a year earlier had knelt a pew behind me, but for my own vocation. I began to fantasize myself as a cold slab of flesh on a steel table. That was something to take to bed, to rub like worry beads.

A day or so later I told my confessor I had been fretting about the death of an ex-schoolmate and that I was finding it hard to pray for him. Far from comforting me, my confessor played on my anxieties, I think. Yes, he strongly hinted, Pat Power might have spurned the gift once given. God, who gave the impulse to say yes, doesn't wish to hear no a little later down the pike. Maybe Pat's violent death was intended as a lesson for me and the others who have stayed, he said. He didn't say any more, nor did he need to. I knew boys got punished for not doing their duty, for squandering rare gifts. I knew about rewards for virtue and punishments for evil.

I have since stood at the Y in the road on Route 10 outside Durand, Wisconsin, where the Corvair that Pat Power was riding in should have made its northward turn onto Route 25. I have since tried to imagine a moment of crunching tin and shattering glass. On the night I was there you could almost hear the corn straining in its stalks.

I have talked at considerable length to one of the survivors of that crash, Dan Grandmaison—husband, father, onetime aluminum-siding salesman, now the largest portrait and wedding photographer in Duluth, Minnesota. Dan Grandmaison told me he had switched seats with Pat Power eighteen minutes before the accident. And nearly every October, on or near the anniversary of the crash, Dan Grandmaison insists he wakes to discover a quarter-sized smear of dried blood on his pillowcase. *Oh, it's there again,* he says, fumbling from sleep. And when he looks in the mirror, he sees his lip is cut. Apparently what happens is that at some point during his sleep, Dan Grandmaison begins unconsciously to gnaw at his mouth until it bleeds.

For two decades the name Pat Power has had peculiar resonance in me. It seemed back then, as it seems now, that a sword, deadly and blinding, had come from a scabbard to take him inexplicably away.

I had begun to de-emphasize sports and to accentuate cultural things, though not in any conscious way. On weekends a half dozen of us would climb into our shiny seminary suits and motor across the diocese with a priest-chaperon-moderator. Father Judge Mission Seminary became known as one of the state's crack debating teams. I remember the girls at Bishop O'Connell high school in Arlington, Virginia, giggling at us and calling us "the black cloud." This was because we stood hunched together, as if in a huddle, during the get-acquainted periods.

A Trinitarian named Shaun McCarty began to emerge in

these years as one of my major influences. Father Shaun had taken over varsity athletics; he also coached us in debating and public speaking. Father Shaun had neither the Vincent Fitzpatrick capacity to create awe and trembling, nor the Brendan Smith gift for throwing open previously dark rooms in an instant. What he had, I think, was a kind of ultimate art of Dale Carnegieism. This sounds left-handed, but I don't mean it to be so. Father Shaun was an achiever and a doer and a charmer. He used every scintilla of his God-given abilities, which were not inconsiderable. What he was in love with, besides his priesthood, was product, and by my third or fourth year I think I had begun subconsciously to ally myself with his goals and philosophy. I suppose I knew down deep I could never be a Vincent or a Brendan, although I might someday be a Shaun. Father Shaun seemed a generalist *extraordinaire* in a field of generalists, and I find that he remains today one of my bigger influences and closest seminary friends. I wrote a letter a while ago to a classmate named Harry Gerken, asking him about Father Shaun. He wrote back: "I like your analysis of Shaun and the 'How to Win Friends' kind of person. I think what distinguishes him in my mind is that he treated each of us as individuals in an institution which promoted conformity. To the best of recollection, other priests seemed to play favorites if one did not conform to their image of what a 'good seminarian' should be, while Shaun looked for the individual potential in each of us. He would not put down, but rather try to motivate in positive ways. You mentioned that he was not the intellectual giant that, say, a Brendan was, but somehow Shaun was far superior in the human skills."

On the basketball court he was very human: he blew up a lot. My own basketball career had peaked at the junior varsity level, and when I came up to the varsity the next season, I was lost promise and failed dream. Father Shaun started me for the first three games of the season, and I think I threw the ball away a dozen times. He benched me, and the next year I didn't go out. One night in study hall, when he was monitoring, he sent for me and said: "How come you didn't go out this year, Hendrickson?"

"I didn't come to the seminary to play basketball, Father," I snapped. Before the air could dry that sentence, he shot up from his desk. "Oh, yes you did, Buster. You came to do it all." Buster was one of his words when he was riled.

At a national seminary conference in Washington in 1963, Father Shaun delivered an eloquent paper in which he asked, "Are adult demands placed on little boys made more of clay than stardust?" The panel Father Shaun was on had been convened to answer the question: Why the dropouts? (As early as '63, the trend nationally had been spotted.) Father Shaun placed as many adult demands on us as any priest in the seminary, and I wonder now if at least some part of it was his own insecurities. He had been sent to the seminary as a teacher immediately following his ordination. He had become prefect of the college department, and in some cases he found himself disciplining people only a few years younger than himself. He never knew that much about basketball, at least as a coach of basketball, and I think he compensated by blowing up.

Once, after I had won a state tournament in extemporaneous speaking, thereby qualifying me for a trip to the National Catholic Forensic League finals in Miami Beach, Father Shaun thought he was going to win it all, I believe. But his prize extemp speaker folded in the stretch like a speed horse at Hialeah with a furlong left. I finished sixth, one notch below the trophies, and Father Shaun's disappointment for me was enormous. On the flight home we talked of a lot of things, although not about the tournament. I think he felt I would burst into tears. I remember his parents met us at National Airport in Washington. We had several hours to kill before catching the train down to the seminary. Father Shaun took the wheel of his dad's car and led me into a ghetto in northeast Washington. He parked the car in an alley and told me to come on, he wanted me to see what some other people's lives were like. I was a senior in high school, and I had never seen a ghetto before, or anything close to a ghetto. Father Shaun's question at the 1963 conference, whether people like himself were placing too many demands on priesthood candidates who were, after all, only little boys, must have amounted to a significant threat to his own system of beliefs. And therein, I think, lay the start of new freedoms. Not long ago I attended his silver anniversary of ordination. Although he has mellowed some, he is still hot for winning. He keeps six or seven irons in two or three fires. I'm not sure he can take a joke the way some people might want him to, but he remains a generous, motivated, spiritual human being. The other evening, on the phone, I was kidding him about never slowing down, and he said, "You know, Paul, there's a thin line between synergism and a diffusion of forces."

Father Constantine, Prefect of Discipline, was still hard as stone when he needed to be. In the spring of my fourth year, eight or ten of us began going outside after lights-out to sit on the fire escape. We sat around every night for maybe forty-five minutes, smoking, breaking Major Silence. Eventually the prefect caught up to us. He got mad out of all proportion, I thought, slapping the lot of us on indefinite jug. He was a hard man to figure out. A year later, when my Kentucky grandfather died and I asked permission to attend the funeral, Father Constantine was not only insistent I go, he personally arranged it, getting up in the middle of the night to wake me and drive me to the train depot. On the platform he pushed another ten bucks at me. "You may need it, gent," he said. I did, too: on the way home, between planes in Washington, I went to see *To Kill a Mockingbird* and afterward had a steak dinner and a bottle of beer. It was a gray winter Sunday in Washington, but I rode around the city on buses feeling like the prince of freedom.

I was still trying to solve emotional conflicts with overly intellectual defenses. And when I didn't do that, I hid it all, even from myself. At one point I hurt my back seriously and had to go into town for electric shock impulses. I had ripped several muscles while playing handball, but the damn thing was, nothing *looked* wrong with me. Nothing was swollen, nothing was black and blue; I just couldn't walk straight. When my walk straightened out, but my back still hurt, I asked the prefect to exempt me from waiter duty and the dishes crew. Roger Recktenwald, for one, ragged me about my "fake injury." I got to where I was afraid to mention it because I knew nobody believed me. The system had taught us not to be needy, not to be different: Grin and bear it. Once, I remember Father Shaun saying, "Hendrickson, you've got too much human respect." What he meant was that I cared too much about what the others thought about me. I craved to be thought "regular."

The seminary was institutionalizing itself. At Holy Trinity a boy's folks could come as often as they wished and stay as long as they cared. Two guest houses had been built at Holy Trinity to house seminarians' families, who were thought to be the Order's most generous benefactors: they had given a son. But in Virginia, in a school built to house 220, such open-door policies for guests were no longer realistic. Now there were specially designated weekends three or four times a year for family visits. The families had to stay in town at the Thomas Motel, or at the Ramada, and come out to the seminary between ten and five. At five a bell rang; it was time for the visitors to clear out. One pickup meal a day was provided whereas before parents had their own private dining room.

And what else was institutionalizing itself, I think, was my old dream of priesthood. The dream was becoming more sober, less wildly glamorous. A distance of space as well as time was making its way in me, though I could barely chart it. I remember Father Benedict's saying once, on a Day of Recollection: "Some boys have a vocation just to come to the seminary." I had never heard anything like this before. Another time I remember him saying: "The reasons you came are not the reasons you stay."

In 1964 my classmates and I began preparing ourselves for our twelve months of novitiate. We would be leaving Father Judge Mission Seminary and returning to Holy Trinity for a special year of prayer and testing. Our class was down to fourteen seminarians. We had picked up two or three seminarians who had come into our class from the outside, which meant there were about ten "originals." As part of the requirements for admission to the novitiate, each of us had to undergo a number of hours of psychological testing and a visit to a psychiatrist. When it came time for my turn in town at the Shrink, I found myself terrified. In his office I could barely make my tongue work. He asked me what in the world was wrong. I said that I was afraid my written tests had revealed something terrible about me. I said it and laughed. "But you did great on these tests," he said, motioning toward a sheaf of papers spread out on his lap. "Didn't you know?" He took up a paper that he said contained basic biographical information as well as evaluations of me by the seminary faculty. "Born in Fresno, California, eh?" he said, trying to get me to say something. "Yes," I shot out. "And I've never been there, either." (What I meant was that my parents had moved on to another air base when I was a month or two old.) He peered over his glasses in his khaki suit.

On my last night in Virginia, I won the *Virtus et Scientia*. It was the school's single highest prize, a kind of Nobel, and they gave it out once a year to the sixth-year seminarian going on to his novitiate who most seemed to embody the ideals of Thomas Judge. The selection was by faculty ballot, and the winner's name was kept secret up until presentation. Father Vincent, as Dean of Studies, made the award on stage in the gym. We were seated behind him, under blue cutout numerals that announced: 1964. I felt any chance I had for the prize was slim, and that Dick Hennessey, who easily had the best mind of us, would surely get it. Father Vincent gave a little speech and then announced my name, turning forty-five degrees toward me and calling me, "Mister Father Judge Mission Seminary, 1964." The place was clapping; people were on their feet. I was proud to get the award, of course, but I was insanely proud that the Old Roman Himself had made the presentation and chosen to call me that. It was as if I had pleased my old man for the whole world to see. It was as if Father Vincent had invited me at last to come forward and sit in a wing chair at the head of some immense table.

Thirteen months later, thirty pounds lighter, anxiety-ridden, I would be gone from the seminary, a vocation vanished. It might have been predicted: the *Virtus et Scientia*, which stands for Valor and Knowledge, seemed to carry a strange jinx. Almost everyone who ever got it ended up leaving not long afterward. Dick Hennessey, who was not an "original" in our seminary class, persevered. In fact, he followed in the Old Roman's footsteps, becoming a patristics and Latin and Greek scholar.

On June 26, 1964, after I had been home in Illinois for several weeks, a letter came to me from the Custodian General of the Order. The letter said: "I am happy to inform you that our General Council has approved your acceptance into the Postulancy. You are to report to Holy Ghost Novitiate, Holy Trinity, Alabama, on Friday, July 24, 1964. This is another step forward in your vocation to the religious life and the missionary priesthood. It is a step which will demand of you a growth in spiritual maturity, and in the virtues which must characterize your whole future as a Missionary Servant. It will call for generosity and a firm sense of commitment to God. But each day will bring you new strength and joy, for you will be sustained by God's loving grace if you ask for it humbly and cooperate with it with fortitude and wisdom."

The Goodbye

———

By 1965 the world, even the narrow one I dwelt in, was
different. And so was I. I was seven years older, for one
thing, a man-child.

I SEE NOW I should have packed up and gotten the hell out
of the seminary within weeks of my entering novitiate in the
summer of 1964, but instead I stayed around for thirteen
months, dropping pounds and confidence nearly by the
week. There is a word of Greek origin, used in monastic life,
which may fit here—*accidie*. It refers to the mental prostra-
tion of recluses induced by fasting and other physical causes.
An *accidie,* a spiritual numbness, an intellectual immobility, a
kind of blazing noonday devil, had seemed to overtake me in
that final year, lodge in my bones. I was forever examining
my conscience for confession. In the end I got over my *accidie,* and out of the seminary, because my bowels seemed to
have razor blades in them. I was always on a toilet, and with
no results. A doctor told me that no amount of medicine he
prescribed would make me well until I could make up my
mind whether I wished to be a priest or not. Finally I went
home to get away from my pain.

If it is true, as some psychologists think, that we move in
the direction of our currently dominant thought, then it was
inevitable I should have left in my seventh year, for all I could
seem to fix on then was me, my problems, my vocation. A
poet has put the neurosis hauntingly: that which we fear the

most we bring upon ourselves. Losing my vocation, the "it," was the thing I feared most. Whatever it was that had pulsed me toward priesthood for six years suddenly, in my seventh, seemed gone, missing without a trace.

For years after I was gone, I blamed my leaving on the Master of Novices. I am not saying now that Father Declan was blameless, far from it; only I may have it a little more in context now. Father Declan's proper title wasn't Master of Novices for nothing. You had to have his permission to write a letter. (In the novitiate we were permitted to write home once a month, that's all.) You had to have his permission to get two aspirin, or a new safety razor, or a bar of soap, from the drug closet. In the minor seminary there was always a number of Christ figures to fear and care for; you could play one strength off another. But in the novitiate there was but one link to reality: the Master of Novices. Novices were kept strictly segregated from the rest of the Order. You had to have the Master's permission to say more than hello to another priest or brother in the community. Father Declan's job was to train us rigorously in the ways of poverty, chastity, and obedience, and in the hands of a madman such mind control could have been awesome. By the time I reached novitiate, Father Declan had been at his post for nearly a quarter of a century. He was the only Trinitarian novice master of any permanence the Order had ever had. I see now it was a cruel thing to leave a man in so intense a position for so long, and they must have done it because this man had been so Christly good at it. But we have histories of sin, and we have histories of grace. There is darkness in the light. Maybe the novice master had simply been at his post too long; an inertia had taken over. In the end something was terribly wrong, with him and with me. As it turned out, our class was the last to have him as Master of Novices. Within weeks after I left, he was reassigned to the missions. He wrote to me himself with the news. That is another of the small mysteries: once I got free of his control, he could only be kind, solicitous. I received several warm letters from him that summer after I went home, when I was fighting with my father and trying to find a university to take me at such a late date. *Why now?* I wondered.

There are novitiate stories of seeming paranoia, of incredible petty meanness, of favoritism, of slamming people into the claustrophobic box of the four "humors," that I suppose could be told here. The novice master believed that any human being on God's earth could be understood as a combination of one or more of the four medieval temperaments: sanguine, melancholy, phlegmatic, and choleric. Part of one's novitiate year was learning the temperaments. Father Declan lectured on them in the classroom; we took notes. He was known for being able to spot what you were, find your "major" and "minor," within twenty-four hours of your arrival to begin the novitiate year. He had me down as a "melancholy-sanguine," which means, I suppose, that I mostly saw the hole of life, though occasionally I could see the doughnut. "Here comes Brother Garret, the little Mel," he'd say, abbreviating melancholy, raising it to a vocation. He spoke with a kind of head-clucking Jersey Irish brogue and liked to sit with us outside during evening colloquy with his hands sheathed in his armpits. He was approaching fifty then and had a growing paunch and looked like a Hollywood version of an Irish country pastor. His face could go deep shades of red when he was suppressing his laughter after he had lightly humiliated you. "Let the Brothers have cigarettes, tet tet," he'd say, as if in a Socratic dialogue with himself, giving us permission to smoke. He was a riveting storyteller, and when he shined his beacon on you during the story, there was nothing like it. He seemed to me as evil as he was saintly and comic and profound in the ways of religious life. Years later, reading *All the King's Men* and Robert Penn Warren's brilliant creation of Willie Stark, the despotic and benevolent Louisiana tyrant, I could only picture Father Declan. As to the temperaments, my classmates could shrug off these crude categorizations, could see them in some way as part of the testing, but I could only seethe inwardly at being fitted into the Master's humors box. I remember saying to a classmate named Bob Doud, who had recently joined our class: "This life is a valley of tears and thorns." I must have said it with some conviction, for Doud shook his head. "Maybe you should get off," he said. We were washing dishes.

Novices were permitted to talk twice a day, at a thirty-minute colloquy after lunch and at another after supper. The rest of the day and night belonged to Major and Minor Silence. Major Silence began after the last hours of the Divine Office, while we stood in chapel and swayed through choruses of *O clemens, O pia.* Oh, merciful, oh, upright. This silence lasted until after breakfast, when the Minor Silence began. Breaking Minor Silence was never as sinful as disturbing the mercy and piety of the night.

Midway through my novitiate year something alarming began to take place. Father Declan came in and accused someone from the class of sneaking into his bedroom when he wasn't there and shifting his clothes and books and personal mementos around. This accusation went on for weeks, his increasing anger and frustration, our bewilderment. Who would be crazy enough to do something like this, we all wondered. The man must be dreaming. Was he trying to turn us against one another, place a Judas among us? If it was a test, he seemed to be carrying it to the hilt. I began to feel isolated by my fear and paranoia. Once, lathered to a fury, the Master came in and held up the Blessed Sacrament and swore by his hand and the power invested in him by the Order's constitutions that he was hereby declaring the culprit's profession of vows to be invalid. You can profess the vows, he screamed, but I announce here and now that they will be invalid. He was awful-faced.

A day or two later Geoff Mischler and I were painting the outside of the refectory. We were working from scaffolding and stood about ten feet apart. It was the Minor Silence, and for once I was keeping it. I had been too upset by the events of the day before. The Master came up the lane from collecting the mail at Sister Basil's post office. I could see him coming from perhaps one hundred yards and turned around to watch him come. When he got close, he said, "Forewarned is forearmed, eh, Brother Garret?" I didn't know what he meant. "I saw you breaking the Silence," he said. I protested that I wasn't. "Now you've got two sins to confess at Chapter of Faults," he said. Chapter of Faults was our weekly public confession. You raised your arms in chapel and told your fellow novices and the Master what infractions of the Rule you were guilty of in the past seven days. At the Chapter, I refused to confess it.

Not too much later I began going into town to see a stomach doctor. The Master had given me permission to go, but once, an hour before I left, he acted out for the benefit of my classmates a little sketch of a person in severe stomach pain. He pretended he was the ulcer and went burrowing and digging through an imaginary stomach lining. His laughter was deep and red and evil.

One of my jobs in novitiate was digging a crawl space beneath the chapel for the termite man. The old building had begun badly to deteriorate, and Father Declan had assigned Bertin Glennon and me to go down under the chapel with pickaxes and shovels and tunnel a hole wide enough so that a man could get from the front to the back with his spray equipment. Bertin and I spent a month down there in that sweltering podzolic soil. Every few hours another novice would bring us iced water in a tin can and we would gulp it dry. I felt like a miner tunneling my way out of religious life.

No matter how awful that year was simply because of the novice master, I think I can see now that had he shown me only sweetness and light, it still probably would not have made any difference in the ultimate outcome. It probably would have just prolonged the inevitable, and in this sense Father Declan did me a favor. I have begun to think lately that it may be time for some healing. In all the research I have done for this book, in all the miles I have traveled to ask the same, repetitive, unanswerable questions, I have never gone to see Father Declan. And I know right where he is. He is less than a two-hour drive from where I write this morning. I guess I feel there is nothing to say, although probably there is much. I suspect that he is an old man in a dry season and that both of us could use the talk. Maybe I'll go tomorrow.

Those last weeks and months of my novitiate seem to me now like an emulsion in my brain on which are suspended millions of shimmering light-sensitive crystals. In early July of 1965, I went into town again to see Dr. Brokerman. I had been to him three or four times since January, and each time he had given me another bottle of chalky green liquid that dried instantly, like miracle paint, on my lips and tongue, but did almost nothing for my aching bowels. This time I drove myself in, in Father Declan's car. In seven weeks I was due to profess the three vows of poverty, chastity, and obedience, and would then go back up North with my classmates, a full-fledged religious, to begin my philosophy studies. On the scale in Dr. Brokerman's office my weight was down to one hundred and thirty-five pounds. The doctor, not gentle but skilled, pushed me flat on the examining table. "Now I'm going to put you to bed out there at that seminary school for a week solid and not let you leave your cell, Brother Garret," he said, almost angrily, and I had jumped a little at the word "cell," though that is a word common enough in religious life. He led me to another room, told me to get into a gown, came back, had a nurse assist him while he inserted a hose in my rectum. He doused the lights, pulled some machinery down from the ceiling, began taking pictures of my lower intestine. Except to tell me when to turn and when I could or could not breathe, he didn't speak. My stomach was hurting fiercely, but even worse, I wanted to jerk the hose from me and fling it at him. Cold air was shooting up the gown on the steel table. None of this was going to do any good. I felt ridiculous. Maybe I'll take the Master's car and instead of going back to the seminary I'll drive down to Florida, lie on the beach in Panama City, I remember thinking. I did nothing of the sort. I lay still. That night the doctor called Father Declan to talk about me, and a few days later I was on a Trailways bus to Canton, Mississippi, to one of the Order's missions. Dr. Brokerman had ordered me to get away from the novitiate for a week.

In Canton, Mississippi, in the summer of 1965, American blacks were struggling for their civil rights. A few months earlier the battle of Selma, Alabama, had been joined at the Edmund Pettus Bridge. CBS film crews had come to Canton that July for the integration of the town swimming pool. In Canton I met a muscled young black man from the mission who told me he was ready to die for his freedom. His name was Junior Chin and he came from a family of civil rights activists. Junior could not have been more than a year or two older than I was; he was married, with a child. He was a deep believer in God, he said. He had been trained in the North in the ways of nonviolence. Meeting Junior and his wife, seeing this strange other world, standing at the fringe of the swimming pool one evening and listening to choruses of "We Shall Overcome" must have released something in me, popped it, like a tear of sweat breaking at your lip. At the end of the week I rode the bus back to Holy Trinity and told Father Declan I had made up my mind to leave, and this time he did not resist. "You may go, Brother," he said.

The next afternoon I got Father Declan's permission to call Illinois and break the news. As I dialed I begged the ceiling my father wasn't on a flight and that he would pick up the phone. He did. He said he had been in the garage working on a mower, and I could picture him wiping his hands on a rag, holding the phone in the crook of his neck, filmy with perspiration. I had tried to put clues in several of my recent letters home about my stomach problems, about the craziness of novitiate. I had not been able to say directly what I was so bothered about, and I wondered now if my parents had picked up my distress signals. I worked to keep a steady voice. I said I was coming home. "Yeah, boy," my father said, which, for him, has always been the highest term of affection. I said I was worried about Mom. "I'll tell her, son. You come on home; we'll be here," he said. I have always been grateful for that response, and yet I don't think I was in the house an hour, two days later, when my father and I were yelling at each other. "What do you mean, you may go back?" he said with disgust. "It's over, Paul. Can't you see that? Get on with something else." He couldn't stand hearing me say it was possible I had made a mistake and that I might reapply for admission the next year. My father seldom left doors ajar, at least then. Before that summer was out, I was fighting with him weekly, and once nearly with my fists, and after this he could say bitterly to my mother that over his dead soul would another child of his go off to a seminary or convent school at fourteen. My little brother Mark, the last of four sons, and my only sister, Jeannie, were coming up. I think he was worried.

Holy Trinity had been an encounter with God, but that was over now. I think I moved through those last hours as though through mayonnaise. I packed, dressed, told Roger and Bertin and the others goodbye, made a visit to chapel. I hung on one knee just inside the door and prayed to find my way. I got into Father Declan's station wagon. He was going to drive me to the train himself. We rode most of the twenty-three miles in silence. At the depot there was a hard half-hour to kill. Finally I was on the train, in my seat, looking through smudged glass at my former novice master. The train lurched north, toward home.

I have a photograph of myself taken a few weeks after I got home. I am all buzz-headed bug-eyed Adam's apple. My wife says I looked like an escapee from Dachau. When I got home to Illinois my brother Eric, then in high school, held up my clerical clothes the way one might hold up a dead skunk. My father gave me forty dollars and told me to go get some normal clothes. I went into Gaede's in Wheaton and bought a loud shirt and a louder tie and a pair of canary-yellow slacks. I still thought white socks were cool and bought several new pairs. Within weeks of getting out, my stomach began to settle down, although it was years before a doctor would take me off Librium and Donnatal. My gut still jumps now and then and I suppose always will.

Redux

I've been up and down and round and round and back
   again
I've been so many places I can't remember where or
   when.

> —Jim Croce,
>   from the song "Age"

We shall not cease from exploration
And the end of all our exploring
Will be to arrive where we started
And know the place for the first time.

> —T. S. Eliot,
>   from *Four Quartets*

A man can claim to be going somewhere only if he has
   come from somewhere.

> —Daniel Berrigan

Those who believe that they believe in God, but without
passion in their hearts, without anguish in mind,
without uncertainty, without doubt, without an element
of despair even in their consolation, believe only in the
God idea, not God Himself.

> —Unamuno,
>   Spanish philosopher
>   and writer

BETWEEN THE ANGER and the torpor, the tune began to slip back in. Somewhere in the mid-seventies I found myself sliding into the last pew of churches when I was out on the road reporting a story for a newspaper or a magazine. I found myself picking up a spiritual book here and there in a bookstore. I found myself wondering what had become of my old schoolmates, my old Christ figures, nearly all of whom I had long lost touch with. There was a void in my life, like a narrow grave.

After I got out of the seminary in 1965, I enrolled in a Jesuit university in St. Louis. I had wanted badly to go to Notre Dame, but the admissions office said I was too late. I remember the night I arrived in St. Louis: the university was holding an outdoor dance. Several thousand undergraduates were writhing a limp night away while loudspeakers blasted over and over the Rolling Stones singing, "I can't get no . . . I can't get no SAT-is-FAC-tion." I had barely heard of the Rolling Stones. I had never heard the song.

There were about three thousand undergraduate women in the school; eventually I began to feel as though I were in a candy store. I was hampered only by my impecuniousness. Girls would say, "But you're so fresh." They didn't mean I was forward. They meant I was behaving like someone who had never held hands before, never paid two admissions to a movie.

Four years went by, and I grew a little, finished graduate school, and fell in love and got married. I was twenty-five in the fall of 1969, chronologically old enough for what I was undertaking, though not much qualified otherwise.

Jane Sunday Barbagallo, at eighteen, had fallen in love with the graduate teaching assistant at Penn State (he had fudged to her at first on his religious past), and vice versa, and both of us were too smitten and immature to see it couldn't possibly work. I was still a technical virgin and knew next to nothing about sexual intimacy. On the night of the day we were married, we drove to Kennedy airport in New York and took a gaudy hotel room. (We were on our way to Bermuda.) We tried to have intercourse, but it was like a segment from a Woody Allen movie.

Ten years later, in the spring of 1979, a decade of newspaper jobs and gritty cities behind me (Detroit, Indianapolis, *et al.*) I got married again, this time to Cecilia Regina Moffatt. We had the ceremony in the parlor of some friends' place in Washington. Fifty people attended, including my ex-wife. We hired a harpist and had the invitations hand-lettered. A priest friend from the seminary was supposed to come but didn't. The Jesuit we asked to officiate wore a stole and an alb, though not a chasuble. He didn't say a Mass but offered instead a Eucharistic liturgy. Ceil and I passed out communion and paid for our own food at the party. The parlor belonged to a female Episcopal priest, and so we asked her to give a blessing. Afterward my father came up and said he was impressed with the simplicity of our wedding, although he had been unfamiliar with the "liturgy." That night Ceil and I and some friends from out of town sat on stools in a bar on Capitol Hill near our apartment and toasted our good fortune.

Ten years elapsed between the first time I got married, in 1969, in a lavish in-law production on the Main Line outside Philadelphia, and the second time, in 1979, in a do-it-yourself, less-is-more approach. I don't think a sanity could have come any sooner. I blink and those ten years are gone. It is no little startling irony to me that the Irish Catholic colleen who became my second wife has her own small connection to Thomas Judge and the Order he founded: Ceil's grandmother on her father's side held an ordination breakfast in her home one day in 1899, in Germantown, Pennsylvania. The guest of honor that morning was a tubercular newly ordained Vincentian—Thomas Judge. I discovered this only a year ago.

Ten years slipped by between the first and second times I tried marriage. In that same period, between '69 and '79, while an inquisitive, semi-disheveled, double-knitted former divinity student sought to find his secular legs, the faith I had grown up in as an altar boy, and pretty much forsaken as a man, seemed to transmogrify itself, permute from the inside. The boat—the one I'm in, and the one my Church is in, and the one my old religious Order is in—seems to be righting itself now, though in distinctly new waters.

And encounters with God go on, in one form or another. Last week I got on an airplane and flew to Ohio and then rented a car and drove to Greene County. I wanted to visit the spot where my infant brother and most of my maternal forebears lay. St. Brigid's Cemetery, out Second Street on the edge of Xenia, Ohio, is a lyrical little spot with leaning fence posts and a gravel lane parting its middle. Firs and maples shade modest stones. My great-great grandfather John Kyne lies here. John Kyne, who fled the dark hole of the Irish potato famine in the middle of the last century, is my earliest ancestor in the New World. He lived to be an old coot of eighty-eight and shake his stick at the new century. He sold an acre here, he bought five there, and when he died, in 1912, he had amassed a small fortune and a big family and seven hundred acres of prime Ohio farmland. John Kyne and his son Bill Kyne and Bill Kyne's son Bernie Kyne and Bernie Kyne's wife—whom I could always call only Nonna— all lie in a graveyard out Second Street in Xenia, Ohio, and so also does my own dead brother, whom I never knew, Baby David Hendrickson. David Hendrickson's stone is flat to the ground and probably about the size of the box that brought him to Ohio from Illinois on the back seat of a Chevrolet piloted by my rueful twenty-nine-year-old father one whitened winter day in 1948. The stone says simply:

Infant
David Hendrickson
January 6, 1948

I drove into the cemetery and stood over my brother's marker. It was a few days before Thanksgiving and the air was cold and keen. I don't quite know what I was expecting. Lightning, maybe? An encounter with God? No lightning came. Xenia winked on. The grass in the graveyard felt spongy beneath my shoes, and I could see that one end of David's stone had buckled up under the earth's softness. I didn't feel sad, particularly. I didn't feel like crying. I had never even known this person whose remains were beneath my feet. I wasn't sure what I felt, or what I should be feeling, though there may have been a small peace, a belief, or at least hope, that suffering can be redeemed. My religious experience, I know now, was a gift, and a gift is not something you are entitled to. My gift came early, and maybe a winter night in 1948 and a brother I never knew had something to do with it. And maybe not. Maybe someday, with a child of my own,

I will understand my own childhood more fully. For now, I must try to love the questions themselves, as the poet Rilke said. In truth, I barely got to experience my gift. Had I stayed on in religious life another six or seven years, I might have gained an entirely different perspective. But I must work with the gift I received. I am grateful to have gotten it.

I still don't know all the reasons why I left the seminary, although I think it had to do with killing off something you love so that one day you might love it again, properly. It also had to do, I suppose, with wanting to get laid, although that was a lesser reason than a secular world wants to believe. But in a sense none of that is important. What is important is knowing what I got out of the seminary experience, knowing what kind of human being it helped fashion me into. I think I see now, standing at the probable midpoint of my life, that leaving the seminary was the most positive moment of an overall positive experience, even if the leaving had to be accompanied by the kind of pain with which I imagine a pro athlete must put away a game he has loved deeply and just as deeply raged against. He must put it away because of age or erosion of skills or change in the rules or some other confluence of causes over which he has not always had control or in which he has not even played the dominant role.

What I think I got out of the seminary was a moral framework upon which to build the rest of a life. There was far too much protection; we were far too isolated. But there were joys in that ghetto. There were deep mysteries. There were camaraderies and values of a transcendent nature that I doubt a "value-free" Self-oriented, Rolfed, est-ed society could ever understand. If we are a record of whom we have loved and those who have loved us, then I think I am a lucky man indeed.

Sometimes I think that all of us who went to the seminary could be defined not so much by what we've done as by what we remember. There is much to remember. The priests who taught us were just people doing the best they could. They taught us, by indirection, that the true value is not what you produce but who you are; that the real goal is not so much to do as to be. It took a while to see that.

I remember sitting in a bar in California one night with Eddie Murphy. Eddie was the kind of scrapping guard on our basketball team I always wanted to be. He had just gotten divorced when I talked with him; he was feeling guilt, especially where his daughters were concerned. He told me that whenever he goes to a bar nowadays and tries to meet a woman, he is nearly always successful—at first. "Then about twenty minutes later I want to start talking serious with her, about philosophy or some goddamn thing." He laughed at himself. He said that he feels he can figure out people in a wink, get to their essences, but that this somehow never stops him from botching relationships. Maybe it's *why* he botches them. He leaned close. "Tell me, do you think you're better than other people?" I laughed and nodded and let it go with a "Sometimes." "I think it's because we've seen some things from the inside, or think we have," he said.

What happened in my seminary, even as it was happening in the outer world, was a huge shift. It was, as a friend of mine said later, a shift no could control, or even understand. A vast and secure and seemingly immobile landscape had altered all at once, almost too subtly to see, and we were all left standing in different spots. My seminary and my Order were caught in the middle of the shift, and in that sense you could say we were trapped by history. Also, with my particular religious group, there may have been a little too much gain too soon. In this the Trinitarians are not unlike America herself, I think. A charism seemed to go away, at least for a time, although this is only the view from arrogant hindsight.

I wonder if men like Vincent Fitzpatrick ever wanted to leave Alabama. Father Vincent could marvel at the new plant up in Virginia, I'm sure, its architectural wholeness and esthetic beauties, but I wonder if he didn't instinctively sense, long before we moved up there, the tyranny of big buildings and new money. The fundamental paradox of my old Order is that just at the point when it became more visible in the Church, more financially secure, less outlaw and outrider, its seminarians and men in vows and even its ordained members began jumping from the boat in alarming numbers. And Vincent Fitzpatrick, the animus, the Tiger, the Old Roman, went alone one day to the splendid new seminary chapel, stood there in a pool of amber filtered light beneath the seventy-five-foot-high gold dome and the specially commissioned stained glass and the Aegean-blue mosaic pillars from Italy and said: "O Lord, why are You rejecting our prayers of stone?" He wasn't a poet, but that is a poet's plea.

It is nearly immaterial to me now whether an ecumenical council or an encyclical on birth control really caused the Church's general disarray a decade and a half ago. That is a question academics and historians can fight out. It will take another half-generation to know, I suspect. Then the little men with the calculators and heavy glasses can come along to tell us what happened. Some will insist it was Pope John's council, that well-meaning attempt at modernization and liberalization, the *aggiornamento*, as it was called back then. Another theory holds that it was really the encyclical on birth control that did in the Church. It is ironic to me that what may have been the biggest swamper of all was not a wave of change but of nonchange, a reaffirmation of an old bankrupt Church status quo: contraception is a mortal sin. In 1966, before the encyclical, the resignation rate of priests in America was practically nil—one half of one percent. In the two years following the encyclical ban on birth control, 1969 and 1970, 3.6 percent of diocesan priests and 5.2 percent of religious order priests in the country departed the rectory and mission. In a book called the *Anatomy of Revolution,* author Crane Brinton pointed out that revolutions usually occur not so much during a time of no change as during a period when changes are coming rapidly and institutions aren't keeping up with the expanding expectations. In some ways I think a blurring of generational time helps explain what happened in this country and in the Catholic Church in the curtain years of the sixties and into the first years of the seventies. Things were simply going too fast, though for some others they weren't going fast enough. It was a runaway school bus, to use Roger Recktenwald's vivid image. The kids were hollering out the window and there wasn't any driver. What was happening in my religious Order and in the rest of the Church was only one wave behind (and sometimes it seemed simultaneous with) what was going on in America as a whole —in Grant Park in Chicago, on the campus of Kent State, and elsewhere. The sixties began, some people have said, on November 23, 1963, with the assassination of John F. Kennedy, and came to a close on August 9, 1974, with the resignation of Richard Nixon, and in between, in the psychic shocks and aftershocks produced by rifle fire on a Memphis motel balcony, on that greensward in Kent, Ohio, a faith in a rational order seemed lost, or at least badly shaken. You can still hear the requiems meandering from the yellowed pages of 1968 calendars, for that was the year that raged and still rages in the imagination. An angry mob whose age was hard to fix roamed in the secular city. There was another indeterminate mob loose in the spiritual city, too, although not so violent or celebrated. This mob was in revolt against things like papal authority, birth control bans, celibacy. At the rise of the sixties the secular city had JFK, the spiritual city John XXIII. As Gary Wills, in his eloquent book *Bare Ruined Choirs,* put it in a description that cannot be bettered: "Under one John professors went to Washington and created the new frontier. Under another, enlightened young theologians went to Rome and created Vatican Two." But the groundwork for future shock, for euphoria and subsequent dismay, had been earlier laid, I think—in the somnabulistic fifties. It now seems clear that Pope John's Vatican Two was merely accelerating, legitimizing, changes that had begun a decade and more earlier. Pope John's council let a secret out of the bag: that a church can change, that a church *has* to change. On that humid, cloudy day in 1963 when they buried Pope John, the *pontifex maximus,* the chunky little visionary who had humbly begun a revolution, the crowds streamed and teemed, far out into the Via del Conciliziaone. John XXIII had wrought something in his brief tenure as the Holy Father which his successor, Paul VI, a pontiff in chains, would not know how to contain. A brush fire that is beaten out in one corner will start in another.

In the past several years, as I have roamed the country looking for answers to deep mysteries, I have stopped often to see my old friend and classmate Bertin Glennon, shepherd of St. Ann's in Manchester, Kentucky. The way you do it is catch a plane to Lexington, get a car, get onto Interstate 75, go past the rich bluegrass horse farms, get onto the Daniel Boone Parkway, and then make your way into the darkening Cumberland coalfields and Appalachian dreams of eastern

Kentucky. There are several dozen Trinitarians from my years in the seminary whom I know well and who remain in their vows, but Bertin Glennon, the once and future roly-poly kid on a train platform in 1958, is the only one of the boys of priesthood who endured. Bertin has special priestly status for me. All the rest of us from the class of '58, at least those of us who were "originals," are gone. It is the mystery of Bertin's commitment, I suppose, that keeps drawing me back to Clay County, as if one last visit will crack the code of why he remains a priest. There are times when I wish to hell he would get out of the priesthood. That would box it up, so to speak. And there are other times when I want to grab Bertin by the pocket watch umbilicaled to the chain in his belt loop and get him to promise me, swear to me, he'll never go. What I invariably end up feeling after an overnight or two with Bertin is a buoyance, not a sense of romantic doom.

The last time I went down to Kentucky, Bertin was still Manchester's priest, but the bishop of Covington had lately put him in charge of one of the diocese's deaneries, which means he is an overseer of other priests in the diocese. And beyond that, his empire had widened to include a satellite mission down in Barbourville in the next county. "Hell, Paul, I'm planning to be Pope," Bertin cackled to me on the phone. Bertin had two nuns and three college-age kids working and living with him this time. I watched the padre in his hulky black V-neck sweater, sitting at the head of supper in the rectory, barking orders, jamming up his glasses with his index finger, presiding over a chaos of fried chicken and green beans with fatback. There were also mashed potatoes and pizza on the table. (Bertin had had a craving for pizza that night and ordered out.) It might have been a scene from a clerical version of *Life with Father*. It might have been one of Father Brendan Smith's old "entertainments" from the seminary. Bertin kept barking orders, and the nuns and three volunteers kept ignoring them. That evening I heard Bertin tell an elderly lady who had come for a religious education class: "There's something about seeing you people believe that makes me want to keep on being a priest. That's why we stay. There aren't any other reasons." Afterward Bertin and I sat dopey for a little while in front of the television.

There is a lever on the side of Bert's recliner rocker, and he operated it as if he were in an earthmover. We watched the news and turned in.

For all the torpor one hears of nowadays, for all the dreary downward statistics about the ability of traditional religion to give meaning and structure to our lives, America nonetheless seems a spiritually hungry place to me. In point of fact, the overall national decline in church/synagogue attendance in America has been arrested, pollsters say. They began picking up something toward the end of the seventies, blips on the radar screen. There were signs, albeit shadowy and contradictory, of a "new flowering" (Gallup), of disenchantment with the self-absorption ethic (Yankelovich), of a return to Church of Catholics in their thirties, particularly those who had attended a college and were of Irish descent (National Opinion Research Center). Maybe it was a "life cycle" phenomenon. Maybe it was generational. Maybe it was just spiritual longing. America was feeling dry-mouthed and empty, the magazine writers said. There was a search out there, not for dogma but for some reason to have belief at all. That was a description of me.

More than a year ago, on a placid summer morning in 1981, I sat in a spare Unitarian church on Lexington Avenue in New York City and witnessed the marriage of my first wife to a George Becker. Ceil, my bride of two years, sat beside me. Ceil was studying a hymnal. She began to giggle. She nudged me. She pointed to the last page of the hymnal in which there was printed up, for the faithful's quick reference, A Gender Sensitive Guide to Hymns for the Celebration of Life. Someone had taken the time to break the hymnal into convenient categories: "Hymns without gender problems"; "Hymns in which the only problem is the personification of a natural object or abstract idea"; "Hymns in which the only problem is reference to God as Lord"; "Hymns in which the masculine reference is obvious because it refers to Jesus."

"We've come to this," whispered Ceil, sighing. My wife is a levelheaded and modern woman who nonetheless knows how to giggle at the sublime when it sounds absurd.

At the reception—in Little Italy, around the corner from the clam house where Joey Gallo got it with a spray of bullets —my former mother-in-law came up to talk and meet Ceil.

Mrs. Barbagallo and I have buried the Tommy gun at last. "It just wasn't in God's plans," she said. "I don't try to understand these things anymore. It just wasn't in God's plans."

Two months previous to that day, on another sunny morning in 1981, I went up to Philadelphia to participate in a meeting of some old friends and priests from the seminary. Seven or eight of us had gotten together to try to determine the answer to a tricky question: Where and how do we still experience a need for one another? Periodic reunions are not the answer, we know. "Reunion" smacks of club ties and frat paddles, of that championship season. We had had something deeper, more equivocal, than that. We talked that day of the possibility of holding regional annual get-togethers, with a liturgy as the focus. All those who believed, and those who didn't, would be welcome. The emphasis would be on shared values, on preserving the threads of a common past. Father Vincent Fitzpatrick, the Old Roman, was there that day. (He opened with a shaky prayer and chiseled notes on a tablet before him.) Father Brendan, my old literature prof and play director, was there. (He dangled an ash and tried to collate mimeographed papers held between his knees.) Father Shaun, my old debate coach, came. Jim Thessin, a Harvard-educated lawyer who was several years behind me, showed up. And so did three former priests from the Order, all of whom had resigned their vows under particular moments of stress and conscience. All three sat together on a sofa, like bulky brothers home for Thanksgiving. Each was married, working for the bread. One of the three, Gus Fagan, runs a sheltered workshop for the retarded in Virginia. Another, Maury Flood, helps build housing for low-income families and retirees in Washington, D.C. The third, Jack Kenny, is a probation officer on Long Island. When I knew him his name was Father Claude, only we didn't much call him that. We called him Cadge. Cadge was a corruption of Cash, which had nothing to do with money but everything to do with attitude, with being *casual*. Maybe his casualness had something to do with his earlier life (he had entered late, after college and a stint in the Army), although I suspect it had more to do with his genes. The Cadge was a priest who had in focus the things that counted. You could tell it by his corrections: he didn't expect you to hang yourself for talking in line. And you could tell it from the way he sauntered down halls flipping at his cincture belt: he looked like a pro jock who had stuck on religious wear.

After he left the seminary faculty, Father Claude volunteered for a South American expedition. He went down to Colombia and Ecuador and met a nun from Canada and ended up falling in love. So he wrote an eloquent, ragged 3,500-word epistle to the Pope, typed by his own hand, with struck-over words and occasional lapses in grammar. "Maybe it is a dream too soon for its time," the Cadge said in his letter, petitioning to marry Phyllis and yet remain a priest who worked amid the poor in the barrios of Guayaquil, Ecuador. "I'm not a hero. I wonder, though, if our mutual love and hopes might be a sign of the times. The priest means well, but what do we know of the burdens of this life? I have found too many persons who have a narrow notion of sin: somehow, it's all sexual."

The Holy Father never wrote back. A friend who read the letter told Father Claude that it was a remarkable document which added up to a lousy petition and a great apologia. Later, planning to marry Phyllis anyway, he had written his twin brother trying to explain: "Love, life, God, and time are sometimes mitigating factors. Stay loose. I am." When he came back from South America with his new bride, a man at a personnel agency in New York said: "First off, Mr. Kenny, you've got to get rid of this do-gooder thing." And now Jack Kenny has two kids and a middle-line job and a folder of probation cases from Nassau County. The first time I went to see him he was worrying about a man who had beaten up his wife with a broom handle.

This day in 1981, Philadelphia, the Cadge had on a sweater with the sleeves jammed past the elbows. At fifty, his belly was tight. (In the seminary, isometrics were a constant text to his sermon on fitness.) Perhaps it was just my bias leaking, but I couldn't help thinking that each of these three former men of God, despite their mufti, was a dead ringer for a priest. Before the meeting was over, Jack Kenny said to the three other men in the room—Shaun, Vincent, Brendan— who didn't leave their vows back then: "Whether any of us wants to admit it or not, you're Church to us. You guys are the first endorsement of what I am."

Why, I have lately wondered, does my life seem to cut so sharp a pattern of exits and re-entries, sometimes when I least expect? I have heard others from the seminary ask this same thing. It is as if we were all destined to leave, on a spectrum from rage to loneliness to desperation, only to find ourselves returning again to old places in new skins, new masks. I remember something my old college prefect Father Ambrose, now Bob Benzing, X-ray equipment repairman, said in conjunction with this. We were talking about the distance of space and time most of us have seemed to come, and he said that he could remember journeying down to Washington years ago, when he was a boy, with his father. It was during World War II, and he and his father had come to visit his sister, Jane, who had joined the WAVES. They visited her at a hotel near Union Station, and years later, passing through Washington again, this time as a seminarian, Brother Ambrose found himself eating lunch in that same hotel. He said he could remember going on a motor trip through the South when he was a boy, stopping off at a church in Charlottesville, Virginia, to take pictures—only to find his once and future priestly self saying Mass there on weekends years later. His grandfather had stood with Grant at Appomattox; the grandson was to be missioned to a seminary faculty only miles from those silent fields. And now Bob Benzing, Father Ambrose no more, is married to a black woman and former nun, and the two are parents to two baby girls. "Sort of like wafting on the winds of providence, eh?" he said. "I don't know what it means, if indeed it means anything at all. It's just a pattern I see."

I remember something John O'Connell said: "It's a leap, Paul. You make it. I'm a great believer in the Lilies of the Field story. God takes care." John now teaches Latin at an academy in Texas. In the hallway of his home in Fort Worth, there is an enlarged framed photograph of John and his parents taken the day before his father died in his sleep of a blood clot. John's father and mother and little brother had been visiting at the seminary that weekend, and the picture was snapped, on the pool deck, toward the end of Sunday afternoon. Afterward John told his family goodbye and the O'Connells drove home to Kennett Square, Pennsylvania. Less than thirty-six hours later, his father was dead. Father

Constantine summoned him to tell him the news. "Brother Basil will take you to the plane in an hour," the prefect said. "But he can't be dead," John said. "I just saw him." On the flight home, the plane flapped viciously in the wind; the son could fix only on his own mortality.

For most of us, I think, leaving was like swimming straight out from shore. It was better not to look back. I think of Will Booth, FBI agent, deep believer, family man. We sat talking one January day in his office in downtown Jackson, Mississippi. Will weighs 240 pounds now, with a neck as big as a Saint Bernard's. He said he left the seminary, after ten years, on the morning he was supposed to profess his final vows. He had no idea where he was going; he just started swimming. They dropped him off in Washington, D.C. He called for a taxi, settled himself against a cracked leather seat, told the driver to take him out to the place where the Washington Redskins play football. He didn't know where that was. He got there as the team was about to begin a practice. He walked through a gate and down a tunnel and straight up to a man in a sweat shirt and a ball cap and a pair of cleats. "Excuse me, sir," Will Booth said in that soft, polite, earnest Vicksburg, Mississippi, voice that always sounded like breezes combing through tupelo trees. "Could I speak to you about a tryout?"

He didn't get a job playing pro football on his first day hatched from religious life, although he did land a four-year college basketball scholarship. (I found the coach who gave him the scholarship and asked if he remembered. "Hell, yes, I remember that boy," he said, coming alive. "Big strong kid with stone hands comes walking in the door one day like a dream. Not so agile, maybe, but immensely coachable. What ever happened to him?") And now, nineteen years later, Will Booth is a federal agent in Jackson, Mississippi, working bank robberies, kidnappings, fugitive cases, motorcycle gangs, white-collar scams run by syndicates out of Chicago. On the day I saw him, he sat behind a desk and rubbed a finger inside his shirt collar, and squashed cigarettes in a tray, and doodled on a legal pad and said this: "It's like the whole process, really. Maybe you're not afraid the way you are when you're facing a shootout. Maybe you're so scared when you go out there that you end up not being nervous. I guess you'd have to be going through it to really know. But anyway, I honestly feel the Lord did it for me."

What brought all of us together, I think, was a search for God. Sometimes I feel we are bonded to each other by strange nodes, mysterious fibers, chains of interlocking grace and paradox and reverie that run from a center I'm still trying to find. In a sense that is an idea stolen from Teilhard de Chardin, the great Jesuit scholar and humanist of this century. I can't prove this invisible network, this spiritual grid. But I feel it. Sometimes, too, I feel as though we've all lost something vague and indefinable in our lives, that something has been swept away. I am not speaking of our "vocation," exactly. I am not precisely sure, even now, what I am speaking of. But of this I feel sure: There is in us a certain longing for home, a spiritual discontinuity, which of course is what millions of other people who didn't go to a seminary also complain of. Only in our case it is complicated by guilt and strong religious overlay and the hard, literal fact that a home closed up. So Roger and Dick Ohrt and the Liteky brothers and I all bring along some old tutorial god, as yet unquiet.

I hadn't particularly planned it that way, but the last time I went down to Virginia to take a look at Father Judge Mission Seminary, which is now a Federal Job Corps Center, with pinball machines in what was once the priests' cloister, I found myself on the evening train out of Washington that we had always ridden in the seminary. It was a pleasant ride on a pleasant Saturday evening. Before I knew it I was there. Lynchburg, Virginia, was dark and quiet. On the platform waited a lone cabbie. I got in the back of his hack and asked about hotels, and he said the place I definitely wanted to be was the new Sheraton out on the highway because that was where the action was. On the ride out I asked if he knew the Reverend Jerry Falwell. In the years since my seminary closed, Lynchburg has become famous, or maybe notorious, as the home base of Falwell and the Moral Majority, a now nearly global enterprise that got started, if you believe legend, one Sunday morning in 1956 in the abandoned warehouse of a Lynchburg soft-drink bottling company. The Reverend Jerry Falwell was a twenty-two-year-old unknown preacher. The floor was sticky with Donald Duck Cola. The preacher extended his hands and prayed for the gift of the Spirit to enter. I said this to the man driving me out to the Sheraton, and he cut in: "You know you can lose a hack license in this town if you so much as have a beer can sitting on your front seat? Reverend Jerry, he wants his drivers clean, he wants this town clean."

The next morning the Reverend Rex Humbard, not Jerry Falwell, was witnessing from the Cathedral of Tomorrow on the television set in my room. I turned down the sound and went back to bed and lay there in silence with much on my mind. I was trying to figure out why Lynchburg generally and Father Judge Mission Seminary particularly have never seemed to attach themselves in my imagination the way Holy Trinity and Russell County always have. I have long wanted to care for the Virginia part of my seminary experience more than I seem able to, somehow. I don't have to try to like Holy Trinity. The place simply exists in my most deeply internalized daydreams. I see copper-red earth and piney woods and the pecan grove across the road and the clover coming up down at Red Level.

Rex Humbard was still preaching on the set in the Sheraton, and Jerry Falwell apparently was not going to come on, so I got up, snapped off the TV, dressed, ate, and went to find a rental car. I drove through Lynchburg. The town was Palm Sunday—dead. I drove into a black neighborhood and came on a boarded-up building with a sign out front:

THE VIRGINIA COLLEGE AND SEMINARY,
FOUNDED 1888.
SELF-HELP AND INDEPENDENCE.

In a jewelry store window I saw a placard that said Thomas Jefferson used to summer in these whale-humped Blue Ridges, trying to escape the pressures of government. I had fried chicken at Lendy's Gazebo in Madison Heights and wrote this in my notebook: "Why is it all so empty?"

In the afternoon I drove out to the seminary. You can still see it for miles, hoisting itself up out of the folds of Tobacco Row Mountain. A year earlier I had stopped by to see the building, and it had been empty then. It wasn't empty today; it was reeling under attack from three hundred black or white, male or female Job Corpsmen, most of them teenagers. At the front gate, where they have put up a government-looking guardhouse, I asked a woman in Security if I could go through. She said it was irregular, and that most of the ex-seminarians who come back to take a look are turned away, but that perhaps an exception could be made in my case since I was writing a book. Her name was Terry and she led me through the buildings. There were padlocks on doors, stenciled lettering announcing "BAY 1," "BAY 17." The library was something else, the rec rooms were something else. There were gouges in the walls and they had put up concrete dividers. Most of the youths in the Center know vaguely of the building's past, Terry said. There is a reverence for the chapel, she said, even though it doesn't much look like a chapel anymore. Government properties are not allowed to hold religious services, so music and theatrics and public programs go on in the chapel these days. But it was the one part of the school that hadn't been chinked and gouged and smudged. It seemed in mint condition, without altar or organ or statuary. "They won't mess it up, they're careful about this room," Terry said. On the outside of the chapel doors, some of the little steel crosses that we used to polish endlessly were missing. "Somebody has been pulling them off," she said. "Security is collecting them." I saw a sculpture of proffered hands, out of which water used to flow into a fountain. The fountain had dried up; there were old leaves in the basin. Out front of the seminary the massive twelve-foot-high bronze statue of Father Judge by famed sculptor Ivan Mestrovic still stood. Terry said the kids won't go near it. "Spooks them," she said. "Whenever anything mysterious happens around here, the first thing the kids say is: 'Father Judge did it.' They think he's buried on the property somewhere." She said that one night a security guard clanged through the halls with chains. Afterward you could have heard a peep, she said. On the way out, Terry said: "We've had two fires here recently. We suspect arson." I was glad to go. The place had nothing for me.

And yet, nothing that is good is ever completely lost, I believe. In other ways Father Judge Mission Seminary is much alive. Perhaps I am thinking just now of evening Benediction when one of the priests would lift a glittering spiked monstrance from the altar, wrap it in the satin cape that was draped around his shoulders and bunched in his hands, turn, and pass our Lord before our eyes while tallow dripped and floor fans whirred and the stillness seemed deafening. The monstrance, encasing the pale host, spangled like sun-whitened gold, and it was at such moments I was sure, and no longer suspected, I was at the epicenter of Something. For now, though, I keep searching.